EXPERIMENTAL DESIGN AND STATISTICS FOR PSYCHOLOGY

To
Lorella and Leonardo
With Love

Fabio

To
Portia, Steven, Martin, Jonathan and Amy
With love

John

FABIO SANI AND JOHN TODMAN

EXPERIMENTAL DESIGN AND STATISTICS FOR

PSYCHOLOGY

A FIRST COURSE

BLACKWELL PUBLISHING
350 Main Street, Malden, MA 02148-5020, USA
9600 Garsington Road, Oxford OX4 2DQ, UK
550 Swanston Street, Carlton, Victoria 3053, Australia

First published 2006 by Blackwell Publishing Ltd

1   2006

Library of Congress Cataloging-in-Publication Data

Sani, Fabio, 1961–
   Experimental design and statistics for psychology : a first course / Fabio Sani and John Todman.
      p. cm.
   Includes index.
   ISBN-13: 978-1-4051-0023-6 (hardcover : alk. paper)
   ISBN-10: 1-4051-0023-0 (hardcover : alk. paper)
   ISBN-13: 978-1-4051-0024-3 (pbk. : alk. paper)
   ISBN-10: 1-4051-0024-9 (pbk. : alk. paper)   1. Psychometrics—Textbooks.   2.
Experimental design—Textbooks.   3. Psychology—Research—Methodology—Textbooks.   I.
Todman, John B.   II. Title.

   BF39.S26 2005
   105′.72′4—dc22

                                                              2005019009

A catalogue record for this title is available from the British Library.

Set in 10/12.5pt Rotis Serif
by Graphicraft Limited, Hong Kong
Printed and bound in India
by Replika Press

For further information on
Blackwell Publishing, visit our website:
www.blackwellpublishing.com

CONTENTS

PREFACE

In this book, we have set out to introduce experimental design and statistics to first and second year psychology students. In writing it, we had three aims in mind.

First, we hoped to turn an area of study that students generally find daunting and feel anxious about into something that makes sense and with which they can begin to feel confident. In pursuing our first aim, we have tried to use a simple, friendly style, and have offered many examples of the concepts that we discuss. We have also included many diagrams summarizing the connections between concepts and have added concise summaries at the end of each chapter, together with a glossary of concepts at the end of the book. Furthermore, we have tried to integrate experimental design and statistical analysis more so than is generally the case in introductory texts. This is because we believe that the concepts used in statistics only really make sense when they are embedded in a context of research design issues. In sum, we are convinced that many of the problems that students experience with experimental design and statistical analysis arise because these topics tend to be treated separately; by integrating them we have attempted to dispel some of the confusion that undoubtedly exists about what are design issues and what are statistical issues.

Second, though we wanted to write a very introductory book that makes minimal assumptions of previous knowledge, we also wanted to avoid writing a *simplistic* account of an inherently rich and complex area of study. In order to achieve this, we have included features referred to as either 'additional information' or 'complications'. These are clearly separated from the main text, thereby safeguarding its coherence and clarity, but complementing and enriching it. We hope that these features will help students to look ahead at some complexities that they will be ready to fully engage with as they gain understanding; these features should also help to maintain the book's usefulness to psychology students as they progress beyond introductory (first and second year) courses. In sum, we hope to share our fascination with the richness and complexity of the topic of this book, but without plunging students too far into controversies that they are not yet ready to deal with.

Our third and final aim was to write a book that is in line with recent technological advances in the execution of statistical analysis. Nowadays, psychology students do not need to make complex calculations by hand, or even by means of calculators, because they can access computers running special statistical programs. As a consequence, we have, in general, avoided giving details concerning the calculations involved in statistical tests. Instead, we have included boxes in which we explain how to perform given statistical analyses by means of a widely used statistical software package called SPSS (Statistical Package for Social Sciences). Our experience of teaching statistics to students has convinced us that they make most progress when they are encouraged to move from a conceptual understanding to computer execution without any intervening computational torture. All SPSS output illustrated in the book is based on Release 12. Details of format may vary with other versions, but the information will be essentially the same.

If you are teaching a design and statistics course, we hope you will find our approach to be 'just what you have been looking for'. If you are a first year psychology student, we hope that the book will help you to learn with confidence, because it all hangs together and 'makes sense'. We hope that it will provide a base from which you can move forward with enjoyment rather than with apprehension to tackle new problems and methods as they arise. Enjoy!

CHAPTER ONE

Scientific Psychology and the Research Process

Psychology and the Scientific Method

To some extent, we are all curious about mental life and behaviour. For instance, we may wonder whether our recollection of a certain event in our childhood is real or just the result of imagination, or why we are going through a period of feeling low, or whether our children should watch a particular television programme or not. That we, as ordinary people, should be interested in these and other similar issues is hardly surprising. After all, we are all motivated to understand others and ourselves in order to make sense of both the social environment in which we live and our inner life. However, there are people who deal with mental and behavioural issues at a professional level: these are psychologists. It is true that, often, psychologists may deal with problems that ordinary people have never considered. However, in many cases psychologists address the same issues as those that attract the curiosity of ordinary people. In fact, a psychologist could well study the extent to which people's memories and recollections are accurate or wrong, or the reasons why people become depressed, or whether violence observed on television makes children more aggressive.

Now, if ordinary people and psychologists are, to some extent, interested in the same issues, then the question is: what is the demarcation line between the psychological knowledge of ordinary people and that of professional psychologists? How do they differ in terms of their approach to issues related to thinking, feeling and behaviour? The main difference between lay people and psychologists is concerned with the method they use to produce and develop their knowledge. Ordinary people tend to make generalizations on mental life and behaviour based on their own personal experience or that of people who are close to them. In some cases, lay people may even accept the view of others on faith, in the absence of any critical examination. Moreover, they tend to cling rigidly to their convictions, regardless of possible counter-examples. On the contrary, psychologists use the **scientific method**.

The term 'scientific method' is a rather broad one, and different scholars may have different views on what it entails. In fact, there exists a discipline, known as the **philosophy of science**, which is devoted to the study of how science should and does work. Philosophers of science discuss the aims, procedures and tools of science, as well as its relation to other forms of knowledge, such as, for instance, religion, art and literature. However, although many aspects of science have long been the subjects of dispute, there is a general consensus on some core features of scientific activity. In particular, scientists agree that their task is to explain natural and social phenomena, and that they should do so by following a two-stage research process. First, they must formulate **hypotheses** concerning the mechanisms and processes underlying the phenomena that they wish to investigate. Second, they must test their hypotheses in order to produce clear and convincing evidence that the hypotheses are correct.

If you want to conduct a psychological study in a scientific fashion, you will have to work in accordance with this two-stage research process. In the next section, we will discuss what these two stages involve.

Additional information (1.1) – The scientific attitude

The term 'scientific method' implies not only the use of specific strategies and procedures, but also a specific type of mental attitude towards the process of investigation and learning. Ideally, scientists should keep an open mind, and be careful not to allow their biases and preconceptions to influence their work. Also, they should never accept findings uncritically, and should always submit them to scrutiny and be very sceptical and cautious in their evaluation. However, it must be said that this is not always easy to achieve. In fact, many philosophers of science believe that complete neutrality and impartiality is not attainable. In their opinion, scientific knowledge is always affected, at least to some extent, by the personal life of the scientists, and by the cultural, political and social climate within which scientists conduct their research.

The Research Process

Formulating hypotheses

The first crucial step of the research process is the formulation of hypotheses about a specific issue. However, before you can formulate your hypotheses you will have to decide the type of issue that you wish to investigate. Clearly, the field of psychology is vast, and there is a great variety of problems that you could potentially address. Ideally, you should study something that you are particularly curious about, and that you consider worthwhile studying.

The decision to study a given issue may be based on two main sources. First, it may be based on your knowledge of existing **theories** in psychology (or in related disciplines). For instance, suppose that there exists a theory postulating that we all have a strong need for security. Also, suppose that, according to this theory, when people feel particularly vulnerable their need for security increases and therefore they become more dependent on figures who are seen as protective and caring. Now, you might find this theory persuasive, but at the same time it could make you think about some aspects that are overlooked by the theory. For example, you might wonder whether a sense of psychological protection and security could be obtained not only by depending on specific individuals, but also by joining a group. As a consequence, you could decide to conduct a study to investigate whether the need for protection may lead to seeking group affiliation.

Additional information (1.2) – The nature of theories

Theories have two main features. First, they organize findings from previous research into a coherent set of interrelated ideas. Consider that every single day psychologists conduct a countless number of studies in their laboratories around the world. If all the results that emerge from these studies were simply included in a very long list of isolated findings, without any form of organization and systematization, psychological research would be a chaotic, unstructured and largely unproductive activity. Second, theories help researchers to think about further implications of the findings and ideas upon which a theory is based. As a consequence, theories can generate new research problems and lead to the formulation of new hypotheses.

When a hypothesis is derived from a theory, then testing the hypothesis implies testing the theory too. If the hypothesis is proved false, then some aspects of the theory will probably need to be revised or, in some cases, the theory will be rejected altogether. On the other hand, confirming the hypothesis would support the theory. However, it would not prove that the theory is true once and for all. It would simply increase our confidence in the capability of the theory to account for certain phenomena.

The second source upon which your decision to study a certain issue may be based is your everyday knowledge and life. You might be intrigued by a behaviour that you have observed in yourself or in other people, or that has been shown in a film that you have seen or described in a novel that you have read. For example, suppose that you have noticed that your mood influences your performance in exams, in the sense that when you are in a good mood during an exam, your performance tends to be good too. You might wonder whether this is just you, or whether this is a typical

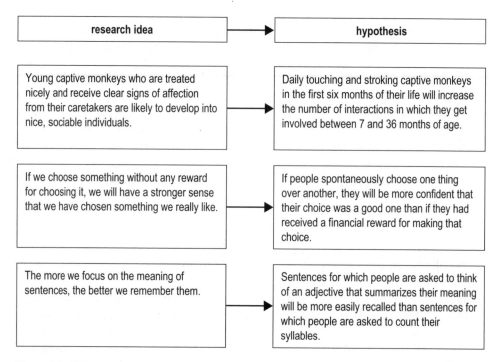

Figure 1.1   From research ideas to testable hypotheses

psychological phenomenon. As a result, you might decide to explore the relationship between mood and performance in exams.

Once you have decided the issue that you want to investigate, you are ready to translate your general and still rather vague ideas into precise hypotheses. For instance, concerning the relationship between mood and intellectual performance, you could put forward the following hypothesis: 'the more positive the mood of people, the better their intellectual performance'. (See Figure 1.1 for some examples on how to move from research ideas to precise hypotheses.)

So, what is a hypothesis then? There are two different types of hypotheses; the type that is exemplified above can be defined as **a formal statement in which it is predicted that a specific change in one thing will produce a specific change in another thing**. In fact, by saying that the more positive the mood the better the performance, you are virtually saying that a specific change in mood (that is, its improvement) will produce a specific change in intellectual performance (that is, its enhancement). That means that by formulating this type of hypothesis you are anticipating the existence of a cause–effect relationship between particular things (in this case 'mood' and 'intellectual performance'). In fact, it can be said that the change in mood is the cause of the change in intellectual performance, or if you like, it can be said that the change in intellectual performance is the effect of the change in mood.

The second type of hypothesis differs from the one we have just discussed in important ways, and it is discussed in Complications 1.1 below. However, let us emphasize that in this book we will mainly be dealing with the type of hypothesis explained above.

Complications (1.1) – When hypotheses make no claim about cause and effect

To be precise, scientific hypotheses do not always take the form discussed above. For instance, suppose that you wish to hypothesize that the higher people's self-esteem the higher the salary they earn. This is a perfectly plausible hypothesis that could be tested empirically. However, this hypothesis does not say that a change in one thing will produce a change in another thing. In fact, it makes no claims concerning which thing causes which: it does not say that a change in self-esteem causes changes in the salary, nor the other way around. This hypothesis simply states that two things (self-esteem and salary) will change together: if one is high, the other one will also be high. In sum, in some cases a hypothesis may be a formal statement in which it is predicted that a specific change in one thing will be associated with a specific change in another thing.

In this book we focus on hypotheses that a change in one thing will produce a change in another thing, because the book is mainly devoted to experiments, and the hypotheses that are tested through experiments are of this kind. Hypotheses in which it is predicted that two things change together are generally tested by means of non-experimental studies, and will be dealt with in Chapter 10.

Remember that a good hypothesis should be expressed in terms that are precise and clearly defined, and should be parsimonious, that is, as simple as possible. This will make it easier for you to set up a study by means of which your hypothesis is tested.

Testing hypotheses

Testing a hypothesis implies devising a study by means of which you can provide convincing evidence that the hypothesis is correct. To be truly convincing, the evidence you will produce must be **empirical evidence**, that is, it must be observable by other people – not just you!

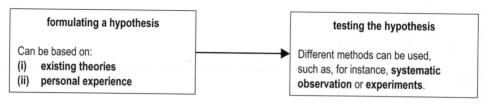

Figure 1.2 The research process

Empirical evidence supporting a postulated causal relation between things can be gathered through the use of various techniques. For instance, you could rely on the **systematic observation** of behaviour. This is what psychologists who are interested in animal behaviour tend to do. Basically, animal psychologists go where the animals live, or create an artificial environment in which animals are placed, and then they observe and record animals' behaviour through the use of established procedures. For example, a psychologist who is interested in, say, the behaviour of chimps could use systematic observation to demonstrate that a high amount of time devoted to 'grooming', that is, reciprocal cleaning and brushing among a group of chimps, leads to more frequent cooperative activities in the group.

However, the technique that is most often used by psychologists – as well as scientists in many other disciplines – is the **experiment**. Experiments constitute a very powerful technique for the investigation of causal links between different things, and this is why they are ideal for testing causal hypotheses. Experiments are typically run in laboratories (although it is possible to conduct them in more natural settings too). Because, as specified above, a hypothesis states that a specific change in one thing will produce (cause) a specific change in another thing, experiments are based on the creation of a situation in which a change in one thing is artificially produced, and the corresponding change in another thing is systematically observed. This book – with the exception of Chapter 10, in which we deal with non-experimental research – is entirely devoted to the use of the experiment as a method of hypotheses testing.

To conclude this chapter, it is necessary to make a further observation on the research process. (See Figure 1.2 for a schematic representation of such process.) While the formulation of good, interesting and clear hypotheses is a very important step – and by no means a simple one – the most taxing part of the research process is certainly the construction of a sound study through which the hypotheses can be tested. This is particularly true with regard to experiments. In fact, although each experiment is unique in various respects, all experiments must be designed according to a set of basic rules.

In the next chapter we will discuss these rules at length, and we will make you familiar with the experimental terminology and jargon. In order to avoid talking in abstract terms, we will explain the experimental rules and present the experimental terminology within the context of a fictitious experiment. This experiment will constitute an attempt to test the hypothesis put forward above, that is, the hypothesis that 'the more positive the mood of people, the better their intellectual performance'.

SUMMARY OF CHAPTER

- Ordinary people and professional psychologists are both interested in mental and behavioural issues. However, while ordinary people gather their knowledge by using a rather casual approach, psychologists use the scientific method.
- The scientific method implies following a two-step research process. First, the researcher must formulate hypotheses – that is, formal statements predicting that a specific change in one thing will produce a specific change in another – concerning the issue that is of interest. Second, the researcher must test the hypotheses, that is, he or she must design a study aimed at producing empirical evidence that the hypotheses are correct.
- The experiment is the method that is used to establish a causal link between events.

CHAPTER TWO

The Nature of Psychology Experiments (I): Variables and Conditions

In Chapter 1, we said that in order to investigate a psychological issue scientifically, you should comply with a two-step research process. First, you must formulate hypotheses. The kind of hypothesis that we will consider in this chapter is a formal statement predicting that a specific change in one thing will produce a specific change in another. We offered the following example of this type of hypothesis: 'The more positive the mood of people, the better their intellectual performance.' The second step consists of testing the hypothesis (i.e., providing evidence that the hypothesis is correct). Finally, we stated that the most commonly used technique for testing these types of hypothesis is the experiment.

To design and conduct a sound experiment is a rather complex task, which implies acting in accordance with a set of very specific rules. In this chapter we will discuss the most important rules. However, we want to base this discussion on a concrete example. Therefore, we will start by describing an experiment that can be used to test our hypothesis about the causal relationship between mood and performance. Then, we will give a detailed explanation of the rules and procedures underlying the experiment.

An Experiment Testing Your Hypothesis

Let us remind you again of the hypothesis that we want to test: 'The more positive the mood of people, the better their intellectual performance.' The experiment that follows is meant to gather evidence that this is indeed the case.

To start with, we recruit 40 **participants** for the experiment. All participants attend at the laboratory at the same time. When they arrive, they are told that they are participating in an experiment on the effects of watching television on performance. This is a **cover story** – a mild deception – designed to prevent them guessing the experimental hypothesis (see the discussion of 'demand characteristics' in Chapter 3, for an appreciation of why cover stories may be necessary). Participants are then asked to enter a specific cubicle labelled with their name, sit in front of a screen, put headphones on and watch a 15-minute video excerpt from a film. Unknown to the participants, they do not all watch the same excerpt. In fact, one group of 20 participants watch a very funny excerpt, and another group of 20 participants watch an excerpt with neutral content, that is neither funny nor dramatic. (Participants had been allocated to two groups before arriving at the laboratory, by means of a random procedure.) Finally, after watching the video, all participants are asked to complete a test, contained in a special booklet, in which they have to indicate the correct solution to 10 logical problems, e.g.:

K N H
F H D
S W ?

(The answer is O because the letter in the second column is always as many letters below that in the first column as the letter in the third column is above that in the first column.)

When participants have completed the test, they leave the laboratory. At this point the experiment is over. Figure 2.1 shows a schematic representation of the structure

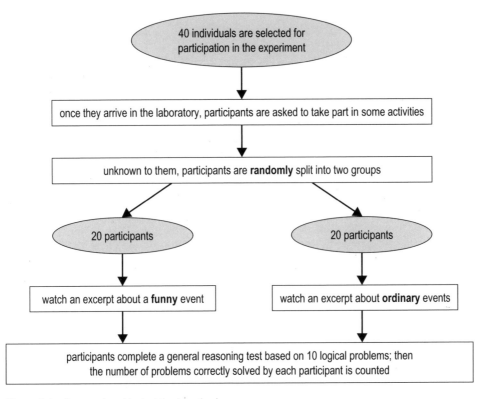

Figure 2.1 An experiment to test the hypothesis

of our experiment. Now, our task is to see whether the **data** we have collected (i.e., individual scores indicating how many logical problems each participant has solved) support our hypothesis.

If our hypothesis is correct, participants watching a funny excerpt should solve a higher number of logical problems than participants watching a neutral excerpt. This is because, while doing the test, participants who had watched a funny excerpt were in a good mood, while participants who had watched a neutral excerpt were in a normal mood. Clearly, to see if our hypothesis is correct, we will simply count the number of logical problems that have been solved by participants in the two different groups.

Complications (2.1) – 'Participants' or 'subjects'?

So far we have used the term 'participants' to refer to the people who take part in experiments. However, until recently it was common to refer to them as '**subjects**'. In fact, the experimental jargon is not yet completely free from this word, which – as you will see in the next chapter – is still used as part of composite terms indicating the forms that the experimental design can take. We refer, for instance, to expressions such as '**within-subjects design**' and '**between-subjects design**'.

So, to recapitulate, we hypothesized that a positive mood would enhance performance on tasks involving intellectual work. To test this hypothesis, we designed and conducted an experiment in which two separate groups of participants were exposed either to a video excerpt that put them in a good mood, or to an excerpt which did not affect their mood at all. Then we observed how participants in both groups performed on an intellectual task, with the expectation that participants whose mood had been enhanced would perform better than participants whose mood had not been altered.

At this point we can discuss our experiment in some detail. What did we really do? And why did we set up the study that way? Addressing these questions will give us the opportunity to discuss the basic rules and procedures involved in psychology experimentation.

Basic Rules and Notions in Experimental Psychology

Independent and dependent variables

As we discussed above, experiments test hypotheses that two things stand in a causal relationship, or, more specifically, that changes in one thing will produce changes in another thing. In an experiment, the things that are expected to change are known as **variables**. Obviously, the term 'variable' reflects the fact that these things can change; it indicates that the level of these things, rather than being fixed, is free to vary. So, considering our case, we hypothesize that specific changes in mood will produce specific changes in performance: that means that both mood and intellectual performance are variables because they may vary from being, say, very bad to very good.

It should be noticed that variability is not a specific characteristic of a limited range of things. On the contrary, virtually all things related to mental life and behaviour can manifest themselves in different degrees, or levels. So, for instance, anxiety, self-esteem, attachment to parental figures, mathematical performance, driving performance, aggression and so on are all aspects of mental and behavioural life whose level may vary from individual to individual or from situation to situation. Thus, different persons, or the same person in different situations, may have different levels of anxiety, self-esteem and so on.

There is, however, an important difference between the two variables in our experiment. Let us consider the variable 'mood' first. We have exposed two groups of participants to different stimuli (i.e., participants watch different video excerpts), so that participants in one group experience a good mood (because they watch a funny video excerpt), and participants in the other group do not experience any alteration in their mood (because they watch an emotionally neutral video excerpt). That means that we have purposefully varied the levels of the variable 'mood'. Or,

Additional information (2.1) – Continuous and discrete variables

There exist two different sorts of variable. Some of the variables we are interested in can vary over a continuous range, like our example of mood, which can vary from very bad to very good. Temperature is another example; it can vary from very low to very high. These are called **continuous variables**. For some, like temperature, we have good quantitative measurements, so we may also refer to them as **quantitative variables**. For others, like mood, we may have only rather approximate indicators, so they may not be very quantitative in practice. But even with a variable like mood that we can't measure very precisely, we can often manipulate it in some way, as in our example, to achieve two or more levels to work with. Other variables can take only whole number values, like our example of the number of logic problems solved, and these are called **discrete variables**. Some discrete variables don't even take numerical values at all; examples would be sex (male or female) and nationality (British, Greek, Chinese etc.). Discrete variables that take values that are not numbers are called **categorical** (or **qualitative** or **classification**) **variables**. Sometimes we use number codes for the categories (1 for male and 2 for female perhaps), but when we do, the numbers are only codes and different numbers would do just as well (e.g., 1 for female and 2 for male).

to put it differently, we have carried out a deliberate **manipulation** of the variable 'mood' (in order to observe how specific variations in the level of mood influence intellectual performance). The variable that is manipulated, and whose changes are supposed to produce changes on another variable, is called an **independent variable** (or IV for short). This is because its variations, and therefore its levels, do not depend on what the participants in the experiment actually do but are predetermined by the experimenter.

Concerning the variable 'intellectual performance', this is not subjected to manipulation, and therefore its levels are not predetermined by the experimenter. On the contrary, the levels of intellectual performance shown by participants in the experiment are hypothesized to depend on the variations of participants' mood (the IV). In fact, we expect that when mood is good intellectual performance will be high, and when mood is neutral intellectual performance will be average. Now, the variable whose levels depend on the levels of a prior variable is defined as a **dependent variable** (DV for short).

Levels of the independent variable and conditions of the experiment

We said that the levels of the IV are manipulated by the experimenter, so that two different situations are created. In one situation we have a group of participants whose mood is enhanced, while in another situation we have a group of participants whose mood is not altered. Because participants in the two groups are treated differently, these situations are referred to as **levels of treatment** of the IV, or, more commonly, as **conditions** of the experiment.

An important difference between the two conditions is that, strictly speaking, participants receive a treatment only in one condition. In fact, in our experiment, it is only in the condition in which participants watch an extract from a funny film that mood is intentionally altered. In the other condition – the one in which participants watch an excerpt whose content is neutral – there is no attempt at mood alteration at all. Basically, in this condition the experimenter makes no attempt to modify the level of mood that participants had when entering the laboratory. Because of the absence of treatment, this condition may be considered as a baseline (or an anchor point). The condition in which the experimenter alters the normal level of the IV is commonly defined as the **experimental condition**, while the baseline condition is called the **control condition.**

However, it is important to specify that not all experiments include a control condition. In some cases, experiments are based on two experimental conditions, each one characterized by a different treatment. In these circumstances it is useful to give a specific label to each condition, because simply calling both 'experimental condition' might cause confusion. For instance, suppose that in our experiment we replace the control condition with a condition in which mood is intentionally lowered by, say, showing participants an excerpt from a very sad film. In this case we could label the two conditions as 'high mood condition' and 'low mood condition' respectively.

Additional information (2.2) – How many IVs and conditions can we have in an experiment?

Although we have designed an experiment with one IV having two conditions, an experiment can be much more complex, involving more than one IV and more than two levels of each IV. In this book, we will deal only with experiments having the same design as the one we are discussing in this chapter, that is, experiments with only one IV, which has only two levels.

Assessing the levels of the DV

While the levels of the IV are predetermined by the researcher, the levels of the DV must be assessed, because, as we said above, rather than being predetermined by the experimenter they depend on variations in the levels of the IV. So the question is: How should the levels of the DV be assessed? We will answer that question by explaining why, in our experiment, we proposed to use performance on a logical test as a way of assessing intellectual performance.

The reason why we decided to look at the participants' performance on a logical test as a way of assessing intellectual performance is twofold. First, performance on a logical test is a plausible type of intellectual performance. Second, it can take precise and objective values; in fact, participants in our experiment can solve correctly a number of logical problems ranging from none to 10, and therefore their performance will take a value somewhere between 0 and 10. This is telling you that, in deciding how to assess the DV, you should remember that the means of assessment must (i) be a plausible, adequate exemplification, or an **indicator**, of the thing represented by the DV, and (ii) provide a precise and rigorous **measure** of the DV. Obviously, using performance on a logical test is not the only adequate exemplification and objective measure of intellectual performance. So, clearly our decision to use this specific task for assessing intellectual performance is a rather arbitrary decision, as we could have used many others. For instance, participants could have written an essay on a given topic, whose quality could have been evaluated by some judges. That means that, in the end, the way in which the DV is assessed is largely a matter of taste and convenience. Anything goes, as long as, as we have stressed, the assessment is plausible and precise. Finally, note that the process of specifying clearly and explicitly the methods (i.e., the operations) used to measure the DV is generally conceptualized as the **operational definition** of the DV.

At this point, we have already presented the core structure of an experiment and the main terms and definitions that are used. In order to form a general picture, you may look at Figure 2.2.

Note that in our experiment we are proposing to use different participants in the different conditions of the experiment. That is, 20 individuals are assigned to the

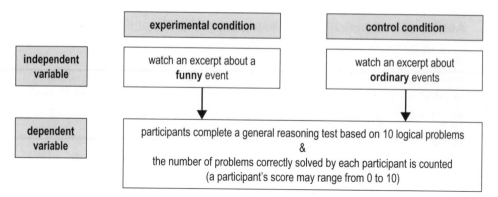

Figure 2.2   Terms and definitions in experimentation

experimental condition (watching funny excerpt) and 20 *different* individuals are assigned to the control condition (watching neutral excerpt). This type of experimental design is called **independent groups design** (or between-subjects design). Now, you must be aware that not all experiments require assigning different people to the different conditions. In some cases it is possible, and even desirable, to use the same individuals in the different conditions. This type of design is called **repeated measures design** (or within-subjects design). The reasons why we may need or want to use one specific type of design rather than the other should become clear in the next chapter.

Additional information (2.3) – Stimulus and response variables

It should be noted that, in our example, the IV consists of exposing participants to a specific stimulus, that is, an excerpt from a film. As a consequence, this IV can be defined as a **stimulus variable**. On the other hand, the DV is constituted by a response (in the form of proposed solutions to a set of logical problems). Therefore, this DV can be defined as a **response variable**. In psychological experiments, this is quite common. That is, IVs are very often stimulus variables (e.g., a video to watch, items to learn or memorize, a specific type of environment to which participants are exposed), while DVs tend to be response variables (e.g., answers to a questionnaire, performance in a test, physiological reactions).

Additional information (2.4) – Manipulation checks

How can we be sure that our manipulation of the IV has worked? In other words, how can we be confident that we truly expose participants to different levels of the IV in the different conditions? So, concerning our experiment, does showing different excerpts to participants really prompt different mood states? Well, it is possible to check whether our manipulation has been successful by means of what is known as a **manipulation check**. This may be defined as a measurement for confirming that the IV took the intended levels in the different conditions. Basically, researchers ask participants in both conditions some questions that may give them a hint about the effects of their manipulation. This is normally done after the DV has been assessed. For instance, in our experiment we could ask participants to define their mood by specifying whether it is, say, 'good', 'neutral', or 'bad'. If we find that in the experimental condition there is a tendency to answer 'good' while in the control condition participants tend to respond 'neutral', then we may assume that our manipulation has worked.

Some further remarks about the nature of independent and dependent variables

We want to conclude this section on the IV and DV by making a further remark on the nature of variables in psychology experimentation. A given variable is not either an IV or a DV by nature, and irrespective of the experiment we are conducting. In fact, a variable that is used as an IV in one experiment may well be used as a DV in another experiment, and vice versa. For instance, while in our study we use intellectual performance as a DV (as we explore how it is affected by mood), in a different study we might investigate the effect of intellectual performance on people's self-esteem, thereby using intellectual performance as an IV. Equally, while in our study we use mood as an IV (as we explore how it affects intellectual performance), in another study we might investigate the effect of doing regular meditation on mood, thereby using mood as a DV. In sum, whether a variable is used as an IV or as a DV is generally based on what hypothesis the experimenter is investigating.

However, there may be some exceptions to this rule. In particular, there are variables such as age, gender and ethnicity that cannot be used as DVs in experiments, because their levels cannot vary as a function of changes in a prior variable. On the other hand, although these variables cannot be used as DVs, they are often used as IVs. In fact, psychologists are very interested in how differences in age, gender and ethnicity affect aspects of human behaviour, thought and emotions.

Additional information (2.5) – Quasi-experiments

Suppose that we want to investigate how being male or female affects musical skills. In this case, we would devise a study in which the gender of the participants constitutes the IV – with two levels of the IV, 'male' and 'female' – and musical skills is the DV. However, by doing so we would not manipulate the levels of the IV, because we would just use the categories that are already available in reality, independent from our intervention. Now, whenever we design a study in which the IV is not truly manipulated, we are not entitled to define the study as a '**true**' experiment. In fact, in this case we would conduct a **quasi-experiment**. This is so because the study closely resembles an experimental design, but it does not involve a real manipulation of the IV. Note that it is more difficult to infer a causal relationship between the IV and the DV from the results of a quasi-experiment. After all, many different experiences may happen to go with being male as opposed to female and any one of these kinds of experience (e.g., socialization experiences) might contribute to a difference in the DV between males and females. (Another important reason for defining a study as a quasi-experiment will be discussed in Chapter 3.)

Conclusions

To recapitulate briefly, in this chapter we have designed an experiment testing the hypothesis that the more positive the mood of people the better their intellectual performance. To see if our hypothesis is correct, we will count the number of logical problems solved by each participant in two different situations, or, more precisely, 'conditions'. Basically, if participants in the experimental condition (mood enhanced) tend to solve a higher number of logical problems than participants in the control condition (mood unaltered), then we can conclude that our hypothesis is correct. On the other hand, if participants in the two conditions solve a similar number of problems, then we must conclude that our hypothesis is wrong.

But can we truly be confident that the scores we obtain will allow us to draw truthful conclusions about the cause–effect relationships between mood and performance? Couldn't our results, regardless of whether they confirm or disconfirm our hypothesis, be misleading because of some shortcoming in our experimental design? In the next chapter we discuss how to increase our confidence that our results will allow us to draw convincing conclusions about the existence, or absence, of the effects of mood on intellectual performance.

SUMMARY OF CHAPTER

- In an experiment, the things that are supposed to stand in a causal relationship are called 'variables', as the levels of these things are free to vary.
- There exist two types of variable. A variable whose levels are predetermined (manipulated) by the researcher is called an 'independent variable' (IV). A variable whose levels depend on, or are affected by, variations in the IV is called a 'dependent variable' (DV).
- Manipulating the IV implies assigning participants to two 'conditions' of the experiment, which differ in terms of the level of the IV to which participants are exposed. In the 'experimental condition' the researcher deliberately alters the normal level of the IV, while in the 'control condition' no attempt is made to make any alteration.
- Assessing variations in the levels of the DV requires devising a plausible indicator of the thing represented by the DV, and a precise way to measure the DV.
- Most variables may be used either as IVs or as DVs, depending on the nature of the experiment. However, some variables, such as age, sex and ethnicity, cannot be used as DVs in experiments, because their levels cannot be affected by variations in the IV.

CHAPTER THREE

The Nature of Psychology Experiments (II): Validity

In the previous chapter we discussed some core concepts in experimental psychology with the aid of an example of an experiment. In this fictitious experiment, we propose to test the hypothesis that people who are in a good mood perform better on intellectual tasks than people who are in a neutral mood. To test this hypothesis, we create two conditions (with participants randomly assigned to these conditions), one in which a group of participants watch a movie excerpt with a funny content (the experimental condition) and one in which another group of participants watch an excerpt with an emotionally neutral content (the control condition). We assume that participants in the experimental condition will end up having a positive mood while participants in the control condition will maintain a neutral mood. Therefore, even though participants' intellectual abilities will probably vary a lot, we expect that participants in the experimental condition will, on average, do better than those in the control condition on an intellectual task. The task requires participants to solve 10 logical problems. To see if our hypothesis is correct we must count the number of logical problems that have been solved by each participant in the two different conditions of the experiment. If participants in the experimental condition (mood enhanced) tend to solve a higher number of logical problems than participants in the control condition (mood unaltered), then we can conclude that our hypothesis is likely to be correct. On the other hand, if the randomly assigned participants in the two conditions solve a similar number of problems, we will conclude that our hypothesis is probably wrong.

But can we be confident that the results of our experiment, irrespective of whether they confirm our hypothesis or not, will allow us to say that we have unveiled the nature of the relationship between mood and intellectual performance? Unfortunately, there are several potential problems.

It could be that what we measure does not adequately reflect what it was intended to measure. That is, it could be that measuring the ability to solve logical problems does not constitute a good strategy for measuring intellectual performance.

Another possibility is that the scores on the DV (intellectual performance) are not really determined by the IV (mood), but by some other variable that we are unaware of. For instance, suppose that the participants in the experimental condition had been tested in the morning and all of those in the control condition had been tested in the afternoon. As a consequence, scores might be higher in the experimental condition than in the control condition because participants in the experimental condition were alert, while those in the control condition were rather lethargic after having had their lunch. In sum, in this case we would obtain higher scores in the experimental condition, as expected, but not because of the effects of the IV; on the contrary, the higher scores in the experimental condition would be due to the effects of a different variable, that is *time of day* (before lunch, after lunch). The same logic would apply if participants in each group had been tested together, but separately from those in the other group. Then, anything that happened in one testing situation, like someone having a coughing fit or a mobile phone ringing, would affect everyone in that group and nobody in the other group, and could therefore account for any obtained difference between conditions on the DV. That is, in this case changes on the DV might be determined by the variable *group testing situation*.

Finally, it could be that what we find in our experiment would not be found in other similar experiments conducted in different contexts, that is, experiments using people whose social class, level of education or nationality and so on is not the same as that of our participants. For example, supposing that in our experiment we use undergraduate students with a Western background, how do we know that our results would also be obtained using, say, fishermen from a Pacific atoll?

In sum, we must be aware of these issues, and do everything we can to make sure that our experimental design is sound and that results will allow us to draw valid conclusions about the effects of mood on intellectual performance. This is equivalent to saying that our experiment must have **validity**. So, how do we deal with validity? Psychologists generally agree that there are three important aspects of validity relating to experiments, namely **'construct'**, **'internal'**, and **'external' validity**. The nature of these three aspects was anticipated in the paragraph above; however, in the next section we will discuss them in more detail, and suggest strategies to increase the likelihood that an experiment is valid in these respects.

Construct Validity

Construct validity is the extent to which a variable actually reflects the **theoretical construct** (i.e., concept, 'thing') that we intend to measure. Basically, if our experiment is meant to inform us about the effects of mood on intellectual performance, then we must be sure of two things. First, that we are really manipulating people's mood, and not either something else or nothing at all. Second, that the way we measure intellectual performance is 'really' a measure of intellectual performance (remember that, when discussing how to measure the DV, we insisted that the measure we use must be a plausible indicator of the DV). In sum, our variables must be a reflection of the things, or theoretical constructs, whose cause–effect relationship we are trying to investigate. In fact, if exposing participants to different excerpts had no effects on their mood, or solving logical problems was not an expression of intellectual performance at all, then, obviously, our experiment would tell us nothing meaningful about the effects of mood on intellectual performance, regardless of the results we may obtain.

Internal Validity

Although our experiment is aimed at exploring the effects of the IV (mood) on the DV (intellectual performance), we cannot exclude the possibility that other variables will influence the DV. The way participants perform in the intellectual task might be influenced not only by their level of mood, but also by the level of other variables. For example, intellectual performance can be affected by 'time of day' and 'particularities of the test situation' (to which we referred earlier), the amount of sleep the participants have taken during the night preceding the experiment, their level of anxiety and so on.

The effects of these variables on the DV may make it difficult to assess the effects that the IV exerts on the DV. This is why we call them **nuisance variables**, though they are also often referred to as **extraneous** or **irrelevant variables** (see Figure 3.1 for an illustration of the conjoint effects of the IV and the nuisance variables on the DV). Also, the effect of a nuisance variable (or NV for short) on the DV is said to cause an **error of measurement**. The effects of an NV on the DV may constitute a threat to the internal validity of an experiment, that is, to the capability of an experiment to show the effects that the IV, and only the IV, exerts on the DV.

NVs can be responsible for two different types of error, namely **systematic error** and **random error**. Systematic error is a very serious threat to internal validity, while random error does not represent a threat to internal validity at all. In the following sections we will explain the nature of systematic error, and the strategies that can be used to prevent it from jeopardizing the internal validity of the experiment. Because turning the systematic error into a random one is one of the strategies that can be used to deal with threats to internal validity, we will also introduce the concept of *random error* in this chapter. However, this will be a very sketchy introduction, because random error will be discussed in detail in Chapter 5.

Systematic error

An NV will cause systematic error when its effects on the DV are mistaken for the systematic effect of the IV on the DV. Suppose again that all participants in our experiment are students in the same university. However, this time suppose that, for practical reasons, participants in the experimental condition (good mood) have been recruited from a specific residence hall in the university campus, and participants in

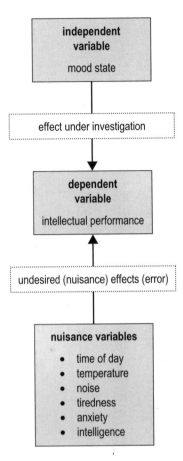

Figure 3.1   The effect of the independent and the nuisance variables on the dependent variable

the control condition (neutral mood) live in a different hall. Now, suppose also that, unknown to the experimenter, the students living in the hall from which participants in the experimental condition have been drawn have had an ordinary night, while the students living in the hall from which participants in the control condition have been drawn have attended a party on the night before the experiment. Now, this implies that a specific NV, that is 'tiredness', would affect the DV (intellectual performance). However, in this case the NV would not affect the two conditions of the experiment to equal extents. On the contrary, it would affect *only* the control condition. In fact, participants in the control condition would be more tired and therefore less concentrated and focused than participants in the experimental condition. (See Figure 3.2 for a schematic representation of how an NV may cause systematic error.)

The implications of this scenario for the participants' scores on intellectual performance can be very negative! Consider what would happen to participants in the control condition: while on the one hand their intellectual performance could be unaffected

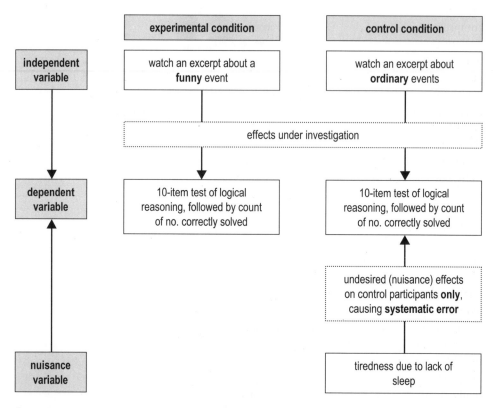

Figure 3.2   How a nuisance variable causes 'systematic error'

by their normal mood, on the other hand it could be impaired by tiredness and lack of concentration. That implies that, if superior scores are obtained in the experimental condition, this might be due to the tiredness of participants in the control condition rather than the good mood of participants in the experimental condition. If this were indeed the case, concluding that our hypothesis about the beneficial effect of good mood has been supported would be a wrong conclusion! In fact, rather than being due to the effects of the IV (mood), differences in intellectual performance in the two conditions might be determined by the fact that an NV has had a negative effect on intellectual performance in the control condition.

In sum, in the example above an NV (tiredness) would affect scores in one condition, that is, the control condition, but not in the other, that is, the experimental condition. In other words, the NV would act as a **confounding variable**, in the sense that its effects would be confounded (inextricably mixed up) with the effects of the IV, that is, mood. In turn, this would make it impossible to tell whether the observed difference between conditions was due to a systematic effect of mood or a systematic effect of tiredness. In other words, in this case the NV offers an alternative explanation for the variations in the levels of the DV in the different conditions, apart from that offered by the effect of the IV. Thus, the internal validity of the experiment has been compromised.

Note that a systematic error not only can create differences between conditions, but it can also eliminate differences where, without the effects of the confounding variable, there would be differences between conditions. For instance, suppose that we are actually correct, and that mood does have an effect on intellectual performance. This means that, in normal circumstances, participants in the experimental condition would solve more of the logical problems. However, this time suppose that the participants allocated to the experimental condition have attended a party on the night preceding the day of the experiment. Now, in this case the performance of these participants would be impaired by the effect of tiredness, and as a consequence participants in the experimental condition might perform no better than those in the control condition. (Basically, tiredness might tend to depress their performance, thereby neutralizing the positive effects of their superior mood.) This would lead us to conclude that we were wrong in predicting that people in a positive mood perform better than people in a normal mood. But obviously, our conclusion would be inaccurate, as in this case the absence of any difference between scores in the two conditions would be due to the effect of the IV being cancelled out by the opposite effect of a **systematic** (confounding) **NV**, that is, tiredness, which has lowered the level of performance of participants in one specific condition, that is, the experimental condition.

Clearly, systematic errors constitute a very serious problem. However, psychologists have devised some strategies that can preserve the internal validity of an experiment. These strategies are part of what is known as **experimental control**, as what they really do is to exert some sort of control over the NVs. So, how do we avoid systematic errors? How can we control potentially confounding variables? It depends on the nature of the NV we want to control. In fact, there are two kinds of NV: **situational variables** and **participant** (or **subject**) **variables**.

CONTROLLING SITUATIONAL NUISANCE VARIABLES

Situational variables are those NVs that are associated with the experimental situation itself (e.g., the experimenter's behaviour, the environment, the instruments used and so on). Two typical situational variables are 'time of day' and 'location'. In fact, these are convenient labels that stand for numerous specific situational NVs, such as noise level and other environmental distractions, temperature, room size, experimenter delivery of instructions and so on. Only the participants at the same location, or those attending at the same time of day, will have their performance affected by the same levels of the various situational NVs. Consequently, systematic error will occur if all of the participants in the experimental condition attend at the same time of day or at the same location and the participants in the control condition all attend at the other time of day or at the other location.

There are two possible ways in which we can try to control a situational systematic NV: we can either try to eliminate the NV, or we can try to turn it into a random NV (which would then produce random error).

Eliminating a systematic NV implies keeping it **constant** throughout the experiment. For instance, suppose we want to eliminate the situational variable concerning 'time of day'. In this case we could keep it constant by simply arranging for participants in both conditions to attend at the same time. However, controlling one potential NV often creates another. For instance, it might not be possible to accommodate all participants in one lab due to lack of space; therefore, in order to run the two conditions at the same time we might have to use two different laboratories and two different experimenters. But if all participants in the experimental condition attended at one laboratory and all of those in the control condition attended at the other, 'location' would become a systematic NV. The crucial point here is that to keep constant all the situational variables that may cause a systematic error is not generally possible.

Complications (3.1) – The 'downside' of eliminating NVs

Exercising control over potential systematic NVs by *eliminating* them, that is, by keeping them at a constant value, has a cost. For example, if only one time of day or only males are used in our experiment, we can never be sure that any effect of mood on intellectual performance that we find would have occurred had we used a different time of day, or had we used females. The more variables we control by eliminating any variation in the values they can take, the more specific the situation becomes and the less we are able to generalize our results to other, or more general, situations. This is the issue of external validity, which will be discussed later in this chapter.

When a given situational variable cannot be kept constant, we can use another form of control, that is, we can try to remove the effect of NVs that may cause systematic error by turning them into **random NVs**.

It is now time to explain what a *random error* is about. Suppose, for instance, that all the participants in our experiment are students in the same university, and that on the day preceding the experiment they have gone to a party where they have had several drinks and stayed until late. Now, because of this, on the following day our participants might, to differing extents, feel tired and have some difficulties concentrating on intellectual tasks. As a consequence, participants might perform worse on the logical problems than they would normally do, some more so than others. That means that the obtained scores on the DV would depend, at least in part, on the effects of the level of participants' concentration (an NV).

However, it should be noted that the effect of this NV would be potentially the same in both the experimental (good mood) and the control (normal mood) condition.

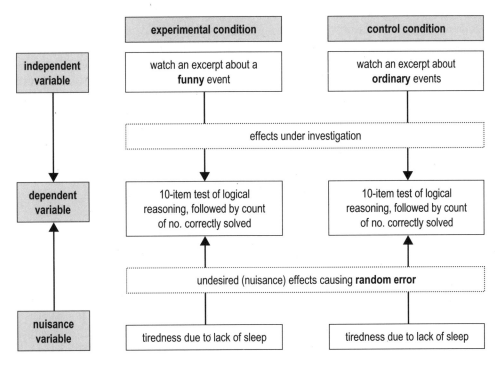

Figure 3.3   How a nuisance variable causes 'random error'

That is, because all participants have attended the party, the intellectual performance of both those in the experimental condition and those in the control condition would have the same possibility of being influenced by tiredness. In sum, in the case of random error the NV has an equal chance of affecting all of the conditions of an experiment. (See Figure 3.3 for a schematic representation of how a nuisance variable may cause random error.)

Random errors normally do not constitute a serious problem for the internal validity of the experiment. Remember that we want to demonstrate that positive mood enhances intellectual performance, and that, as a consequence, we expect people in the experimental condition (good mood) to perform better than people in the control condition (normal mood). Now, the fact that the NV affects participants in both conditions in the same way will tend to lead to lower scores in both conditions. Therefore, differences between scores in the two conditions, which should emerge if our hypothesis is correct, will tend *not* to be eliminated. Of course, it may just happen that participants in the control condition are, on average, more tired than participants in the experimental condition, but it could just as easily be the other way round. In sum, the random error represented by the effect of the NV on the DV would constitute a *disturbance*, in that it would modify the scores that we would obtain without its effects, but would not undermine the logic of our experiment.

On the other hand, it should be noted that random NVs make the scores of participants in both conditions more variable. This is because NVs happen to affect each participant in either a positive or negative direction as a matter of chance. This variability of scores in both conditions acts like 'noise', making it harder to see clearly the effects of the IV on the DV. However, there are statistical techniques that can help us to overcome this problem and see the extent to which the IV is affecting the DV. In sum, dealing with random NVs is a *statistical* issue. This topic will be discussed in detail in Chapter 5.

Complications (3.2) – When random error matters

In some cases, random error can be more than mere 'disturbance', as it can obscure the effects of the IV on the DV completely. For instance, if participants were all extremely tired and unable to concentrate when they arrive in the laboratory, because of their attendance at the party, their performance could be the worst possible one, regardless of the condition to which they are allocated. That could lead the researcher to conclude that mood does not affect performance because there are no differences between the two conditions in terms of the scores produced by participants. On the contrary, the problem would be that the effect of the IV has been obscured by an NV that caused a random error.

Now that you know what a random error is about, you may appreciate why turning a systematic error into a random error constitutes a good strategy for dealing with the threats to internal validity posed by a systematic error. Obviously, the random NVs may still have effects on the DV, as discussed above. However, these effects will not be systematic, and therefore will not undermine the logic of the experiment. That is, you don't have to worry about the experimental design any longer. Once there are not NVs that can potentially cause a systematic error, all you have to worry about is to use the correct statistical tests, which will help you to overcome the problems resulting from NVs that can cause random errors.

How do we turn a systematic error into a random one? Let us return to an example we used previously. Suppose that we wanted to test the experimental group in the morning and the control group in the afternoon, but we have reason to believe that participants in the experimental group may be systematically advantaged as a group, and that, therefore, 'time of day' will function as a systematic NV that threatens the internal validity of the experiment. In this case we want to control the potentially systematic effects of 'time of day'. A possible strategy would be testing each participant individually, with times of testing randomly allocated to participants regardless of which condition they were in. This would ensure that the effects of 'time of day' would not *systematically* affect one condition differently from the other. Indeed, it will have become a *random* NV.

CONTROLLING PARTICIPANT NUISANCE VARIABLES

We can now discuss the other type of NV that can cause a systematic error, namely 'participant variables'. These NVs are associated with the characteristics of the participants (e.g., their personality, intelligence, previous experience etc.), and are always in play, as participants in experiments obviously carry with them their own particular characteristics. What is more, these variables can easily become confounding variables and give rise to systematic error. For instance, suppose that participants in the experimental condition of our experiment have some previous experience of logical problem solving, not shared by participants in the control condition. In this case there would be a participant NV affecting only one condition of the experiment. Also, this variable would certainly cause a systematic error, in that participants in the experimental condition might end up performing better than those in the control condition irrespective of whether their good mood had any effect.

How do we control participant variables? Often, instead of using different participants in each condition we simply use the same participants in both conditions, thereby assuring that there are no differences between conditions in terms of the individual characteristics of participants. For instance, we could have used the same participants in both conditions of our experiment on mood and intellectual performance. We would have arranged things so that 20 participants saw a funny video and then attempted to solve some logical problems, and on another occasion saw a neutral video and attempted to solve the same number of logical problems. In this way, participants may be said to 'act as their own control'.

An experimental design using the same participants in the two conditions of the experiment is described as a repeated measures design. Note that one advantage of using this design is that we may need only half the number of participants (20 instead of 40 in our example) to give us the same number (20) of scores in each condition as there were in the independent groups design.

Despite being effective for controlling participant variables, a repeated measures design may cause problems. Consider our experiment. Suppose the participants watch the neutral video (control condition) first and attempt some problems. Then, when they come to watch the funny video and attempt some more problems, they could capitalize on the practice and experience gained when they took the same type of test in the control condition. Therefore, if in the experimental condition we obtained a better performance than in the control condition we would not know whether this was due to the fact that in the experimental condition participants had a positive mood, or to the fact that they had more familiarity with the test. This problem is known as an **order effect**, which means that scores on the DV in each condition may depend on which condition comes first and which comes second. It is, of course, a particular type of confound.

Randomly constituted groups	Times available for repeated presentations to participants	
	Time 1	Time 2
Group 1 (randomly selected half of participants)	experimental (E) condition presented	control (C) condition presented
Group 2 (randomly selected other half of participants)	control (C) condition presented	experimental (E) condition presented

Figure 3.4 Schematic representation of control of order effects by counterbalancing

The best way to deal with order effects is to use **counterbalancing**. This involves giving the two conditions of the experiment in different orders to two randomly selected halves of the participants. That is, we should make sure that half of the participants (Group 1) do the control condition first and the experimental condition second, and that half of them (Group 2) follow the reverse order. We can represent the order of presentation of the experimental (E) and control (C) conditions, rather abstractly, as:

Half participants (Group 1)   E C
Other half participants (Group 2)   C E

See Figure 3.4 for a more detailed schematic representation of how counterbalancing works.

In some cases, for example in an experiment measuring reaction times to a warning sound presented in a noisy environment (the experimental condition) or in a normal environment (the control condition), many presentations of each condition may be possible, and there may be no problem with switching repeatedly between the experimental and control conditions. In that situation, we usually refer to each presentation as a **trial**. Counterbalancing can then be extended to the order of presentation of, say, 10 trials, with five in each condition. Then, we can represent a counterbalanced order for the 10 trials as:

Half participants (Group 1)   E C C E E C C E E C
Other half participants (Group 2)   C E E C C E E C C E

An alternative (and, in principle, preferable) solution for dealing with order effects when there are a number of trials, as in the last example with 10 trials, is to generate a different random order for presenting the five experimental and five control trials for each participant. However, with 20 participants, and therefore 20 different orders, instead of just the two required for counterbalancing, the administration of the experiment may become more complex than is desirable.

Complications (3.3) – Asymmetrical order effects

The preceding discussion of repeated measures designs has treated order effects as being symmetrical, but this is not always the case. Order effects in repeated measures experiments are *symmetrical* if the effect on performance in the control condition, after having already been exposed to the experimental condition, is the same as the effect on performance in the experimental condition, after having already been exposed to the control condition. In other words, if counterbalancing is applied to deal with order effects, when the second condition is presented, the effect on the DV of having already experienced the first condition is the same whichever condition comes first (experimental or control condition) for participants. This would be the expectation if there were a simple effect of practice in the first condition, which elevated scores in the second condition (or a simple effect of fatigue arising from the first condition, which lowered scores in the second condition). Counterbalancing will ensure that symmetrical order effects do not threaten the internal validity of the experiment. Sometimes, however, we may encounter **asymmetrical order effects**. For example, in a repeated measures version of our mood experiment, it is possible that if the neutral film was seen after the funny film, it would seem boring, whereas if it was seen first, it would just seem 'normal'. If, on the other hand, participants' reactions to seeing the funny film did not vary depending on whether it was seen first or second, there might be an overall bias against the neutral film (boring for half of the participants, plus normal for the other half), which would not have arisen if only one or the other film had been seen (i.e., an independent groups design). In this circumstance, counterbalancing would not entirely remove the threat to internal validity posed by the (asymmetrical) order effects.

Another problem that sometimes arises with a repeated measures design is that, by controlling for participant effects, we may introduce a new NV. For instance, in the example above, it was necessary to have two different sets of logical problems (it would be silly to ask participants to solve the same problems twice – on the second occasion they would remember many of their solutions from the first occasion). The two sets of problems are unlikely to be exactly equivalent in difficulty, so 'problem set' becomes an NV. In order to ensure that it is not a systematic NV, it is necessary to try to make the two sets as near equivalent in difficulty as possible, then to arrange for half of the participants to be given one set of problems after the funny video and the other set after the neutral video, and vice versa for the other half.

As we saw above, using a repeated measures design can be a very effective way to control participant systematic NVs, but in some cases it can actually create new problems. So, the question is: When is it a good idea to use a repeated measures design rather than an independent groups design? There is no cut-and-dried answer to that question but there are several considerations that may help you to come to a decision.

1. The closer the task is to requiring a simple response to a simple sensory stimulus (as when responding by pressing different keys when sounds of differing frequencies are presented), the more likely it will be that order effects will be small and that multiple trials will be possible. With multiple trials, order effects are likely to be better controlled.

2. In some experiments, individual differences among participants are likely to have bigger effects on the DV than in other experiments. For example, differences in reaction time may be expected to have a substantial effect on performance in a simulated driving task. The bigger the likely effects of individual differences, the more worthwhile it will be to try to control these differences between participants if a repeated measures design is feasible on other grounds.

3. If a participant is likely to be permanently changed by exposure to one of the conditions of the experiment, he or she should not be exposed to the other condition; this is because, in an important respect, you would effectively be dealing with a 'different' (i.e., changed) participant. This is most likely to occur when the task set for the participant is cognitively or socially complex, as when some sort of complex learning takes place or there is a meaningful social interaction that influences the way a participant construes a situation.

Applying these criteria to our mood experiment, although individual differences in, say, intelligence may be important in that study (#2 above), order effects are likely to be large and multiple trials would probably not be feasible (#1 above). Additionally, the mood experiment is cognitively complex and exposure to one condition is likely to alert participants to what the experiment is about, which might well affect their mood reactions to the videos (#3 above). The mood experiment is not, therefore, a likely candidate for a repeated measures design. For an additional reason for coming to this conclusion, see Complications (3.3).

At this point, it is worthwhile to provide an example of an experiment for which a repeated measures design might be a more appropriate choice. Suppose that we want to test the hypothesis that people with symmetric facial features are perceived as more attractive than people whose features are asymmetric. To test this hypothesis we could simply design an experiment in which the IV is the nature of the facial features of some target people, whose pictures are shown to participants, and the DV would be the rated level of attractiveness of the target people. Basically, we could create two conditions, one in which participants judge the attractiveness of people with symmetrical facial features, and one in which participants judge people with asymmetrical features. Now, in this experiment, individual preferences are quite likely to be important and order effects and multiple alternating trials would be unlikely to be problematic. We might well conclude, therefore, that we would not need to use different participants in the two conditions. In fact, the same participants could judge both the symmetrical and the asymmetrical faces. By doing so, we would make sure that, if we obtained the expected differences in ratings (i.e., the symmetrical faces are rated as more attractive than the asymmetrical ones), results would not be affected by participant variables.

We can see from the preceding example that a repeated measure design is a way of controlling participant systematic NVs that is substantially based on the idea of making them *constant*. In this respect, it has parallels with one of the strategies that can be used to control situational systematic NVs (i.e., elimination of the NV) that we discussed earlier.

If a repeated measures design is not feasible, some control of relevant participant variables can be achieved in a modification of an independent groups design, in which roughly equivalent people are allocated to the two conditions. Basically, we can match each person in the experimental condition with a specific person in the control condition, by assuring that they are equivalent on age, sex, occupation, intelligence, or any other variable that could potentially affect scores on the DV. The way that this would be done if we wanted to match participants on, say, intelligence, would be to administer an intelligence test and use the results to rank the participants. The two occupying the first and second ranks would then be assigned, one to each condition, using a random procedure (e.g., a coin toss) to decide which one went into each condition. This would be repeated for the pair occupying the third and fourth ranks and so on down to the lowest scoring pair. This design is known as a **matched subjects design**, and constitutes an attempt to approach the control of participant variation achieved in the repeated measures design. However, this design is not always practicable. While matching people on variables such as sex and age is straightforward, matching them on variables such as personality, intelligence, background and so on may be complicated and very time consuming. In addition, if there are several variables on which it would be desirable to match participants, it can be difficult to find pairs who are a reasonable match on all of those variables.

When it would be inappropriate or impractical to use a repeated measures or matched subjects design, the *independent groups design* is always an option. Recall that this is the type of design upon which our example experiment is based. You will have noticed that we assigned different participants to the two different conditions on the basis of a strictly **random procedure**. We did not specify at the time what sort of random procedure we used in our experiment. Well, a possible strategy would be to put 40 cards with the participants' names written on them into a box, and then pick 20 cards out without looking in the box. A coin might then be tossed to decide whether those 20 participants would be allocated to the experimental or control condition. By allocating participants at random we expect the groups to be fairly well matched on all possible participant variables. Obviously, randomization does not ensure that the two groups will be *perfectly* matched on any particular participant variable. On the other hand, we can be confident that a systematic error produced by participant

NVs will be avoided, because, for any participant NV, there is an equal chance of either condition containing a preponderance of people either high or low on that variable (see Chapter 5 for a detailed discussion of the importance of randomization). Recall that a systematic NV implies that there is a pre-existing bias making it likely that *one particular condition* will contain more people who are high on the variable.

To summarize this section on the control of participant NVs, consider that although all three methods outlined above can eliminate systematic differences between conditions as far as participants' characteristics are concerned, they differ in the amount of random variation which remains to obscure the experimental effect. Basically, the repeated measures design will remove all the random variation between the participants (though we saw that this is at some cost). The matched subject design will remove only some random participant variation (usually just for one or two variables, and then not completely). Finally, the independent groups design will not remove any random participant variation (but in this design participant variation can be very effectively randomized).

CONTROLLING SYSTEMATIC NUISANCE VARIABLES AS A DESIGN ISSUE

To conclude, we must emphasize that the effects of systematic NVs is a design issue, and, contrary to what we do in order to deal with random NVs, we cannot use statistical procedures to deal with them. In fact, the ideal solution is to change the design of the experiment to eliminate the confounding NV or convert it into a random NV. However, as we saw above, either elimination or randomization may not always be possible. In that case, we would have a quasi-experiment rather than a true experiment (see Additional information (3.1)).

Additional information (3.1) – More on quasi-experiments

We saw in Additional information 2.5 that one reason for a study being labelled as a quasi-experiment is when the IV is not actually manipulated by the researcher (as with 'age' or 'ethnicity'). However, there is another reason; that is, when either the participants, or the available times for them to attend, are not *randomly* allocated between the experimental and control conditions. Obviously, if the participants in one condition attend together at the same time and those in the other condition attend at a different time, any differences that there happen to be between the two occasions will affect the two groups in systematically different ways. To summarize, a true experiment requires that levels of the IV are set by the researcher and that participants (and the times available for them to be treated) are randomly assigned to the two treatment conditions. In a case where these conditions are not met, we have a quasi-experiment rather than a true experiment, and the conclusion we can draw from our results is much weaker.

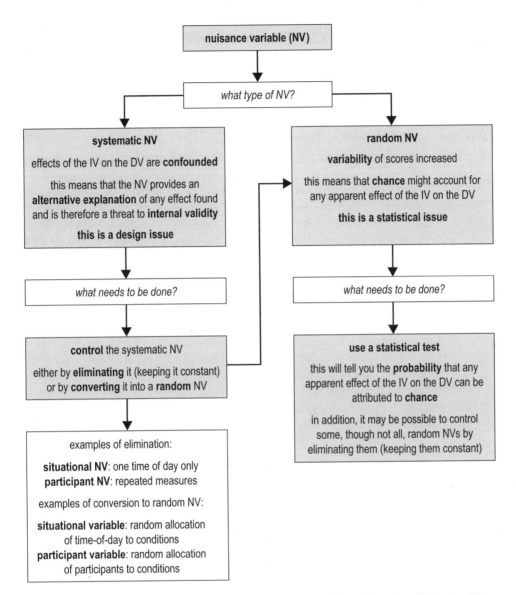

Figure 3.5 Effects of systematic and random nuisance variables and the safeguarding of internal validity

See Figure 3.5 for a summary of effects of systematic and random NVs and how internal validity can be safeguarded by dealing with systematic NVs.

Additional information (3.2) – Three common threats to experimental validity

Three particular categories of threat to the validity of experiments have received much attention and are frequently mentioned as a group in discussions of experimental validity. These are the effects of **social desirability**, **demand characteristics** and **experimenter expectancy**.

Social desirability is the extent to which people's behaviour appears acceptable to other people. It can lead participants to behave in ways that they perceive to be desirable to the researcher. This is probably best viewed as a threat to construct validity. What was intended as a measure of, say, aggressiveness, may in fact be, at least in part, a measure of what the participant believes to be 'socially correct'. Threats to the construct validity of experiments due to social desirability can be reduced by not making the measures too obvious.

Demand characteristics are cues that convey an experimental hypothesis to participants. They are most readily construed as threats to internal validity, leading participants to behave in ways that will confirm the hypothesis in order to please the experimenter. They are therefore confounded with the IV, providing an alternative explanation of any effect on the DV that may be found. Threats to internal validity due to demand characteristics can be reduced by creating a *cover story* (you may remember that we told participants that our experiment is about the effect of watching television on performance, when actually it was about the effect of mood on performance).

Experimenter expectancy is the tendency of the experimenter to construct and/or conduct an experiment in such a way that it is more likely to support the hypothesis. As with demand characteristics, experimenter expectancy effects seem to best fit the category of threats to internal validity. They are confounded with the effect of the IV, so providing an alternative explanation of any experimental effects found. Threats to internal validity due to experimenter expectancy can be reduced by making sure that the experimenter has no knowledge of the hypothesis to be tested (i.e., he or she is 'blind' to the hypothesis), or by preventing participants from interacting with the experimenter.

External Validity

External validity is the extent to which the relationship between the variables observed by the researcher in the context of the experiment can be generalized to different contexts and individuals. Obviously, external validity is threatened by any feature of the experiment that makes it somehow unique, and therefore unrepresentative of what is found in other (external) situations. Remember that there are limits to how far external validity can be achieved within an experiment. This is because we need to deal with many NVs by holding them constant (i.e., deliberately making the experimental situation 'unique'). The requirements of reducing variability in the data and making the situation representative of the 'real world' pull in opposite directions! Nonetheless, it is always worthwhile considering ways in which external validity can be improved without increasing the threat to internal validity or introducing so much random variability into the data that it becomes difficult to demonstrate a systematic effect of the IV on the DV. Remember that external validity is useless if an experiment lacks internal validity (i.e., no causal effect can be inferred) or random variability is too great for an effect of the IV on the DV to show up statistically (see Chapter 5). External validity may be subdivided into three specific types: **ecological validity**, **population validity**, and **temporal validity**.

Ecological validity

Ecological validity is the extent to which our findings can be generalized to settings other than the one we have experimentally created, especially natural settings. Basically, the question is: does the experimental setting that has produced some findings adequately reflect what normally happens in real life? For instance, consider again the study of facial attractiveness that we discussed in the previous section. This study was intended to test the hypothesis that people with symmetrical facial features are perceived as more attractive than people whose features are asymmetric, and did so by showing participants pictures of people with either symmetrical or asymmetrical facial features, and asking them to rate these people for attractiveness. But is this way of judging facial attractiveness a fair reflection of the ways in which we judge facial attractiveness in real, everyday life? In fact, in real life people's faces tend to change expressions, to be highly dynamic rather than static. This might put into question the ecological validity of the experimental setting and findings.

Population validity

Population validity refers to the extent to which experimental findings can be generalized to people who differ in some important respects from those who participated in the experiment. For instance, a typical aspect of psychology experiments is that of using university undergraduate students as participants, because it is easy to recruit them. However, there are many aspects of students' thinking and behaviour that cannot be generalized to other groups (e.g., manual workers, uneducated people, elderly people). What is more, the students used in experiments very often have a Western background. This is a further problem, as people from an Eastern culture may differ from Western people on many crucial psychological dimensions. This has been demonstrated by cross-cultural research showing, for instance, that people in Western and Eastern cultures describe and understand themselves in radically different ways. While Western people understand themselves in terms of personality traits and dispositions (e.g., 'I am hardworking', 'I am extrovert'), people from Eastern cultures emphasize roles and category membership (e.g., 'I am a father of two', 'I am Chinese').

Temporal validity

Temporal validity has to do with the extent to which findings can be generalized to other time periods. Are the psychological processes that we observe today in our laboratories the same as those that characterized people in the near or long past, or as those that will characterize people in the future? People's ways of perceiving the world, thinking and behaving may undergo changes over history. For instance, what we said above about the existence of different ways of self-description and self-conception in different cultural areas of the world could be true of different epochs as well. In fact, social scientists generally agree that the contemporary Western obsession with personality traits and inner dispositions is a relatively recent development, which has replaced a traditional understanding of self exclusively based on inter-personal connections and shared membership of groups.

See Figure 3.6 for a summary of what you should be wary of when dealing with validity issues.

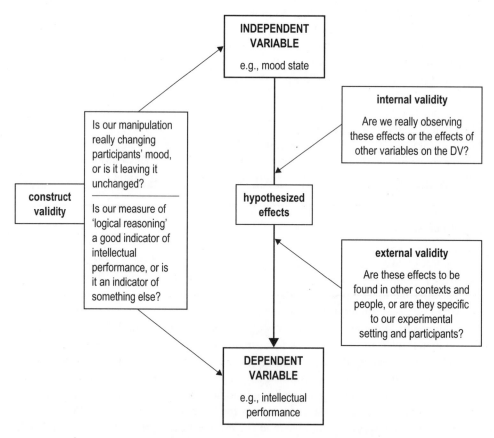

Figure 3.6   Questions you should ask yourself in order to deal with issues of 'construct', 'internal' and 'external' validity

Conclusions

To conclude, how could we summarize the logic of an experiment in a very concise fashion? Well, we could say that an experiment is a technique that allows researchers to collect evidence to demonstrate the effect of one variable upon another. The researcher manipulates the IV (i.e., deliberately changes its levels), does his or her best to ensure that all nuisance variables are held constant or made random, and then observes how the DV changes. In a well-designed and well-conducted experiment, changes in the DV can only have been produced by the manipulation of the IV. That means that, if changes in the DV were indeed observed, they could be ascribed to changes in the IV; in other words, if changes in the DV were observed we could infer a cause–effect relationship between the IV and the DV.

SUMMARY OF CHAPTER

- Experiments may have shortcomings that prevent us from using the obtained results to draw valid conclusions about the hypothesized cause-effect relationship. Therefore, researchers must ensure that the experiment is designed in a way that confers validity. There are three types of validity that researchers must pursue: 'construct', 'internal', and 'external' validity.

- Construct validity refers to the extent to which our IV and DV adequately reflect the theoretical constructs whose cause–effect relationship we want to investigate.

- Internal validity is the extent to which we are really observing the effects that the IV exerts on the DV. Because the DV is normally influenced by variables other than the IV – defined as 'nuisance' variables (NVs) – psychologists must use various strategies to safeguard the internal validity of an experiment.

- When an NV affects scores in one condition of the experiment, but not in the other, we have a 'systematic error'. This constitutes a serious threat to internal validity because the effects of the NV on the DV are confounded with the effects of the IV on the DV. In this case it is necessary to control the NV; this is achieved by modifying the experimental design.

- How systematic errors are avoided depends on whether the NV that could cause the error is a 'situational' variable (i.e., concerning aspects of the experimental setting) or a 'participant' variable (i.e., inherent to participants' characteristics such as personality, intelligence etc.).

- Situational variables may be prevented from causing systematic errors by maintaining the experimental situation constant across conditions or by allocating participants to the different conditions at random, thereby turning the systematic error into a 'random error' – which does not threaten internal validity. We have random error when an NV has an equal possibility of affecting each condition of the experiment.

- The best way to prevent participant variables from causing systematic errors is to use the same participants in both conditions of the experiment (repeated measures design) or, alternatively, to use participants who are matched on relevant characteristics (matched subjects design). If neither of these two options is practical, participants can be randomly allocated to conditions (independent groups design).

- External validity is the extent to which the relationship between the variables observed by the researcher in the context of the experiment can be generalized outside the specific context and participants of the experiment.

CHAPTER FOUR

Describing Data

In Chapter 2, we explained how to design and conduct an experiment aimed at demonstrating the hypothesized effect of one variable upon another. To exemplify, we showed you how to run an experiment that would test the hypothesis that 'the more positive the mood of people, the better their intellectual performance'. Basically, we proposed to create two conditions, one in which a group of participants watch a movie excerpt with a funny content (the experimental condition) and one in which another group of participants watch an excerpt with an emotionally neutral content (the control condition). We reasoned that participants in the experimental condition will end up having a positive mood while participants in the control condition will maintain a neutral mood, and that, as a consequence, participants in the experimental condition will perform better than those in the control condition. We also decided to 'measure' the level of intellectual performance by asking participants to solve 10 logical problems. That means that each participant would end up with a score ranging from 0 (meaning that the participant has not solved any of the 10 problems) to 10 (meaning that the participant has solved all the problems).

Let us go on using the same experiment as an example. Now we have two sets of scores. Because we used 20 participants in each condition of the experiment, we have one set of 20 scores produced in the experimental condition and one set of 20 scores produced in the control condition (see Table 4.1 for hypothetical sets of scores). These scores are still in the form of **raw data**, because no attempt has yet been made to make sense of them. Now the question is: How can we use these scores to demonstrate that participants in the experimental condition performed better than those in the control condition? Well, there are some procedures to be followed and statistical tests to be used, which will be discussed in detail in the following chapters. However, before we try to draw any inference from our data, we must give a good, clear and thorough description of the raw data. This is what **descriptive statistics** is about, and this is what we will discuss in this chapter, using our main example throughout.

Data description comprises two operations: (i) organizing data and (ii) summarizing data. So, let us discuss the different ways in which our raw data can be organized and summarized.

Table 4.1 Hypothetical raw data. The scores (minimum = 0, maximum = 10) are based on number of logical problems solved, and were obtained by participants in the 2 conditions of the experiment

Experimental condition	Control condition
Participants tried to solve the problems after watching a funny excerpt, so they performed in a *positive mood*	Participants tried to solve the problems after watching a neutral excerpt, so they were in an *neutral mood*
7	6
8	4
7	6
6	5
4	5
6	4
7	7
5	6
8	2
7	3
9	4
6	8
7	6
8	5
7	7
9	6
7	5
7	6
5	5
6	7

Organizing Data

If we simply look at our data in the present form, we find it hard to make any sense of them. A cursory inspection will reveal that the highest score in the experimental condition is 9, and the lowest is 4. On the other hand, the highest score in the control condition is 8, while the lowest is 2. This is an interesting aspect of our data. However, we cannot tell anything about the spread of the data in the two conditions. For instance, are they spread evenly between the minimum and the maximum score, or clustered around some specific value? To gain a better idea of the nature of our data we can start by giving them some form of organization by putting them in a more comprehensible and economical format.

Frequency distributions

If we take a closer look at each set of scores we will realize that, while some values occur only once, others appear more than once. For instance, if we focus our attention on the experimental condition, we can see that there is only one participant who solved four logical problems, but that eight participants solved seven logical problems. Now, the frequency of occurrence of the scores in our raw data is in itself an interesting aspect of the data and constitutes useful information. Therefore, the first thing we can do to organize our data is to count how many times each value occurs, that is, to find out the frequency of each score. Taken together, these frequencies comprise a **frequency distribution**, which may then be reported in a table such as the one in Table 4.2.

As you can see, in Table 4.2 we have four columns of numbers. The first two columns, starting from the left, concern the experimental condition and show the scores that have been produced by at least one participant, starting from the lowest score (first column), and how many times (i.e., how frequently) each score has been produced (second column). The remaining two columns are concerned with the control condition and, again, show the scores produced by at least one participant (third column) and the frequency with which each score has been produced (fourth column). Also, at the foot of each of the two columns reporting frequencies you can see the total number of participants in the condition (i.e., 20), indicated by the letter N (clearly, N is equivalent to the sum of the frequencies).

By means of this table of frequency distributions, the characteristics of each set of scores, as well as the nature of the relationship between the two sets, are presented in a more concise fashion. For instance, we can see that in the experimental condition there are two participants scoring over 8, which is the highest score in the control condition. We can also see that in the experimental condition the score of

Table **4.2** Reorganization of raw data reported in table 4.1, in the form of frequency distributions of scores produced by participants in the two conditions

Experimental condition		Control condition	
Score	Frequency	Score	Frequency
4	1	2	1
5	2	3	1
6	4	4	3
7	8	5	5
8	3	6	6
9	2	7	3
		8	1
	(N = 20)		(N = 20)

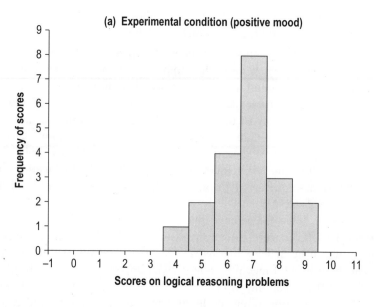

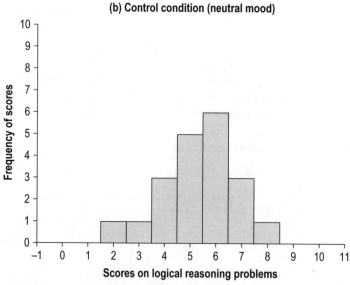

Figure 4.1 Histograms showing data in the two conditions of our experiment: (a) experimental condition (positive mood); (b) control condition (neutral mood)

7 is by far the most frequent score, while in the control condition scores tend to cluster around two central values, that is 5, which is obtained by five participants, and 6, which is obtained by six participants.

In order to obtain a more vivid impression of the nature of the data produced by participants in an experiment, it is possible to display frequency distributions in graphical ways. There are many different techniques that can be used to display frequency distributions pictorially. These include techniques such as box and whisker plots, and stem and leaf diagrams, but in this book we will focus on the two most commonly used techniques, that is, the **histogram** and the **frequency polygon**.

The histogram

The histogram is based on a set of columns (i.e., vertical boxes) that lie on a horizontal axis. Each single column represents a specific score that occurred at least once in the data. The height of a column corresponds to a value on a vertical axis indicating the frequency with which the score represented by the column occurred. The more frequent a score (i.e., the more often a score occurred) the higher the column.

The histograms shown in Figure 4.1 display data obtained in the two conditions of our experiment. If you compare the two histograms, you can spot at a glance the different distribution of scores in the two conditions. For instance, it is clear that, as expected, scores in the experimental condition (positive mood) are generally higher than scores in the control condition (neutral mood).

SPSS operations (4.1) – Creating a histogram

To produce the histograms in Figure 4.1 you should proceed as follows. If the scores for each condition have been entered in a separate column as they are shown in Table 4.1 (this is how they would be entered if we had a repeated measures design):

(i)   Go to the menu at the top of the screen and click on *Graphs*, then click on *Histogram*.
(ii) Click the variable (condition) that you are interested in and move it into the *Variable* box.
(iii) Click on *Display normal curve* (see note below) and then *OK*.

If the scores for both conditions have been entered in a single column and there is another column indicating (e.g., by entry of 1 or 2) to which condition the score in that row belongs (this is how they should be entered for an independent groups design):

(i)   Go to the menu at the top of the screen and click on *Data*, select *Split File*, click the radio button *Organize output by groups*, select the variable that indicates which condition scores belong to, move that variable into the *Groups Based on* box and click *OK*.
(ii) From the top menu, select *Graphs*, and then *Histogram*.
(iii) Select the variable containing the scores and move it into the *Variable* box.
(iv) Click on *Display normal curve* (see note below) and then on *OK*.

Note that by clicking on *Display normal curve*, a line will be superimposed over each histogram, showing how a normal curve for that distribution would look (we will be discussing 'normal distributions' in a later section of this chapter).

Complications (4.1) – Histogram or 'bar chart'?

Some researchers use the term 'bar chart' instead of 'histogram'. So, don't worry if in another textbook you see a figure like our Figure 4.1 described as 'bar chart'. However, most researchers use the term 'histogram' for the type of graphical representation we have discussed above, and 'bar chart' to indicate a specific type of graphical representation that is like the histogram except in one important respect: the bars are not contiguous (i.e., they do not 'touch' one another, they are separated). This type of chart is used when the DV is categorical.

Suppose that we are investigating the effects of two different types of environment (say, either a classroom or a public garden) on children's 'style of play' when they are in a group, and that we therefore observe a group of 20 children playing in a classroom and, on another occasion, the same group of 20 children playing in a public garden. Also, suppose that, on the basis of systematic observation, the general style of play of each child is judged as being either 'cooperative', or 'competitive', or 'individual'. Finally, suppose that we find that, concerning play in the classroom, nine children are cooperative, five are competitive and six play individually. In this case, the classroom data can be represented with the bar chart in Figure 4.2. As you can see, the bars on the horizontal axis are not contiguous because if they were the graph would give the (wrong) impression that the bars are part of a continuum going from low to high values, while they actually represent different categories or classes of behaviour.

The frequency polygon

The frequency polygon is in many ways like a histogram. However, here the columns are replaced by dots plotted at the midpoint of the top of each column. In addition, the dots are joined up with straight lines and, at each end of the polygon, the line goes down to touch the horizontal axis at the midpoint of the next empty unit (unless there are no further units, in which case the line will end at that point).

The histogram and the frequency polygon are both effective ways of displaying data. However, consider that if you want to display two sets of data simultaneously, then the frequency polygon is more effective than the histogram. In fact, as you can see in Figure 4.3, the frequency polygon for the experimental condition and the frequency polygon for the control condition can be accommodated within the same pair of axes. Not only do these two polygons not interfere with each other visually, but by overlapping them you can make useful comparisons.

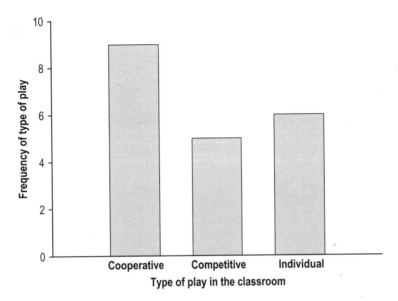

Figure 4.2 Bar chart for a hypothetical study of children's style of play in different environments

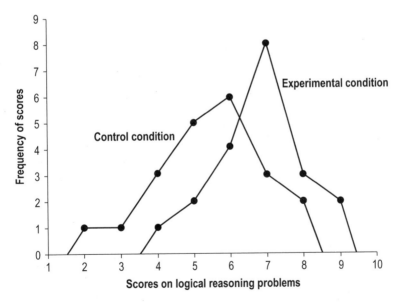

Figure 4.3 Frequency polygons for the data in the conditions of our experiment

Summarizing data

The methods described above help to organize data by showing underlying structures and patterns that are not easy to spot in raw data. However, it is also possible, and desirable, to make a summary of a data set, by extracting single indices or measures from the data. These measures may concern two specific aspects of the data set, that is (i) the average, most representative score (these are called measures of **central tendency**), and (ii) the extent to which the scores are spread on either side of the average value (these are called measures of **dispersion**, or measures of **variability**).

These measures are very useful for forming a better idea of the general features of a set of data. In fact, we often use these measures in our everyday life, without realizing that we are dealing with 'descriptive statistics'! For instance, if a supporter of Dundee United football club was asked how many people attend the home games, he or she would probably say something like 'well, I guess most of the time there are around 4,000 spectators, but when Dundee United plays Rangers or Celtic, there may be as many as 10,000. On the other hand, when the team does really badly the number can go down to about 2,000.' Clearly, what this description does is to provide both information about the typical number of spectators (a measure of central tendency), and information about the extent to which that number may stretch or shrink (a measure of dispersion). In the next sections we will discuss the most useful measures of central tendency and dispersion.

Measures of central tendency

As we said above, a set of data may be represented by a single index (a measure of central tendency) that constitutes the average, most representative score in the data. The most commonly used measures of central tendency are the **mean**, the **median**, and the **mode**.

THE MEAN

The 'mean' is equivalent to what most people understand by the term 'average'. However, the term 'mean' is technically more precise than the term 'average', as there are various types of 'average', while the term 'mean' has a very specific meaning.

The mean of a specific set of scores is the sum of all the scores in the set divided by the number of scores. Although you may use statistical packages to calculate the mean (see SPSS operations (4.2), below), it may be useful for you to calculate the mean of the set of scores obtained in the experimental condition in our experiment in order to get more familiar with this important measure. So, to start with, you calculate the sum of the 20 scores, that is: $7 + 8 + 7 + 6 + 4 + 6 + 7 + 5 + 8 + 7 + 9 + 6 + 7 + 8 + 7 + 9 + 7 + 7 + 5 + 6 = 136$; then, you divide the sum by the number of scores, that is: $136/20 = 6.80$. It is worth noting that participants in the experiment could not solve 6.8 logical problems! That implies that the mean may not occur as a value in the data set; nevertheless, it gives a good idea of the central tendency of the set. At this point, it may be interesting to know that the mean score of participants in the control condition is 5.35. This is telling you that, as expected, participants in the experimental condition (positive mood) have solved more problems than participants in the control condition (neutral mood). This piece of information is useful, but remember that we cannot use it to take for granted that our hypothesis is correct: we need to use a statistical test (discussed later on in this book) to draw that conclusion.

Formulae (4.1) – The mean

The procedure for finding the mean, which is described above, can be translated into a mathematical formula. As with all formulae, it makes use of symbols; however, once you know the meaning of the symbols you'll have no problems in appreciating the meaning of the formula. This is what the formula looks like:

$$\bar{X} = \frac{\Sigma X}{N}$$

And this is what the symbols mean:

X = any score in the data set
$\bar{X}$ = the mean
Σ = sum of
N = the number of scores in the data set

If you now have another look at the formula in the light of your knowledge of the symbols, you will be able to understand that it means the following: the arithmetic mean is equal to the sum of the scores in the set, divided by the number of scores in the set.

We now must deal with a little complication. You need to know that statisticians make a distinction between **populations** and **samples**. A population is generally a wide, or even infinite, set of something (e.g., students at Dundee University, trees in Scotland, elephants in Africa, stars in the Milky Way). Populations should always be well defined, but are quite often ill defined in practice. A sample is a subset of a population. For example, suppose the 40 students we used for our experiment were all students at Dundee University. In this case the 40 students would constitute a sample, while all the students at Dundee University would be the population from which the sample has been selected.

Now, in order to indicate the mean we are using the symbol $\bar{X}$, because we are referring to the mean of a sample. However, if you were referring to the mean of a population, you would be using a different symbol, that is the Greek letter μ (pronounced 'mew').

The mean is an excellent measure of central tendency, and – as you will appreciate in the following chapters – is very useful because it is used in other types of statistical analysis. However, it has a serious limitation: it is a very 'sensitive' measure. This is because some unusual scores – or even just one – may dramatically change its value, thereby giving a very distorted image of the central tendency of a set of scores. Imagine, for instance, that you want to calculate how much, on average, the members of your family watch television in a week. Suppose that there are 5 members in your family, and that every member watches television 6 hours per week, except your little brother, who watches television 28 hours. If you decide to use the mean as a measure of central tendency, you will end up with 10.4 hours per week. Now, if you stated that in your family people typically watch 10.4 hours per week of television, you would be arithmetically accurate, but would give a very misleading impression of the real situation! After all, 10.4 hours is very much above 6 hours, which is the number of hours spent in front of the television by the large majority of the members of your family.

THE MEDIAN

The median is that value of a data set that has as many scores above it as below it. In other words, if you organize a set of scores from the smallest to the largest, the median is the score in the middle. So, suppose that you must find the median of the following set of scores: 4, 2, 7, 6, 7, 3, 8, 4, 7. You will operate as follows. First, put the scores in order of magnitude, that is: 2, 3, 4, 4, 6, 7, 7, 7, 8. Then, take the score falling exactly in the middle. This will be the score 6, as this specific score has four scores falling below it and four scores falling above it.

In some cases things can be slightly more complicated. Note that the set we used in the above example comprised an odd number of scores, that is, nine scores. However, a set might comprise an even number of scores. So, suppose that you have the following set: 2, 4, 6, 3, 7, 3, 7, 5. Now, by putting these scores in order from the smallest to the largest you will obtain the following: 2, 3, 3, 4, 5, 6, 7, 7. In this case it is impossible to find one score that falls exactly in the middle. In fact, this cannot be 4, as this score has three scores below and four scores above; nor it can be 5, as this score has four scores below and three scores above. All we can conclude is that there are two most central scores, but none of them is truly in the middle. So, which is the median in this case? It is a hypothetical number that falls halfway between 4 and 5. This number can be expressed in terms of the mean of the two central scores, that is (4 + 5)/2, which is equal to 4.5.

However, note that with some sets comprising an even number of scores, finding the median does not require calculating the mean between the two most central scores. Consider for instance the set of 20 scores produced by participants in the experimental condition of our experiment. If you put the scores in order of magnitude you will obtain the following: 4, 5, 5, 6, 6, 6, 6, 7, 7, 7, 7, 7, 7, 7, 7, 8, 8, 8, 9, 9. Now, the two most central scores are both 7. In this case the median is simply, and obviously, 7!

Note that, contrary to the mean, there is no symbol for the median. This is simply identified by the word 'median' (although, very occasionally, psychologists use the abbreviated word 'Md').

A strength of the median is that, unlike the mean, it is totally unaffected by extremely high or low scores. So, for instance, in our experimental condition the median would still be 7, even if the lowest score in the set were 0. On the other hand, when a set of scores has a rather unusual pattern of distribution, the median may not indicate the typical score at all. Suppose that a teacher has a small class of 9 pupils, and that they get the following grades in a maths test (where the grades range from 0 to 20): 9, 10, 10, 10, 10, 15, 17, 18, 20. In this case the median would be 10: hardly a good representation of the typical grade! The mean, which is 13.2, would certainly constitute a better index in this case.

THE MODE

The mode is the value that occurs most frequently in a set of scores. So, with regard to our experiment, the modal value in the experimental condition is 7, while the modal value in the control condition is 6.

Like the median, there is no symbol for the mode. This is identified by the word 'mode', though some people may indicate it by the abbreviation 'Mo'.

The mode represents a very simple criterion for extracting a typical score from a set of data – as when it might be stated that the typical shoe size for adult males in Britain is size 9 – but it has some serious limitations when used for very small data sets. For instance, to say that 6 is the most frequently obtained score in the control condition is technically correct, but at the same time it is not a very good representation of typicality, in that the score 5 occurs almost as frequently as 6. That also implies that if only one of those participants who resolved six logical problems had actually resolved five problems, the mode would have moved from 6 to 5. This shows that the mode may be an unreliable measure of central tendency.

Measures of dispersion

A set of data may be summarized by a measure indicating the extent to which data . are 'spread out', or dispersed, around the central value. There are several measures of dispersion; however, we will deal only with the three most commonly used ones, namely the **range**, the **variance** and the **standard deviation**.

THE RANGE

The range is the simplest measure of dispersion. To find the range you just calculate the difference between the highest and the lowest score. So, the range of the set of scores in the experimental condition of our experiment is calculated as follows: 9 (the highest score) − 4 (the lowest score) = 5. Unfortunately, while this measure is easily calculated and understood, it tends to be too crude. Consider, for instance, the following two sets of 15 scores. Set A: 3, 3, 4, 5, 5, 6, 6, 6, 7, 7, 7, 8, 8, 9, 9. Set B: 3, 5, 5, 5, 5, 6, 6, 6, 6, 6, 7, 7, 7, 7, 9. Now, both sets have the same range (set A: 9 − 3 = 6; set B: 9 − 3 = 6); but does that mean that scores in these two sets are

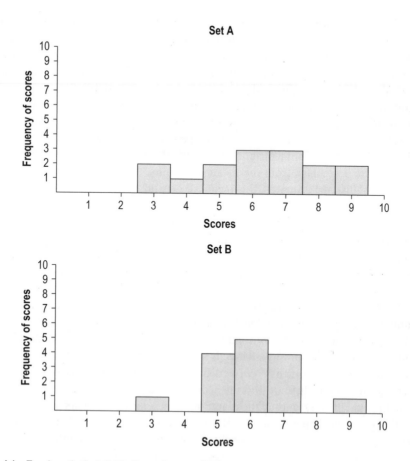

Figure 4.4 Two hypothetical distributions of scores, having the same range

equally dispersed? It clearly does not! In fact, while the scores in set A are very much spread out on both sides of the central value, the scores in set B tend to be bunched tightly around the mean. (The difference between the distributions of these two sets of scores can be better appreciated by looking at Figure 4.4.) As you can see, the big limitation of the range is that it tells us nothing about the positioning of the scores in between the minimum and the maximum ones, and about how much they generally differ from the mean. Fortunately, statisticians have devised more plausible and useful measures of dispersion, which we will discuss in the next two sections.

THE VARIANCE AND THE STANDARD DEVIATION

The variance and the standard deviation (often abbreviated as 'SD') are very important measures of dispersion. In order to appreciate the meaning of these two measures, it is necessary to discuss briefly the notion of **mean deviation**.

The mean deviation is a rather intuitive measure of dispersion of a set of data. It refers to how much, on average, scores deviate (are different) from the mean. For instance, consider the following two sets. Set A: 3, 5, 8, 11, 13; Set B: 6, 7, 8, 9, 10. Now, while the two sets have the same mean, that is 8, it is obvious that scores in Set A tend to deviate from the mean more than scores in Set B. But how much do the scores in the two different sets deviate from the mean, on average? What is the typical deviation? To answer this question you can simply find the deviation of each score from the mean (i.e., the difference between each score and the mean, ignoring the direction of the difference), and then find the mean of the deviations. So, in Set A, the score 3 deviates from the mean by 5 units, the score 5 deviates by 3 units, the score 8 is just the same as the mean score and so it deviates by 0 units, the score 11 deviates by 3 units, and the score 13 deviates by 5 units. The sum of these deviations is $5 + 3 + 0 + 3 + 5 = 16$ and their mean is $16/5 = 3.2$. If you follow the same procedure for Set B, you will find that in this case the mean deviation is 1.2. In sum, the typical distance of a score from the mean is 3.2 in Set A, and 1.2 in Set B. Note that if the direction of each deviation had been retained, they would always sum to zero, as the positive and negative deviations are always equally balanced on either side of the mean. To understand why this is so, consider the four numbers, 2, 3, 6 and 1. They add up to 12 and their mean is $12/4 = 3$. Now, look at the deviations of the four numbers from their mean (i.e., -1, 0, 3 and -2) and add them up. They sum to zero and, because of the way the mean is calculated, this will be true of the sum of the positive and negative deviations of any set of numbers around their mean.

At this point, it is easy to understand what the *variance* is about: the variance is like the mean deviation, apart from the fact that, instead of ignoring the signs of the deviations, they are all converted into positive values by squaring them (when a negative value, say -2, is squared, the answer is always a positive value, in this case 4). The sum of the squared deviations is obtained and then divided by the number of scores in the set minus 1 (the reason for subtracting 1 from the number of scores is explained in Complications 4.2). So, considering the above example, the variance can be found with the following operations: $(-5)^2 + (-3)^2 + 0^2 + 3^2 + 5^2 = 25 + 9 + 0 + 9 + 25 = 68$, then $68/(5 - 1) = 17$. Unlike the mean deviation, the variance has no obvious intuitive meaning: it is simply an abstract measure that increases as the amount of dispersion in the data increases. The more varied the scores, the larger the variance. The variance happens to have some useful mathematical properties when we come to making statistical inferences from our data, and therefore it is much more commonly used than the mean deviation.

Thinking about the meaning of the average *squared* deviation of a set of scores is awkward. One solution is to simply take the square root of the variance. This yields a measure of dispersion called the *standard deviation*, which is usually preferred over the variance when summarizing data (i.e., descriptive statistics). So, if we refer to the above example again, the standard deviation of the set of five data will be $\sqrt{17} = 4.12$.

Formulae (4.2) – The variance and the standard deviation

The formula for the variance, whose symbol is s^2, is as follows:

$$s^2 = \frac{\Sigma(X - \bar{X})^2}{N - 1}$$

This amounts to the following operations: (i) square the differences between each score and the mean, (ii) calculate the sum of the squared differences, and (iii) divide this by the number of scores in the set minus 1 – see Complications (4.2).

Given that the standard deviation is simply the square root of the variance, its formula is this:

$$s = \sqrt{\frac{\Sigma(X - \bar{X})^2}{N - 1}}$$

It may be useful to note that the variance and the standard deviation both have a **computational formula**, that is, a formula that retains the same mathematical characteristics as the defining formula, but is easier to use for calculations done by hand or with a calculator. Different textbooks tend to suggest different computational formulae, but obviously they all lead to the same result. So, we will suggest our own favourite ones, but do not worry if this does not strictly correspond to what you might find in other textbooks:

$$s^2 = \frac{\Sigma X^2 - \dfrac{(\Sigma X)^2}{N}}{N - 1}$$

$$s = \sqrt{\frac{\Sigma X^2 - \dfrac{(\Sigma X)^2}{N}}{N - 1}}$$

Here you must be careful not to confuse ΣX^2, which means that you first square the scores and then add those squares together, and $(\Sigma X)^2$, which means that you first add all the scores and then square the total.

Remember that the mean for a sample and the mean for a population have different symbols – as discussed in Formulae 4.1. Now, this is true also for the variance and the standard deviation. Basically, the symbols s^2 and s indicate the variance and the standard deviation of a sample, but the variance and the standard deviation of a population are indicated as σ^2 and as σ respectively (σ is also a Greek letter, pronounced as 'sigma').

Finally, it might be useful to know that the formulae for the variance and standard deviation of a population are slightly different from the formulae for the variance and standard deviation of a sample. More precisely, to find the variance and the standard deviation of a population you do not need to subtract 1 from N in the denominator – for an explanation, see Complications (4.2). So:

$$\sigma^2 = \frac{\Sigma(X - \bar{X})^2}{N}$$

$$\sigma = \sqrt{\frac{\Sigma(X - \bar{X})^2}{N}}$$

Complications (4.2) – N − 1 and N in the denominators of variance and SD formulae

Before starting, let us warn you that you might have trouble following this. If so, don't worry. It is okay just to accept that we use N − 1 in the denominator for sample variance and SD 'because it works'.

The reason for dividing by N − 1 instead of N to get the average of the squared deviations from the mean (i.e., the variance or SD) for a sample is that the mean of the sample is just an estimate of the population mean. Once you have estimated the mean and used it to calculate all deviations but the last one (i.e., in the calculation of $\Sigma(X - \bar{X})$, the last difference must be the value that makes the positive and negative deviations from the mean add up to zero. So, adopting the same example that we used previously, if the numbers, 2, 3, 6 and 1 were a sample from a larger population of scores and we used them to estimate the mean of the population, our estimated mean would be 3. If we then obtained any three of the deviations of the scores from this mean, say the first three (−1, 0 and 3), the only value that the last deviation could have would be −2. So, the last remaining deviation, after N − 1 of them have been specified, is not 'free to vary'. We say that there are N − 1 **degrees of freedom** (*df*s) for the deviations to vary independently. The final, remaining deviation is 'fixed'. It is completely determined by the N − 1 other deviations. This fact is recognized by excluding one of the N scores from the denominator of the formula used to calculate the average of the squared deviations (i.e., for the variance or SD of the sample).

In the case of the population variance or SD, however, we have a complete set of data and the actual mean is known. Unlike when calculating the sample variance or SD, where we lost one df because of the need to estimate the population mean, no estimate is required when calculating the population variance or SD. Therefore, no dfs are lost and the denominator is N.

SPSS operations and output (4.2) – Mean, range, standard deviation and variance

We will use the scores in Table 4.1 to illustrate these descriptive statistic operations in SPSS. If the scores for each condition have been entered in a separate column, as they are shown in Table 4.1 (this is how they would be entered for a repeated measures design):

(i)   Go to the menu at the top of the screen and click on *Analyze*, then click on *Descriptive Statistics*, then *Descriptives*.
(ii) Click on the variable(s) that you are interested in and move it into the *Variable* box.
(iii) Click on the *Options* button, then click on *Mean*, *Range*, *Standard deviation*, and *Variance*.
(iv) Click on *Continue*. Finally, click on *OK*.

If the scores for both conditions have been entered in a single column and there is another column indicating (e.g., by entry of 1 or 2) to which condition the score in that row belongs (this is how they would be entered for an independent groups design, which is in fact the case for the data in Table 4.1):

(i)   Go to the menu at the top of the screen and click on *Analyze*, then on *Compare Means* and *Means*.
(ii) Select the variable that contains the scores and move it into the *Dependent List* box.
(iii) Select the variable that indicates (with entries 1 and 2) the condition to which the score in each row belongs and move it into the *Independent List* box.
(iv) Click on *Options* and then, in the *Statistics* box, select in turn *Range* and *Variance* and move each of them into the *Cell Statistics* box to join *Mean*, *Number of Cases* and *Standard Deviation*.
(v)   Click *Continue* and then *OK*.

Whichever way the data were entered, the main output, shown under the heading, 'Report', would contain essentially the same information, though details of formatting may vary.

Report

SCORE

CONDIT	Mean	N	Std. Deviation	Range	Variance
expt	6.8000	20	1.2814	5.00	1.642
control	5.3500	20	1.4609	6.00	2.134
Total	6.0750	40	1.5424	7.00	2.379

The Normal Distribution and its Properties

Let us now go back for a moment to the issue of frequency distributions. An important thing to note about frequency distributions is that they have a particular shape. For instance, if you look at Figure 4.1 or Figure 4.3 again, you will notice that the shape of those distributions tends to be symmetrical, in that the continuous imaginary line of the polygon has a peak around the middle, and two approximately equal tails at the ends. A distribution with this type of shape is said to approximate to a **normal distribution**, one that has a very specific mathematical definition.

This type of distribution is extremely common as it characterizes many human variables (both physical and psychological). Think, for instance, about people's height. Presumably, if you measured the height of, say, British people, you would realize that there are few very short and very tall people, a good few relatively short and relatively tall people, and a lot of people who are more or less average. If you represent the distribution of the height of British people with a histogram, you end up with the typically symmetrical shape of the normal distribution. Many other variables, such as other physical measurements, size or error in skilful performance, mental measurements and so on, also have approximately normal distributions. But the normal distribution is not just common: it has some important specific properties.

Before discussing these properties, let us stress that distributions may take many shapes, and they are not always approximately normal. Two relatively common shapes are the positively and the negatively skewed ones. The crucial feature of a **positively skewed distribution** is that the tail on the right side of the peak, where the bigger values lie, is longer than the tail on the left side, where there are the smaller values. On the contrary, a **negatively skewed distribution** is characterized by a longer tail on the left side of the peak. (See Figure 4.5 for histograms of normal and skewed distributions.)

The normal distribution and the position of the mean, median and mode

In the above sections about the mean, the median and the mode, we saw that these three measures of central tendency do not always coincide. The manner and the extent to which these measures differ from one another depend on the way in which the scores are distributed, that is, on the shape of the distribution.

The normal distribution has the same mean, median and mode, and samples from a normal distribution will have similar mean, median and mode values. For instance, suppose that we have the following set of eleven scores: 4, 5, 6, 6, 7, 7, 7, 8, 8, 9, 10. This is a set with a perfectly symmetrical distribution around the central value (this is a rare occurrence in real experiments, but it could happen). If you find the mean, median and mode of this set, you will realize that they all take the same value, that is, 7.

However, the scores may form a skewed distribution. In this case the values of the mean, median and mode can be very different from one another. Interestingly, in skewed distributions the value of the median is always between the value of the mean and that of the mode. However, whether the biggest value is that of the mean or that of the mode depends on the way in which the distribution is skewed. In a positively skewed distribution, the biggest value will be that of the mean, while in a negatively skewed distribution the biggest value will be that of the mode.

For instance, suppose that we have the following data set, constituting a positively skewed distribution: 5, 6, 6, 6, 7, 7, 8, 9, 10, 11, 12. In this case, the mean takes the

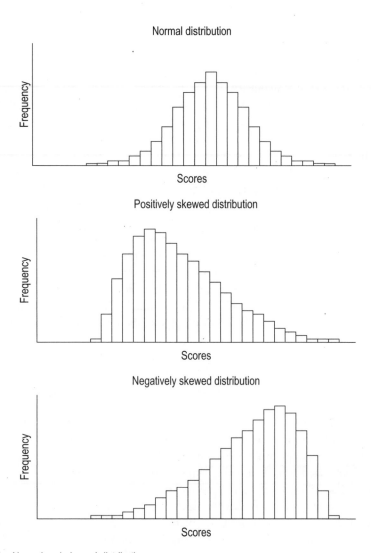

Figure 4.5 Normal and skewed distributions

biggest value, that is, 7.9, the value of the median, which is 7, is in between the mean and the mode, and the value of the mode is the smallest one, that is, 6. Now consider the following set, constituting a negatively skewed distribution: 5, 6, 7, 8, 9, 10, 10, 11, 11, 11, 12. This time, the biggest value is that of the mode, which is 11, followed by the value of the median, which is 10, followed by that of the mean, which is 9.09.

See Figure 4.6 for a graphical representation of the position of the mean, median and mode in the ideal normal distribution and in positively skewed and negatively skewed distributions; for simplicity, we show the curve, but not the histogram.

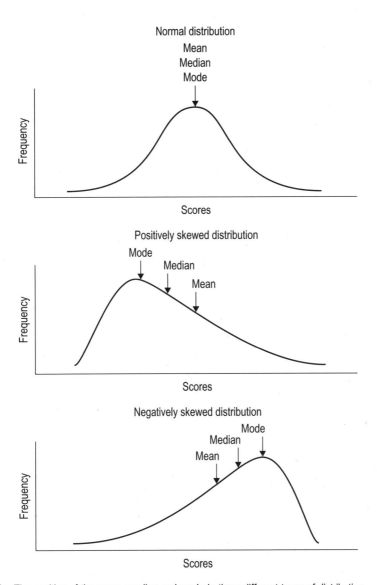

Figure 4.6 The position of the mean, median and mode in three different types of distribution

The area under the curve of the normal distribution

We now move to discuss a property of the normal distribution that is extremely important for the statistical analysis of psychology data.

Let us start by making a very simple observation. Given that the normal distribution is symmetrical and samples of data from a normal distribution will approximate
this symmetry, if we draw an imaginary line down the middle through the central

point of a normal distribution corresponding to the value of the mean, the median and the mode, we know that 50% of scores fall on one side of this line, and 50% of scores fall on the other side. Now, the very interesting thing about the normal distribution is that it is possible to draw a line down through *any* point, and know the percentage of scores falling on each side of the line. What is more, we can draw lines down through any two points, and know the percentage of scores falling between them. At this point you may ask: How is that possible? To answer that question, we must discuss the relationship between the normal distribution and one of the measures of dispersion discussed above; that is, the standard deviation.

The normal distribution and the standard deviation

Once again, consider the scores produced by participants in the experimental condition of our study, which approximate to a normal distribution. If you calculate the standard deviation you will find that it is 1.28. Now, in accordance with statistical terminology, we can say that, concerning the specific set of scores in our experimental condition, the value of 1.28 is equivalent to *one* standard deviation. As a consequence, the value of 2.56 is equivalent to two standard deviations, the value of 3.84 is three standard deviations, and so on.

At this point, let us go back to the issue of the percentage of scores falling under a specific portion of the curve of the normal distribution. First, let us draw a line down the middle through the mean value which, as we saw above in the section on the mean, is 6.8. Then, let us draw another line down the value that corresponds to one standard deviation above the mean, which is 6.8 + 1.28 = 8.08. Now, the mathematical characteristics of the normal distribution allow us to know that the portion of the distribution falling between the mean value (6.8 in this case) and one standard deviation *above* the mean value (8.08 in this case) includes roughly one-third (34.13%, to be precise) of all the scores in the distribution. Because the normal distribution is symmetrical, the same is true for that portion of the distribution falling between the mean and the value corresponding to one standard deviation *below* the mean (which in this case is 6.8 − 1.28 = 5.52). To make full sense of this, look at Figure 4.7, which illustrates an ideal normal distribution. This figure will also make it easy to realize that, on the basis of elementary arithmetic, the portion of the distribution falling between one standard deviation below the mean and one standard deviation above the mean comprises 68.26% of the scores in the distribution. Also, we can deduce that the portion of the distribution that is lower than 1 SD below the mean and the portion that is higher than 1 SD above the mean each comprise 15.87% of the scores.

We can now say how it is possible to draw a line down through any point and know the percentage of scores falling on each side of the line, and how it is possible to draw a line down through any two points and know the percentage of scores falling between the two points: it is possible thanks to the special relationship between the normal distribution and the standard deviation that we have just discussed. We will explain this idea in the following section.

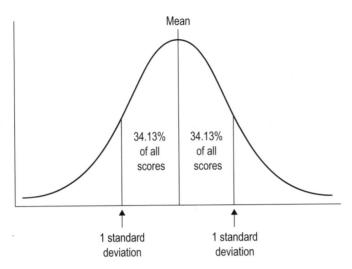

Figure 4.7 Proportion of scores under the normal curve, between the mean and one standard deviation above and one standard deviation below the mean

Z-scores

Suppose we know that adult British people are normally distributed in terms of the amount of time they spend in front of television every day. Then, suppose that the mean of this distribution is 92 minutes, and the standard deviation is 16 minutes. Finally, suppose that we are interested in finding out how many British people spend more than 2 hours (i.e., more than 120 minutes) per day watching it. (Note that this is like taking a histogram representing our distribution, then drawing a line down through the point 120, and then wanting to discover how many values there are to the right of that line.) How do we proceed?

First of all, we must find out how far 120 is from the mean (i.e., 92), and that value is 28. Second, we need to know how much is 28 in terms of standard deviations. To put it differently: if, concerning this specific distribution, 16 is equivalent to 1 standard deviation, how many standard deviations will 28 be equivalent to? To know this, we divide 28 by the value of the standard deviation. This will be: 28/16 = 1.75. That means that the value 120 is equivalent to 1.75 standard deviations. (You need to know that values expressed in standard deviations are called **z-scores**. So, 1.75 is a z-score.) The third and final step is very simple. Statisticians have worked out the percentage of scores falling above or below any z-score (not just those corresponding to 1, 2 or 3 standard deviations) and have arranged this information into a special table (see partial version of Statistical Table 4.1). Therefore, all you need to do at this point is to look at the table and find out the percentage of values falling above 1.75. To do that, you enter the table at row 1.7 and column 0.05 (for the 2nd decimal place), and see that the value at their intersection is 0.0401 (i.e., 4%). In sum, that means that there are

Statistical Table 4.1   Probabilities associated with values as extreme as observed values of *z* in the normal distribution (partial table – full table in Appendix 1)

z-value	2nd decimal place of observed *z*-value									
	0.00	0.01	0.02	0.03	0.04	0.05	0.06	0.07	0.08	0.09
0.0	0.5000	0.4960	0.4920	0.4880	0.4840	0.4801	0.4761	0.4721	0.4681	0.4641
0.1	0.4602	0.4562	0.4522	0.4483	0.4443	0.4404	0.4364	0.4325	0.4286	0.4247
0.2	0.4207	0.4168	0.4129	0.4090	0.4052	0.4013	0.3974	0.3936	0.3897	0.3859
0.3	0.3821	0.3783	0.3745	0.3707	0.3669	0.3632	0.3594	0.3557	0.3520	0.3483
0.4	0.3446	0.3409	0.3372	0.3336	0.3300	0.3264	0.3228	0.3192	0.3156	0.3121
0.5	0.3085	0.3050	0.3015	0.2981	0.2946	0.2912	0.2877	0.2843	0.2810	0.2776
0.6	0.2743	0.2709	0.2676	0.2643	0.2611	0.2578	0.2546	0.2514	0.2483	0.2451
0.7	0.2420	0.2389	0.2358	0.2327	0.2296	0.2266	0.2236	0.2206	0.2177	0.2148
0.8	0.2119	0.2090	0.2061	0.2033	0.2005	0.1977	0.1949	0.1922	0.1894	0.1867
0.9	0.1841	0.1814	0.1788	0.1762	0.1736	0.1711	0.1685	0.1660	0.1635	0.1611
1.0	0.1587	0.1562	0.1539	0.1515	0.1492	0.1469	0.1446	0.1423	0.1401	0.1379
1.1	0.1357	0.1335	0.1314	0.1292	0.1271	0.1251	0.1230	0.1210	0.1190	0.1170
1.2	0.1151	0.1131	0.1112	0.1093	0.1075	0.1056	0.1038	0.1020	0.1003	0.0985
1.3	0.0968	0.0951	0.0934	0.0918	0.0901	0.0885	0.0869	0.0853	0.0838	0.0823
1.4	0.0808	0.0793	0.0778	0.0764	0.0749	0.0735	0.0721	0.0708	0.0694	0.0681
1.5	0.0668	0.0655	0.0643	0.0630	0.0618	0.0606	0.0594	0.0582	0.0571	0.0559
1.6	0.0548	0.0537	0.0526	0.0516	0.0505	0.0495	0.0485	0.0475	0.0465	0.0455
1.7	0.0446	0.0436	0.0427	0.0418	0.0409	0.0401	0.0392	0.0384	0.0375	0.0367
1.8	0.0359	0.0351	0.0344	0.0336	0.0329	0.0322	0.0314	0.0307	0.0301	0.0294
1.9	0.0287	0.0281	0.0274	0.0268	0.0262	0.0256	0.0250	0.0244	0.0239	0.0233
2.0	0.0228	0.0222	0.0217	0.0212	0.0207	0.0202	0.0197	0.0192	0.0188	0.0183

Source: The entries in this table were computed by D.R. McDonald at the University of Dundee.

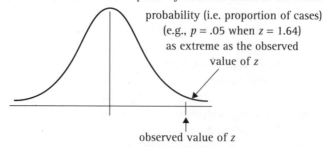

probability (i.e. proportion of cases) (e.g., *p* = .05 when *z* = 1.64) as extreme as the observed value of *z*

observed value of *z*

only 4% of British people watching television for more than 2 hours per day, and, obviously, 96% watching television for less than 2 hours per day. Finally, consider that, when you have a negative *z*-score (i.e., a score that is smaller than the mean), the value that you find in the table refers to the percentage of values falling below that score.

The *z*-scores are a form of **standard score** that allow us to compare scores that were originally obtained as values on quite different scales. For example, a score of 60 on a test with a mean of 50 and an SD of 10 would be equivalent to a score of

115 on a test with a mean of 100 and an SD of 15. Both scores are 1 SD above the mean, that is, they exceed the scores of 84.13 of people taking the test. The z-scores are also useful when it comes to making statistical inferences from data, as we shall see in later chapters.

SUMMARY OF CHAPTER

- Data description comprises two operations: (i) organizing and (ii) summarizing data.
- To organize a set of raw data we can create a table specifying the frequency distribution of the scores (i.e., how many times each value occurs), and we can display frequency distributions pictorially, by means of a histogram or a frequency polygon.
- To summarize a set of data implies extracting single indices or measures from data. These measures may concern either the most typical value (measures of central tendency), or the extent to which the scores are spread on either side of the average value (measures of dispersion).
- The most commonly used measures of central tendency are the mean, the median and the mode. The mean of a set of scores is the sum of all the scores in the set divided by the number of scores. The median is the score that has as many scores above it as below it. The mode is the score that occurs most frequently.
- The three most commonly used measures of dispersion are the range, the variance and the standard deviation. The range is the difference between the highest and the lowest score. The variance is the average of the squared deviations of each score from the mean, and the standard deviation is the square root of the variance. Both the variance and the standard deviation are abstract measures that increase as the amount of dispersion in the data increases, and so have no obvious intuitive meaning.
- Frequency distributions may have many different shapes. However, many real distributions tend to have a roughly symmetrical bell-like shape, and distributions with this shape are approximations to what are referred to as 'normal distributions'.
- The normal distribution has some specific properties. First, in a normal distribution the mean, the median and mode will have the same value. Second, in a normal distribution the area under the curve has a special relationship with the standard deviation, in that it is possible to know the percentage of scores falling under specific portions of the curve, provided that scores are expressed in units of standard deviation (known as z-scores).
- To convert a score into a z-score we must subtract the value of the mean from the score, and then divide the result of this operation by the value of the standard deviation.

CHAPTER FIVE

Making Inferences from Data

To introduce the issue that is at the heart of this chapter, we will use our imaginary experiment again. In this experiment we want to test the hypothesis that people who are in a good mood perform better on intellectual tasks than people who are in a neutral mood. To test this hypothesis, we create two conditions. In one condition a group of participants watch a movie excerpt with humorous content (the experimental condition), and in the other condition a different group of participants watch an excerpt with an emotionally neutral content (the control condition). We expect that participants in the experimental condition will perform better on an intellectual task than those in the control condition, because of a mood change induced by the experimental condition. The level of intellectual performance is measured by presenting participants with 10 logical problems. To decide if our hypothesis is correct we must count the number of logical problems solved by participants in each condition of the experiment.

Now, suppose that participants in the experimental condition generally solve more logical problems than participants in the control condition (e.g., the *mean* number of logical problems solved is higher in the experimental condition). This indicates that our hypothesis 'might' be correct. However, finding that participants in the experimental condition tend to solve more problems than those in the control condition is insufficient to lead us to the conclusion that mood *really* has an effect on intellectual performance. As we saw in Chapter 3, no meaningful conclusions can be drawn from the results of an experiment if we have not previously ensured that our experiment has *validity*. That means three things. First, we must make sure that our IV and DV really measure 'mood' and 'intellectual performance' (construct validity). Second, we must ensure that we are really observing the effects of the IV on the DV, and not those of systematic NVs (internal validity). This is extremely important because if there are systematic NVs affecting the DV, then we cannot claim to have a *true experimental design* (we will discuss this notion at greater length later in this chapter). Third, we must ensure that the effects of the IV on the DV that we observe can, as far as possible, be generalized to other people and situations (external validity). (See Figure 3.6 for a schematic illustration of what these three types of validity are about.)

At this point, suppose we find the differences that we were expecting, *and* we are confident that our experiment has validity. Will this be sufficient to conclude that people who have a good mood perform better than people in a neutral mood? Unfortunately it will not! The fact is that once we have reached this stage we have to do still more things with our data. This is because there are still *random* NVs that can affect our DV (intellectual performance) because they can *never* be completely eliminated. Therefore, we need to use procedures that can ensure that random NVs are not responsible for differences between scores in the experimental and control conditions. Put differently, we need to deal with our data in a way that will allow us to *infer* whether scores in the two conditions are sufficiently different to justify the conclusion that the hypothesis is correct. These procedures concern the domain of **statistical inference**.

Given that statistical inference is essentially about inferring that differences in scores between conditions are *not* due to random NVs, it is important to discuss the nature of NVs and the effects they may have on scores on the DV. In doing so, we will necessarily repeat some of the ideas already expressed in Chapter 3.

Random NVs and their Effects on Scores in the DV

To explain the nature of random NVs, consider again the example used in Chapter 3. Suppose that all the participants in our experiment come from the same university, and that on the day preceding the experiment they attended a party where they had several drinks and stayed until late. On the following day our participants might find it difficult to concentrate on intellectual tasks and, as a consequence, they might generally perform worse on the logical problems than in normal circumstances. Clearly, this implies that the scores on the DV would partly depend on the effects of the level of participants' concentration (that is, an NV).

Note that the effect of this NV would be potentially the same in both the experimental (good mood) and control (normal mood) conditions. This is because, all participants having attended the party, the intellectual performance of both those in the experimental condition and those in the control condition would have the same possibility of being influenced by tiredness. Therefore, it can be said that NVs are 'a nuisance' because they introduce **variability** into the data, which makes it harder to see the effects of an IV on scores on the DV.

Let us explain this notion more carefully. Imagine that the IV had no effect on the DV, and that there were no random NVs affecting our DV. Then all scores in both conditions would be the same (see Figure 5.1a for an example). If there were still no NVs, but the IV did have an effect, we would have two possible scores, one for each condition (see Figure 5.1b). In this case it is rather obvious that the IV has affected scores in the two conditions differently. If there were no random NVs, our data would always be clear like that, and there would be no need for inferential statistics. Unfortunately, that is cloud-cuckoo land. There are always potential random NVs and they make it harder to tell whether our IV has had an effect. In Figure 5.1c

(a) | expt. condition | control condition |
|:---:|:---:|
| 2 | 2 |
| 2 | 2 |
| 2 | 2 |
| 2 | 2 |
| mean = 2 | mean = 2 |

(b) | expt. condition | control condition |
|:---:|:---:|
| 4 | 2 |
| 4 | 2 |
| 4 | 2 |
| 4 | 2 |
| mean = 4 | mean = 2 |

(c) | expt. condition | control condition |
|:---:|:---:|
| 2 | 2 |
| 5 | 1 |
| 5 | 0 |
| 4 | 5 |
| mean = 4 | mean = 2 |

Figure 5.1   Effects of random NVs on scores: (a) no effect of IV and no random NVs; (b) effect of IV but no random NVs; (c) effect of IV and effect of random NVs

you can see an example of what random NVs can do to the scores in the two conditions of the experiment. Here, due to the effect of the IV, the difference between means for the two conditions is the same as in Figure 5.1b but, because there are also random NVs operating, this difference might have been caused by (1) the IV, (2) random NVs just happening to pile up in favour of the experimental condition on this particular occasion, or (3) some combination of the two. How can we decide whether we should be persuaded that the IV had an effect? The clue is in how much variability there is between scores *within* a condition. The variability within a condition cannot have been caused by the IV, because every participant within a condition received the same treatment (i.e., the same level of the IV). So, the variability within conditions must have been due to the chance effects of random NVs. Therefore, the more differences there are within conditions compared to the mean difference between conditions, the more likely it is that random NVs that caused the differences within each condition could also have caused the difference between conditions.

What we really need to know is, given the amount of variability among scores within each condition, just how likely it is that the obtained difference between means (say, in Figure 5.1c) might have been entirely due to the effects of random NVs. This is where a statistical test will help. It will tell us either that it is unlikely that random effects could account for the data we obtained, in which case we will infer that our IV probably did contribute to the difference, or that it is not that unlikely, in which case we will conclude that the difference between means might well have been due to the cumulative effects of random NVs just happening (by chance) to pile up in favour of the experimental condition on this particular occasion. In the latter case, we could not claim that our experiment had shown there to be an effect of the IV (look back at Figure 3.5 for a summary of the effects of systematic and random NVs).

But there is another very important point to consider: Whichever way the evidence points, it is never conclusive. For example, we might conclude that the evidence is not strong enough to persuade us that the IV had an effect, but that does not mean that the IV definitely had no effect. It might just not have been big enough to show up clearly against all of the variability produced by the random effects. At this point, we need to be clear that we do not reach a cut-and-dried conclusion that the IV definitely did or did not have an effect. Our conclusion is necessarily **probabilistic**. We conclude that random effects *probably were not* sufficient to have caused the difference between means (supporting an effect caused by the IV) or, alternatively, that random effects *probably were* sufficient to have caused the difference (not supporting an effect caused by the IV).

Also, remember that we cannot just assume that potential NVs will be random in their effects. We saw in Chapter 3 that NVs can have systematic effects; that means that they can affect only one condition of the experiment, thereby providing plausible explanations of a difference between scores in the two conditions of the experiment, which compete with the explanation that it is the IV that caused the difference. We also saw that potential systematic NVs should be controlled by holding them constant, effectively eliminating them as variables, and, when this is not possible, they should be controlled by *turning* them into random NVs. Once systematic NVs have been *made* random, then they can be dealt with using inferential statistics. (Figure 5.2 recapitulates the main points in this argument that were made in detail in Chapter 3.)

So, how do we ensure that potential systematic NVs are made random? We must use a procedure known as **random allocation**. However, at this point it is necessary to make it clear that this procedure is logically distinct from another important procedure, which is known as **random sampling**. Now, since random allocation is often confused with random sampling, and since, as we said, random sampling is an important issue, let us clarify what it is about, before we discuss random allocation.

Random sampling

In order to be able to say that the results of an experiment apply (can be generalized) to the population from which the sample of people who participate in the experiment is drawn, it is necessary that the participants are **representative** of the population. (This is the issue of external (population) validity introduced in Chapter 2.) How can we ensure that this is the case? In principle, a representative sample of participants can be obtained by random sampling from a defined population. For example, we might want to draw conclusions about all first year psychology students in our university. This would entail putting the names of all of those students in a metaphorical

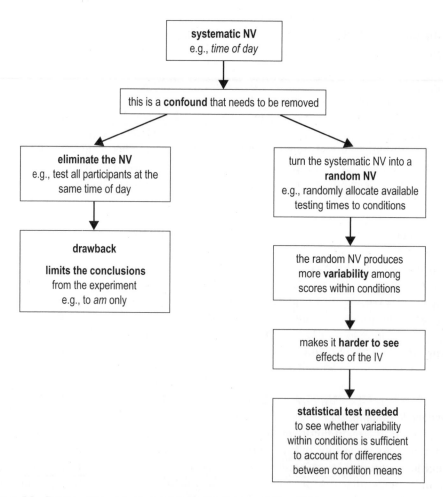

Figure 5.2   Dealing with systematic (confounding) nuisance variables (NVs)

hat and pulling out the required number (the sample size) while blindfolded. A more realistic alternative would be to assign a unique number to each student and then use a random number table to select the required number of students. The point is that every student must have an equal chance of being selected. The reality is that random sampling from a defined population presents some difficulties (see Additional information (5.1)), with the result that it is more an ideal than a procedure that is commonly adhered to.

Having clarified what random sampling is about, let us return to the issue of random allocation, which, as we specified above, is a procedure used to ensure that potential systematic NVs are made random, thereby allowing us to infer whether the IV can account for the difference between DV means in the two conditions.

Additional information (5.1) – The unreality of random sampling in experiments

Random sampling procedures tend to be quite time consuming and are often difficult to implement. For these reasons, they are rarely carried out in practice. If a sample of first year psychology students were required, it is much more likely that an **opportunity sample** (e.g., volunteers from a class) would be used. The difficulty of obtaining a random sample from a population of all first year psychology students in UK universities would obviously be even more problematic, and imagine the difficulty of trying to obtain a random sample of all UK undergraduates. The broader the population of interest, the less likely it is that a random sample will be obtainable. In fact, the extent to which generalization to other people is possible is much more dependent on **replication** of the results (i.e., showing that we get similar results) with different participants, than on the existence of a random sample from a population. We would also like to be able to generalize our conclusions to other specific *situations* (e.g., viewing alone, with familiar others, with unfamiliar others, in a relaxed environment, in a formal environment etc.). In this case, the argument about generalization being based on replication applies even more strongly, because there is usually no attempt to randomly sample from a population of possible situations of interest.

Random allocation

The random allocation of experimental units (participants and test occasions) to conditions is the hallmark of a 'true' experiment. A true experiment is one in which the only thing that differs systematically between conditions is the experimenter's manipulation of the level of the IV (e.g., mood-raising video versus control video). Other NVs, such as individual characteristics of participants and particular environmental conditions, will also affect the scores obtained on the DV, but we know that so long as these do not affect one condition in a systematically different way than they affect the other condition, they will not be a threat to the internal validity of the experiment. Provided that any potential NVs are *random* in their effects, that is, they have an equal chance of affecting scores in favour of either condition of the experiment, any systematic effect can only have been the effect of the IV.

Random allocation of participants (and test occasions) to conditions is a way of ensuring that the particular characteristics of participants (e.g., motivation, suggestibility, alertness etc.) have an equal chance of affecting the mean score in either condition. It is not the case that random allocation guarantees that the participant characteristics in the two conditions will be equal. In fact, that is extremely unlikely. More of the highly alert participants will probably be allocated to one or other condition, but the point is that it could be either condition that benefits.

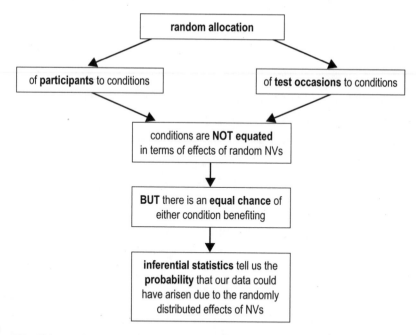

Figure 5.3   Using random allocation

The same argument applies to the allocation of available testing times to conditions (see Figure 5.3). Unless participants will all be tested on the same occasion, each available testing occasion should be allocated at random (e.g., by tossing a coin) to one of the two conditions. The need for this aspect of random allocation is frequently overlooked. Thus, experiments are often, incorrectly, carried out with participants in the two conditions being tested in separate groups. That leaves open the possibility that any systematic effect that is inferred from the data could have been due to particular characteristics of the two test situations.

Additional information (5.2) – More on random allocation in experiments

Suppose we have a sample of 20 people who are going to take part in our experiment. We can expect that they will differ from one another in all sorts of ways that might affect their scores on our logical reasoning test (i.e., there will be NVs). Now suppose that there is really no effect of our IV (*type of video*). Then, if there were no NVs, we would expect everyone in the sample to get the same score. But there *are* NVs, so that the participants get different scores from one another, even though there is no effect of the IV. Now suppose that the scores obtained by the sample of 20 people were:

Person	1	2	3	4	5	6	7	8	9	10	11	12	13	14	15	16	17	18	19	20
Score	23	26	17	24	31	19	33	25	27	21	21	18	17	12	30	22	16	23	20	17

Then, suppose that the first 10 people had been randomly allocated to the experimental (good mood) video condition and the remainder to the control (normal mood) condition. The means for the two conditions would have been:

Experimental mean = 24.6
Control mean   = 19.6

We can see that the mean score in the experimental condition would have been higher, but remember that the differences were due solely to NVs and not at all to the different videos. Furthermore, if the people with the first 10 scores had been put in the control condition, the mean score in that condition would have been higher by the same amount. So, it is clear that, if there is no effect of the IV, random NVs are equally likely to result in a higher or lower mean for the experimental condition. That is not all – depending on which people were randomly allocated to which condition, the difference between means in the two conditions (in whichever direction) would vary. With most allocations, individual differences would tend to roughly balance out across conditions, so that the difference between means would be relatively small, but, with some allocations, the difference would be relatively large. For example, if it just happened that the ten people with the highest scores had all been in the experimental condition, the means for the two groups would have been:

Experimental mean = 26.4
Control mean   = 17.8

This looks like quite a strong advantage for the experimental condition, but we know that in this case it was just due to NVs (e.g., individual differences among the sample) and, as usual, if the allocation had been reversed, the apparent advantage would have been for the control condition.

Random allocation is the best way to ensure that there is an equal chance of the advantage going to either condition. Whatever the outcome, we know that the effects of the NVs will be randomly distributed between conditions, so that if there is really no effect of the IV, any apparent effect we see will be due to chance. Our statistical analysis uses the fact that most differences between means caused by random NVs are relatively small to tell us how confident we can be that an obtained difference between means is large enough to make it unlikely to have been caused by random NVs (chance), and was therefore probably due to the systematic effect of the IV (provided there are no confounding variables) (see Figure 5.3).

The Process of Statistical Inference

At this point, we are ready to discuss the details of the process of statistical inference that allows us to decide whether, on the basis of the data we have collected, a hypothesis is *probably* correct or not. So, we will now discuss what you should do in order to decide whether differences between conditions are due to chance (i.e., the effects of random NVs), or to the effects of the IV, as predicted. Let us start by introducing some technical terms that will allow us to provide a formal explanation of this process.

Experimental hypothesis and null hypothesis

In Chapter 2, we discussed that what is meant by a hypothesis, in the context of an experiment, is a prediction about an effect of an IV on a DV. We will call this the **experimental hypothesis**. We can also talk about a contrary hypothesis, one that predicts that the IV will *not* have an effect on the DV. This is referred to as the **null hypothesis**.

Statistical significance

Another important concept is that of **statistical significance**. We talk about a difference between means being statistically significant when there is a low probability that it could have arisen as the result of *random error*, that is, the chance effects of random NVs. But what do we mean by a low probability? Total certainty that random error was responsible would be represented by a probability of '1' and total certainty that random error was not responsible would be represented by '0'. By convention, we take 'low probability' to be a 1 in 20 chance (that is 5 in 100, which is a probability of .05) or, if we are feeling more conservative, a 1 in 100 chance (which is a probability of .01) or, if we are feeling really conservative, a 1 in 1,000 chance (that is, 0.1 in 100, which is a probability of .001). These levels of confidence are described as **alpha (α) levels** and the α level you are willing to accept as evidence of an effect is supposed to be set before data are collected. Then, if the probability level obtained when a statistic is calculated (more on this later) is below the designated α level, we can conclude that the null hypothesis can be rejected and the effect of our IV is said to be *statistically significant*. (Note that researchers prefer to say that 'the null hypothesis can be rejected', rather than say that 'the experimental hypothesis can be accepted'; see Additional information (5.5) for an explanation of why this is the case). Thus, if α has been set at .05 and the obtained probability (p) when a statistic is calculated is .04, we can claim that the effect of our IV was statistically significant but, if p is .06, we have to conclude that the effect was not statistically significant (the effect is then usually described as being 'non-significant').

Complications (5.1) – Reporting the lowest *p*-value possible

Not everyone agrees that a pre-defined significance level (i.e., α level) should be set, and the null hypothesis rejected if the probability of obtaining the data when the null hypothesis is true is less than the pre-defined α level. There is a view that focusing narrowly on whether the probability is below (reject null hypothesis) or above (fail to reject null hypothesis) the critical α value is too crude. For example, with α set at .05, a probability of $p = .049$ would be reported as significant (i.e., $p < .05$), whereas a probability of $p = .051$ would be reported as non-significant (i.e., $p > .05$). As the consequences of finding an effect to be statistically significant or non-significant can be considerable – not least in determining whether a study is published in a journal – we might question the logic of this all-or-none decision. Another example may help you to see the problem. Suppose, once again, that α is set at .05. Then, probabilities of $p = .051$ and, say, $p = .87$ would both be reported as non-significant, with no distinction made between them. Similarly, probabilities of $p = .049$ and $p = .0001$ would both be reported as significant, again with no distinction made between them. An alternative is to focus on the actual value of the probability. In this view, $p = .0001$ would be reported as 'highly significant' or perhaps as 'significant $(p < .001)$', and $p = .051$ might be described as 'approaching significance'. Against this argument, some researchers regard it as 'suspect' to decide what level of significance to report after seeing the result of the analysis. Nonetheless, it is common for researchers to report the lowest conventional level (.05, .01, .001 etc.) of probability that their analysis permits. The justification claimed for this is that the probabilities are best treated as 'indicative' of levels of confidence rather than as rigid decisions. There does seem to be a gap between the classical (predetermined α level) approach expounded in most statistic texts and what many researchers actually do.

Imaginary distributions

Now, we come at last to an explanation of how the statistical decision is reached. First, you need to make an imaginative leap. We have only done the experiment once, of course, and we got a particular set of data, with a particular mean for each of the two conditions. If we could wipe out all memory of the experiment and do it again, we would almost certainly get a different set of data and different values for each of the condition means. Now, the imaginative leap. Imagine that we were able to repeat the experiment thousands of times in this way. Each time we would get

Additional information (5.3) – An intuitive rationale for the conventional alpha levels

What is the rationale for adopting $p < .05$, $p < .01$ etc. as the critical values that we use to decide whether to reject the null hypothesis? The answer is that they are really convenient, and ultimately, arbitrary, conventions. They do, however, map reasonably to our intuitive notions about chance events. Let's do a mind experiment about when you decide that some outcome is more likely to have resulted from some systematic effect than from the operation of chance (random effects). Imagine that I show you 10 coins and bet you that I can toss them so that more of them come down 'heads' than 'tails'. You take on the bet, reasoning that you have an even chance of winning, and we agree that I will give you 10p for every coin that comes down tails and you will give me 10p for every coin that comes down heads. I toss the first coin, it comes down heads and you hand over 10p. The same happens with the next coin, and the next, and so on. After how many heads in a row would you become *suspicious* that this was not a game of chance? After how many would you become *convinced* that something systematic was causing the run of heads – that I really did have the knack of tossing coins so that they came down heads or, more likely, that I had a set of weighted coins? When we have asked these questions to classes of students, there has always been a majority that become suspicious after five heads in a row and convinced after seven in a row. The probabilities of two, three, four etc. up to 10 heads in a row are shown in Figure 5.4. There you can see how students' intuitions map on to the conventional values of $\alpha = .05$ and $\alpha = .01$. The probability of a run of heads drops below .05 for the first time when there have been five in a row and below .01 for the first time when there have been seven in a row. Of course, if the stakes were higher you might be inclined to challenge me sooner or, if there was a penalty for an incorrect challenge, you might wait for the probability to drop lower. These are analogous to the deliberations that lead a researcher to choose a higher or lower α level for statistical significance.

No. heads in a row	Probability		Conventional significance levels
1st head	$p = .5$		
2nd head	$p = .5 \times .5$	$= .25$	
3rd head	$p = .25 \times .5$	$= .125$	
4th head	$p = .125 \times .5$	$= .063$	
5th head	$p = .063 \times .5$	$= .031$	← $p < .05$
6th head	$p = .031 \times .5$	$= .016$	
7th head	$p = .016 \times .5$	$= .008$	← $p < .01$
8th head	$p = .008 \times .5$	$= .004$	

Figure 5.4 An intuitive rationale for the conventional levels of statistical significance

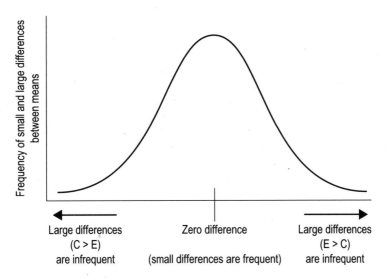

Figure 5.5 Hypothetical distribution of differences between means when the null hypothesis is true

different specific values for the experimental and control means. For either condition, we could imagine plotting the frequency with which different mean scores were obtained. These would be frequency distributions like those discussed in Chapter 4 and illustrated in Figure 4.3, but they would of course be imaginary (or hypothetical) distributions, because we did not really repeat the experiment thousands of times.

Now, imagine what the means for the two conditions would be like if the null hypothesis were true, that is, the difference between the means was entirely due to the chance effects of random NVs. Most often, the means would be very similar but sometimes the chance effects would happen to pile up in favour of one or other mean and, occasionally, the chance effects would pile up to create a really big difference between the means. Just as we could plot imaginary distributions for each mean, we could also plot the frequency of various sizes of *difference* between the two means – that is, a **hypothetical distribution of the differences between means**. If we did that, and the null hypothesis were true, we would be likely to see something like the distribution of means shown in Figure 5.5. This shows the frequency with which various values for the difference between means might be expected just on the basis of chance effects of random NVs; that is, it is based, not on real data, but on our understanding of chance effects, as they occur, for example, in coin-tossing experiments. The most frequent differences would be very close to zero, and the frequencies would decrease for progressively larger differences in either direction.

A COIN-TOSSING ANALOGY

Let's pursue the analogy of a coin-tossing experiment, to stand in for an experiment in which there happen to be *only* random (chance) effects operating. Suppose you and I each have 10 coins, which we can assume are 'unbiased', that is, they are equally likely to come down heads or tails when flipped. If we each flipped our 10 coins thousands of times and each time recorded the number of heads, the most frequently obtained difference between number of heads and tails would be zero, with small differences in either direction also being relatively frequent and large differences being infrequent. In fact, if the frequencies were plotted we would have an approximately *normal distribution* very like the one shown in Figure 5.5 (and earlier, in Figure 4.6). Suppose now that I provide each of us with a new set of 10 coins and bet you that I can use my telekinetic powers to make all of your coins come down one way and all of mine the other way. You take on the bet and we flip the coins and, lo and behold, all mine come down heads and all yours come down tails. When you get over the surprise, you will probably conclude that you just witnessed a systematic effect rather than a random (chance) effect, because you (rightly) believe that the chances of a difference of 10 heads between us, in the absence of some systematic biasing effect, would not be zero but would be extremely low. Of course, you will probably soon begin to entertain the unworthy thought that the systematic effect may have been biased coins rather than my telekinetic powers!

THE IMAGINARY DISTRIBUTION OF A NEW STATISTIC

Now, we have already explained that if the probability of getting a difference between means as great as that we obtained, just by chance (given the amount of variability among scores within each condition), is lower than the α value specified (e.g., .05), we should conclude that the difference is statistically significant (i.e., we should reject the null hypothesis at the .05 level of probability and conclude that the experimental hypothesis is supported). So, if the obtained difference between means is among the 5% largest possible differences in the distribution in Figure 5.5 (i.e., 2.5% largest in either direction), we conclude that the difference in means is statistically significant at the 5% level. This is actually a slight over-simplification. The 'difference between means' is a **statistic** – a value calculated from a sample of data, just as a mean of a sample of data is a statistic – but we use a slightly more complex statistic in practice, because, in this case, for example, we need to take account of the *variability among scores within conditions* as well as the difference between means for the two conditions. The reason why we take account of the variability of scores within conditions is that the bigger the effects of random NVs, the greater the variability they create among scores within each condition and the more plausible it becomes that the random NVs *alone* could account for the difference between means (i.e., without there being any effect of the IV).

There are a number of different statistics available. Which one it is appropriate to use depends on details of the experimental design and the type of data we are collecting. These statistics will be introduced in later chapters, but the point to hang on to now is that they are all used in the same way to summarize the data (just like the difference between means) in order to see whether the value of the statistic is extreme enough to make it unlikely (e.g., probability < .05) that it would have arisen just by chance when the null hypothesis is true. Just how each different statistic tells us what the probability is of chance having produced the difference between conditions will be dealt with in the following chapters.

Statistical inference – a concrete example

In order to make the argument about statistical inference more concrete, we will repeat it using the example of the experiment from Chapter 2 – that was the example about the effect of viewing a *mood-enhancing video* (compared with viewing a *neutral video*) on performance on a test of *logical reasoning*. Participants are randomly allocated to one of the video conditions and all participants are shown the relevant video and then tested on the set of logical problems at the same time in the same laboratory. This means that situational variables have been largely eliminated (not entirely, of course – one participant may have an uncomfortable chair or be sitting in a draught, for example). Individual difference variables, on the other hand, will clearly have an effect (some participants will simply be better than others at solving logical problems irrespective of their moods, some will be more motivated to do well, and so on).

Individual difference variables (and any remaining situational differences) will, however, function as random NVs. This is because participants were randomly assigned to conditions and (although this was not explicitly stated) participants should have been randomly allocated seating positions in the laboratory. When participants' scores have been recorded, the means for the two groups are obtained and a statistic is calculated from the data. An appropriate statistic in this case would be the independent groups (or unrelated) t-statistic. This statistic will be explained in Chapter 9. For the moment, all we need to know is that the value of the statistic gets bigger as the difference between the means increases and the variability among scores within each condition (due to the random NVs) decreases. The distribution of values of the statistic when the null hypothesis is true can be specified for each possible sample size (number of participants). The distributions for a small, medium and large number of participants (say $N = 5$, 30 and 100, per group) are shown in Figure 5.6. When, in the calculation of t, one mean is subtracted from the other to obtain the difference between means, the value will be positive or negative depending on the direction of the difference (which mean was larger).

You can see in Figure 5.6 that both large negative and large positive values of t will be rare when the null hypothesis is true (i.e., the tails of the distribution). If the value for t that we obtain in our experiment falls in one of the tail areas, we can conclude that the mean difference between problem scores in the two video conditions was statistically significant, that is, the null hypothesis (that the mean difference was due to chance effects of random NVs) can be rejected with a known maximum probability (the value at which α was set) of being mistaken. If the value of α (the level

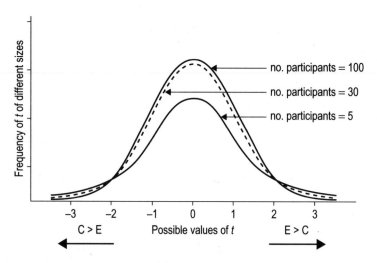

Figure 5.6 Hypothetical distribution of *t* for a small, medium and large number of participants when the null hypothesis is true

of statistical significance sought) was set at .05, and the obtained value of *t* falls within the .05 (5%) most extreme values in the tails (.025 at the end of each tail), the difference between means will be statistically significant at the 5% level. If the obtained value falls closer to the centre of the distribution than that (i.e., outside of the **rejection regions** in the tails), we will have to conclude that the null hypothesis cannot be rejected at the 5% level; that the difference between means is non-significant at that level of confidence. Figure 5.7 illustrates how statistical inferences about the null hypothesis and, indirectly, the experimental hypothesis are arrived at. The left-hand side shows a value of *t* that falls in one of the 'tails' of the hypothetical distribution and is therefore statistically significant. The right-hand side shows a value of *t* that falls outside of the tails (i.e., closer to the mean of the distribution) and is therefore non-significant. Tables giving the minimum size of *t* that will fall in the 5%, 1% or .1% most

---

Complications (5.2) – The truth about the null hypothesis

It is quite common for students (and researchers, for that matter) to refer to the probability of the null hypothesis being true. This is a misconception. The null hypothesis is either true or it is false. It refers to a 'state of the world'. There are no 'probabilities' associated with the truth or falsity of the null hypothesis. The probability that statements about statistical significance refer to is the probability that the data we obtained might have arisen just by chance when the null hypothesis is true.

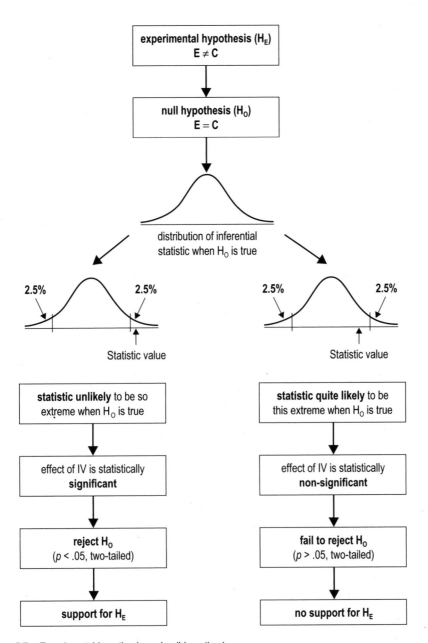

Figure 5.7 Experimental hypothesis and null hypothesis

extreme areas of the tails are available for different numbers of participants (i.e., the minimum t values needed for statistical significance at various α levels). Such a table is provided in Appendix 1 and also in Chapter 9, where t-tests will be considered in detail. Discussion of how to use the table will be held over to that chapter.

Additional information (5.4) – Statistical inferences from samples to populations

A formal treatment of the inference process we have been describing asks the question: How likely is it that our two samples of scores were drawn from populations with the same mean? In order to understand how an answer to this question is sought, we need to be clear that a population refers to all of the possible objects of a particular kind. It does not necessarily refer to people (e.g., the population of first year university students in the UK) or even to tangible entities of any kind (e.g., stars in the Milky Way, traffic lights in London). It can refer to an entirely imaginary set of all possible scores that could have been obtained by an infinite number of participants in an experiment. When we carried out our experiment, however, we only had a small number of participants and the scores they obtained are regarded as a **random sample of the population of scores** that we could have obtained if we had tested an infinite number of participants with the same characteristics as our sample. We can acknowledge that our sample of participants is unlikely to be a random sample from the population of possible participants that we are interested in, but this does not affect our (reasonable) assumption that the obtained scores are a random sample of the **imaginary distribution** of all possible scores (i.e., the imaginary population of scores). In fact, we have two samples of scores in our experiment, one sample for each condition. If the null hypothesis is true, the means of the populations of scores from which these samples are drawn will be equal; there will be, effectively, a single population of scores with a single mean. Still assuming that the null hypothesis is true, we have two random samples from the same population and the means of the samples will differ by chance alone. The means of some pairs of random samples (sets of scores obtained in particular experiments) would happen to differ a lot, so that they would *look like* samples drawn from two populations with different means. A statistical test ascertains the probability of getting, just by chance, two samples of scores that differ as much as those we obtained in our experiment. If the probability is below the value we set for α, we will conclude that it is unlikely that the two samples came from the same imaginary population, and that it is more likely that the null hypothesis is false and the samples came from two different populations of scores (one for each condition) with different means; that is, there was a statistically significant effect of our IV on our DV.

Additional information (5.5) – Why test the null hypothesis instead of the experimental hypothesis?

It does seem tortuous to set up a null hypothesis and subject it to a test to see if we can reject it rather than setting up the research hypothesis and testing it directly. The reason for testing the null hypothesis is that it is a **specific hypothesis** (the difference between the means of two populations of scores is zero). That allows us to construct an imaginary sampling distribution, showing the probabilities of obtaining a statistic of various sizes when that hypothesis is true. The research hypothesis, on the other hand, is a **non-specific hypothesis**. If you wanted to test the hypothesis that the difference between means is 1 on our DV scale, you could set up a sampling distribution and test that hypothesis, just as you could for any other specific difference between means. The problem is that you do not usually have a particular value in mind. To test all of the possible differences between means that you might wish to consider, you would need to set up a sampling distribution for each one. So, we end up setting up the specific null hypothesis, seeing if we can *reject* it at some level of probability, thereby allowing us to infer that the means do differ.

Statistical decision errors

When we make a statistical decision, we recognize that it might be mistaken. After all, the statistical inferences are all statements of probabilities rather than certainties. There are two ways we can be mistaken. First, we might reject the null hypothesis when it is in fact true, that is, there was no systematic effect – the difference between means in the two conditions was entirely attributable to random NVs. Because the difference between means created by the combined effects of the random NVs happened to be large – a difference that would happen, say, less than 5% of the time by chance – we were led to conclude that the difference was probably caused by a systematic effect (of the IV, we hope), whereas, assuming we set α equal to .05, it was in fact one of those 5% of occasions when a large difference was due to chance. This kind of mistake is called a **Type I error** and the probability of making it is known (i.e., the value at which we set α).

The other mistake we can make is to fail to reject the null hypothesis when it is in fact false, that is, there was a systematic effect but we failed to detect it. This may happen when the variability of scores within conditions is large relative to the difference between means, so that we are misled into concluding that random error was probably great enough to account for the difference between means. This kind of mistake is called a **Type II error** and the probability of it occurring is denoted by the symbol β. As with α, we can, in principle, set the value of β at a level that suits us. A level that, by convention, is often thought acceptable is .2 (20%). That is, we accept a 20% risk of failing to find a significant effect of the IV when it does in fact have an effect. The fact that most researchers are prepared to accept a considerably bigger risk of missing a real effect (20%) than of finding an effect that is really just due to chance (5%) reflects a general belief that the theoretical (and maybe, practical) consequences of concluding that an IV has an effect when it does not are more serious than the consequences of missing an effect.

Just as there are two ways of being mistaken, there are two ways of being right. You can correctly reject the null hypothesis - the probability of this outcome is $1 - \beta$ (that would be $1 - .2 = .8$, or 80%, using our example above). This value $(1 - \beta)$ is known as the **power** of the statistical test, that is, the likelihood of the test finding a significant effect when one does in fact exist. In practice, it is usually this *power* probability that is decided on by the researcher, and this automatically determines the value of β, the probability of a Type II error. The other way of being right is to correctly fail to reject the null hypothesis. The probability of this outcome is $1 - \alpha$

Complications (5.3) – What to conclude if you fail to reject the null hypothesis

If the statistical decision is to reject the null hypothesis, the inference is clear. The value of the statistic that was calculated (based, for example, on the difference between means and the variability of scores within conditions) is sufficiently extreme to persuade us that it is unlikely to have occurred by chance (random NVs) alone. We therefore conclude that the data probably arose at least partly as a result of an effect of the IV. In other words, we have found support for our experimental hypothesis.

If the statistical decision is to fail to reject the null hypothesis, the situation is less clear. Does that mean that the null hypothesis should be assumed to be true? The answer is 'no'. The null hypothesis might still be false, but the effect of the IV might be small relative to the effects of NVs and, therefore, hard to discern. The null hypothesis states that there will be zero difference between population means of the two conditions. With a small difference between population means, we would be unlikely to identify a significant difference from our sample data, unless we had extremely good control over random NVs and/or a very large sample of scores, in which case we might well be finding an effect that is too small to be of interest. This is not unlikely, since the null hypothesis is almost never *exactly* true.

Although people sometimes talk about accepting the null hypothesis when it cannot be rejected, it is probably safer to refer to '*failing to reject the null hypothesis*' or '*retaining the null hypothesis*' (i.e., provisionally).

Additional information (5.6) – The power of a test

The power of a test to find an effect when one actually exists depends on a number of factors

- Our ability to control random NVs. The more they are controlled (kept constant), the less variability there will be within each condition and the easier it will be to attribute a difference between means to the IV.
- The size of effect that we do not want to risk missing. The larger the effect, the easier it is to reach statistical significance. To some extent, a researcher can maximize an effect by selecting values for the IV that are relatively extreme. For example, it would be much easier to find an effect of age on time to run 50 metres if we compared 6-year-old and 10-year-old children than if we compared 6-year-olds with 6.1-year-olds! Similarly, we are more likely to find an effect of viewing different videos if the experimental one is really hilarious rather than mildly amusing.
- The α level set. Everything else being equal, it is easier to reach statistical significance with an α value of .05 than a value of .01.
- Whether a one- or two-tailed test is used (a distinction that we will explain in the next section). To anticipate, if you opt for a one-tailed test and your directional prediction is correct, a lower value of the statistic calculated will be needed for statistical significance at a given level of probability.
- Whether a parametric or non-parametric statistical test is used. This distinction will be discussed in subsequent chapters.
- The number of participants included in the experiment. The more participants per condition, the more powerful the test will be. It is beyond the scope of this book but, if you continue to study psychology, you will learn about how to get an estimate of how many participants you will need to achieve a given power.

(that would be $1 - .05 = .95$, or 95%, using our example above). This is the likelihood of the test failing to find a significant effect when one does not in fact exist. The relationship between the decision that is made when a statistical test has been carried out (reject or fail to reject the null hypothesis) and the reality of the situation (the null hypothesis is true or it is false) is illustrated in Figure 5.8.

One- and two-tailed tests

Usually a researcher has a view about the likely direction of a difference between means that will occur. It is likely, for example, that an experimenter conducting

Decision made using inferential statistic	The reality (H_0 is either true or false)	
	H_0 is true	H_0 is false
Reject H_0	Type I error probability $= \alpha$	Correct decision probability $= 1 - \beta =$ Power
Do not reject H_0	Correct decision probability $= 1 - \alpha$	Type II error probability $= \beta$

Figure 5.8 Possible decisions about the null hypothesis (H_0)

the video-viewing experiment would expect scores to be higher in the '*funny*' video condition (E > C; where E stands for 'Experimental condition' and C for 'Control condition'). However, it is possible that people's moods might be worse after being shown the funny video, perhaps because they felt they were being 'manipulated'. If that happened and they scored lower on the logical reasoning test than those shown a neutral video, should the researcher conclude that the experiment showed an effect of the type of video? It all depends on the precise prediction that the experimenter made before collecting the data. If the researcher decided that, although a difference in favour of the funny video was expected, a difference in the opposite direction would be of interest, a **non-directional prediction** should be made; that is, the alternative to the null hypothesis (E = C: i.e., no significant difference) would be that there would be a significant difference in either direction (E > C or C > E). Then, if α was set at .05, we would be looking for an extreme positive or negative value of our statistic (independent groups *t*, in this case) at either end of the distribution of possible values when the null hypothesis is true; more specifically, a value among the .025 most extreme in either direction (see Figure 5.9a). If the value of the statistic falls in either tail (the *rejection regions*), we would conclude that the null hypothesis could be rejected at the 5% level and that there was a significant ($p < .05$) effect of the type of video viewed in a **two-tailed test** of the hypothesis. Sometimes, a two-tailed test is the only sensible option, as when you have two competing experimental conditions, rather than one experimental condition and one control condition.

If, on the other hand, the researcher decided that a difference in the non-expected direction would simply mean that the experiment had failed and was therefore of no interest, a **directional prediction** might be appropriate (e.g., E > C). In that case, if the *t*-statistic were among the .025 most extreme values in the 'wrong' tail (the one representing extreme differences in favour of the neutral video), the decision would be to fail to reject the null hypothesis and to conclude that the video effect was non-significant ($p > .05$) in a **one-tailed test** of the hypothesis. The gain from making the more specific directional prediction is that, if the difference between means is in the predicted direction, a lower value of the statistic (*t* in this example) will be needed

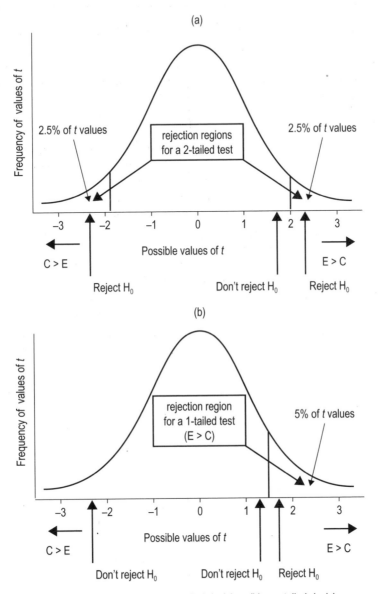

Figure 5.9 One- and two-tailed decisions: (a) two-tailed decision; (b) one-tailed decision

to achieve statistical significance. This is because the region for rejection of the null hypothesis will be the 5% most extreme values in the predicted direction (i.e., all .05 most extreme values are in one tail instead of being split .025 in each tail). This is illustrated in Figure 5.9b.

Complications (5.4) – The decision to do a one- or two-tailed test is 'set in stone'

It should be stressed that a decision to use a one-tailed test *must* be taken before the data have been collected. It is not acceptable to decide on a one-tailed test after you have seen what the data look like. In that case, a smaller value of the statistic would be needed to achieve significance, but it would be 'cheating'! Similarly, once a decision is made to do a one-tailed test, it would be unacceptable to change the decision (i.e., to do a two-tailed test) after it is seen that the difference went in the non-predicted direction. Once again, that would be 'cheating' – you would be looking at a rejection region of $p = .05$ in the originally predicted tail *plus* a rejection region of $p = .025$ in the originally non-predicted tail, so the real probability of the data being obtained when the null hypothesis is true would be .075, not .05! In view of the uncertainty about the stage at which a decision is made to opt for a one- or two-tailed test, some researchers take the view that the statistical test reported should *always* be two-tailed.

SUMMARY OF CHAPTER

- Knowing that an experiment has validity and that there are differences between DV scores in different conditions is not enough to infer that the IV has an effect on the DV. We still have to consider the possibility that these differences are determined by random NVs.
- Random NVs (i) do not pose a threat to the internal validity of an experiment; (ii) cannot be eliminated; (iii) increase the variability of scores on the DV within each condition; (iv) may occasionally pile up in favour of one condition to produce a large effect.
- In order to infer that differences in DV scores between the two conditions are so large that they cannot be due to the effects of random NVs (and therefore the hypothesis is correct), we make use of 'statistical inference'.
- Statistical inference consists of setting up a 'null hypothesis' (an hypothesis of 'no effect of the IV') and seeing whether it can be rejected as a likely explanation of any difference between scores in the two conditions. If it can be rejected at some level of confidence (probability), we infer that the difference between conditions is statistically significant at that level of probability.
- To test the null hypothesis we calculate a statistic from the data (different statistics are calculated depending on the research design) and we see whether it is among the most extreme values that would occur with a given probability (say, $p < .05$) if the null hypothesis were true and the experiment was repeated thousands of times.
- The statistical inference may be mistaken. We may find an effect when the null hypothesis is in fact true (Type I error), or we may fail to find an effect when the null hypothesis is in fact false (Type II error – this may mean that the experiment has insufficient 'power' to reveal an effect).
- If a directional prediction is made (e.g., 'scores will be higher in the experimental condition'), we can use a 'one-tailed' test, which requires a smaller value of the statistic to reach significance. If a non-directional prediction is made (i.e., 'scores in the two conditions will differ'), a two-tailed test must be used. The decision to use a one- or two-tailed test must be made before collecting the data.

CHAPTER SIX

Selecting a Statistical Test

In the last chapter, we talked about the general logic underlying the use of statistical tests for making inferences from our data. In this chapter we will discuss the criteria that you should consider when deciding which specific test to use. Subsequent chapters will focus on details to do with each of the specific tests that we mention in the present chapter. At the outset we need to be clear that there are many more tests available than those we will be dealing with. We will be confining ourselves to the most commonly used tests that are applicable to experiments, or quasi-experiments, with one IV with no more than two levels (or conditions), and to non-experimental studies concerned with the strength of relationship between two variables (**correlational studies**).

The Nature of the Research Question

To start with, you need to be clear whether you are looking for evidence of a difference between scores in two conditions (which may support an inference of an effect of an IV on a DV), or between scores of a single group and a known population mean, or of a relationship between two DVs.

Effect of an IV on a DV

Evidence may be sought for either a *causal* or *non-causal* effect of the IV on the DV. The first consideration in deciding if a causal effect can legitimately be sought is whether you actually manipulated levels of the IV, randomly assigning participants to the two levels. If you did, and provided there were no plausible confounding variables, you would have a 'true experimental design' and you could infer that any effect found was a causal one. If, on the other hand, you selected participants with pre-existing levels of an IV (e.g., age), you would have a 'quasi-experimental design' and you would not be able to infer that any obtained effect of, say, age was a causal one, though some researchers seem to be unaware of this limitation! Having said that, regardless of whether you have an experimental or a quasi-experimental design, you will be asking whether the means of scores in the two conditions are significantly *different* from one another. The appropriate statistical test may well be the same one for both designs. The difference does not lie in the statistical test used, but in how strong the inference of a causal effect may be if the difference between means is found to be statistically significant. The inference is *much* weaker in the case of selection (a quasi-experiment) than in the case of random allocation (a true experiment) of levels of the IV (see Additional information (2.5) for a discussion of quasi-experiments).

A difference between a single set of scores and a known mean

Sometimes, rather than comparing one set of scores with another, a researcher may want to compare a *single* set of scores on a DV with a mean value that is already known. For example, you might want a sample of participants that is *typical* of a population on some variable, such as 'intelligence' or 'extroversion'. Then, provided that *normative* data exist (i.e., a *representative* sample of the population has been measured previously on that variable), the mean score for any new sample can be compared with the mean of the normative sample. If the mean of the new sample does not differ significantly from the normative value, then we can assume that the sample is representative of the population of interest. (Technically, we would say that we could not reject the null hypothesis that the participants we have selected comprise a random sample from the specified population.) On another occasion, a researcher may want a sample that scores *higher or lower* than the normative sample; on extroversion, for example. In all of these situations, a **one-sample *t*-test** can be used to test whether a sample of participants differs significantly from a normative sample on a DV of interest. There is obviously no question of a causal effect in this case.

Relationships between variables

In some studies, researchers just want to seek evidence of a non-causal relationship between two DVs. For example, you might obtain scores on an intelligence test and on a creativity test because you are interested in whether people who are more intelligent tend also to be more creative. In this case, rather than investigating the effects of one variable (the IV) on another (the DV), we are investigating the strength of the relationship (or correlation) between two DVs, and whether that correlation is statistically significant. The degree of relationship between two variables is calculated as a statistic called a correlation index (**Pearson's *r*** or **Spearman's r_s**), which can vary from −1 (a perfect negative relationship, such that, for example, the person who scores highest on intelligence, scores lowest on creativity), through zero (no relationship, such that a person with a high score on intelligence is equally likely to have a high or low score on creativity), to +1 (a perfect positive relationship, such that the person who scores highest on intelligence also scores highest on creativity). The interpretation of correlation indices will be taken up in more detail in Chapter 10.

Type of Experimental Design

In the sections above we saw that you need to decide whether you are looking for (a) a difference between means in two conditions, (b) a difference between the mean of a single sample and the known mean of a normative group, or (c) a correlation between two variables.

If you are dealing with an experimental (or quasi-experimental) study in which different levels of an IV (the conditions of the experiment) are hypothesized to have an effect on the DV scores, you will need to decide which of two types of design is being used; these are an independent groups design or a repeated measures design.

In an independent groups design, there are different participants in each condition. In a true experiment they will have been randomly allocated to conditions, and in a quasi-experiment they will have been selected as people representing the conditions (e.g., people at two different age levels). From the point of view of the statistical analysis, it makes no difference whether you have a true or quasi-experimental design. In an independent groups design, the appropriate test will be either an **independent groups** *t*-test (also known as a **unrelated** *t*-test) or a **Mann–Whitney** *U* **test**. If you have a repeated measures design, in which the same participants are used in the two conditions, the appropriate test will be either a **related** *t*-test or a **Wilcoxon (Matched-Pairs Signed-Ranks)** *T* test.

The next two sections will discuss how to decide between an independent groups *t*-test and a Mann–Whitney *U* test or between a related *t*-test and a Wilcoxon *T* test. Details of the Mann–Whitney *U* test and the Wilcoxon *T* test are given in Chapter 8 and details of the two *t*-tests are given in Chapter 9.

Additional information (6.1) – Matched pairs design

In Chapter 3 we discussed the matched pairs (or matched subjects) design, in which participants in the two conditions are different, but specific procedures are used to match each participant in one condition with a participant in the other condition. Now, despite including different participants in each condition, this design is analysed in the same way as the repeated measures design: that is, using a related *t*-test or a Wilcoxon *T* test. For the purpose of the statistical test, matched pairs of participants are treated as though they were the same person. If the variable on which participants are matched really is an important potential NV, that is, it has a marked effect on DV scores, it will be easier to get a significant result than if matching had not been carried out (i.e., the matched pairs design will be more *powerful* than the independent groups design). If, however, the effect of the matching variable on the DV is minimal, the matched pairs design will be less powerful.

Type of Measurement Used

As emphasized in Chapter 2, in order to assess differences in the levels of DV it is important to devise a plausible indicator of the thing represented by the DV, and a precise way to measure the DV. Measurement is a process of assigning numbers to observations, but numbers are not always assigned in the same way. We can think of a hierarchy of **measurement scales** (or **levels of measurement**), with additional properties of the numbers being added as we move up the hierarchy. We will begin by naming the types of scale that are usually distinguished and indicating briefly what their properties are. The hierarchy is shown in Figure 6.1.

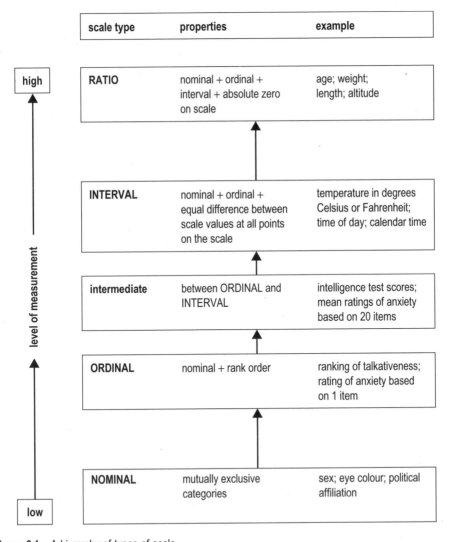

Figure 6.1 A hierarchy of types of scale

Nominal measurement

The 'simplest' type of scale is a **nominal scale**. This amounts to assigning numbers to mutually exclusive categories that differ in some qualitative way. For example, in order to do some statistical analysis in SPSS, we might assign 1 to females and 2 to males, or 1, 2 and 3 respectively to people of British, French and German nationality. These numbers are really just labels for these qualitative or categorical variables and the numbers could be assigned differently (e.g., 1 to males and 2 to females) because there is no 'right' order for the categories; they are all just different. It would make no sense to carry out arithmetic calculations on these numbers, such as calculating their means. Often, though, we count the number of instances in each category and may be interested in differences in the frequencies in different categories. Particular cases of the independent groups and repeated measures (or matched pairs) design have a DV that is measured on a nominal scale. In the case of an independent groups design, this arises when, instead of participants being able to get a range of scores, there are only two possible scores; like *pass* or *fail* or choosing *left* or *right*. Similarly, in the repeated measures design, we may only be interested in knowing in which of the two conditions each individual (or members of a matched pair) scores highest. Studies involving nominal data will be considered in Chapter 7 but, for the moment, it is sufficient to know that there are two additional tests that can deal with these situations. These are the **Chi-Square test** (often written as χ^2) and the **Sign test**.

Ordinal measurement

The next level in the hierarchy is an **ordinal scale**. This has the same property of mutually exclusive categories as a nominal scale, plus the additional property of *ranking* (or ordering) observations in order of magnitude. The numbers assigned express a 'greater than' relationship. The most obvious way that ordinal measurement arises is when people are asked to directly rank a set of people or objects on some dimension. For example, participants might be asked to rank a group of their peers on 'talkativeness' or they might be asked to rank a set of paintings from oldest to most recent. They would end up with a set of 'ordinal numbers' such as 1st, 2nd, 3rd etc. It should be fairly obvious that the difference between the person ranked highest on the talkativeness scale could be just a little more talkative than the person ranked 2nd highest or a great deal more talkative. Generalizing from this, we can see that the differences in talkativeness represented by adjacent numbers at different parts of the scale (e.g., between 1st and 2nd, 5th and 6th or 9th and 10th) cannot be assumed to be equal. We can assume that a higher number always implies *more* of the variable being measured, but we don't know *how much* more. As the intervals between numbers cannot be assumed to be equal, operations like calculating the mean are likely to result in misleading conclusions.

It is possible to create an ordinal scale even when participants are not asked to rank things; for example, when participants are asked to rate things. Suppose individuals are presented with the statement and labelled boxes shown below and asked to tick the box that best indicates their level of agreement or disagreement with the statement. Depending on which box an individual ticked, they might then be assigned a number (1 to 5) on a computer anxiety scale. An individual who ticked the 'strongly agree' box (5) would be considered more computer anxious than one who ticked the 'agree' box (4). However, we cannot infer anything from those scores about *how much* more computer anxious one was than the other. So, strictly speaking, we again have an ordinal scale and the same limitations apply.

Thinking about using a computer makes me feel nervous.

strongly disagree	disagree	neutral	agree	strongly agree
☐	☐	☐	☐	☐

The same argument applies in other situations where, for example, participants perform some task and end up with a score representing, say, number of correct responses. Consider our 'mood and performance' experiment. It might well be that some of the problems were intrinsically more difficult than others, so that solving an additional (easy) problem at the low end of the scale might not represent as big a difference in performance as solving an additional (difficult) problem at the high end of the scale.

Interval measurement

The next level in the hierarchy is an **interval** (or, more descriptively, an **equal interval**) **scale**. This has the same property as an ordinal scale, in that larger numbers imply more of whatever is being measured, and the additional property that the intervals between numbers are assumed to represent *equal* differences in the variable being measured at all points on the scale. A clear example of an interval scale is degree of temperature measured on the Celsius scale. For example, a difference of ten degrees represents the same change in degree of hotness whether it is a difference between −16 and −6 or a difference between 70 and 80. When we add up a number of temperature recordings on an equal interval scale of this kind, we are always adding the same amount of temperature change for each additional degree Celsius, so the arithmetic operation of calculating a mean makes sense. There is still a limitation to what we can infer from scores on an interval scale. It is not possible to speak meaningfully about a ratio between two measurements. What this means is that we cannot assume that a number (say, 80 degrees Celsius) that is twice the size of another number (say, 40 degrees Celsius) represents twice as much of whatever is being measured (temperature in this example), even though the first number is twice as far above 0 degrees as the second number. This is because '0 degrees' does not represent *zero* degree of hotness. The fact that 80 degrees Celsius is not twice as high a temperature as

Complications (6.1) – Dealing with scales intermediate between ordinal and interval levels

Some researchers suggest that the level of measurement attained should strictly determine what statistics it is permissible to use on the data. Others say that the level of measurement is irrelevant; statistics are carried out on numbers, and the numbers are always just numbers, so the result is always 'correct'. We think that both views are unhelpful. What matters is that we can *interpret* the results of an inferential statistical analysis in a way that is *meaningful* in relation to the variable we have measured. In reality, we are not interested in the numbers as abstractions; we are interested in something that they are assumed to *stand for* in the real world. Bearing this in mind, we can now consider what role levels of measurement should play in our decisions about which statistic to use.

If our data were obtained by using ratings, as in the example above used to illustrate ordinal scales, it would probably not be acceptable to perform averaging operations on the data and this would preclude the use of parametric statistics, which always involve such arithmetic operations. However, if, instead of obtaining a rating for just one statement, we got ratings for 20 statements about positive and negative feelings concerning computers, it would be highly likely that there would be more than just ordinal (greater than) information in our data. The intervals between scores could not be assumed to be equal, but a case can be made for expecting them to be *approximately* equal. Our scale would likely be somewhere between ordinal and interval and the more items that were rated, the closer it would probably approach an equal interval scale.

Many researchers, including us, take the view that, if a case can be made for supposing that a scale that is intermediate between ordinal and interval levels is closer to being interval measurement than being limited to ordinal measurement, it is acceptable to assume an approximation to an interval scale. That means that parametric statistics can be used on the data, provided the formal parametric assumptions are reasonably met, applying the same criteria as for a truly interval scale. This might well apply to the recall data in the other example we used above to illustrate ordinal scales. As another example, parametric statistics are frequently applied to test data, such as data from an intelligence test, even though the measurement does not strictly qualify as an interval scale. In the end, what matters about using parametric statistics is whether it results in a statistical inference about an effect on the DV that is both accurate (the probability statement is correct because the parametric assumptions are met) and *makes sense*. 'Making sense' is a matter of being satisfied that treating intervals between scores as equal – which is implicit in the computation of a parametric statistic – is a reasonable approximation to the reality.

40 degrees Celsius is obvious if we convert these temperatures to degrees Fahrenheit (176 and 104 degrees Fahrenheit). To take a psychological example, suppose for a moment that we have an intelligence scale that represents a close approximation to an interval scale. If someone scored zero on the scale, that would not mean they had *no* intelligence. If there had been a few easier questions on the test, they might have scored above zero. The absence of a *true zero* on the scale makes it meaningless to assert that someone scoring 100 is twice as intelligent as someone scoring 50.

Ratio measurement

The final level in the hierarchy is a **ratio scale**, which shares the properties of all of the other types of scale and has the additional property of having a **true zero** point. Although the distinction between interval and ratio scales is important because the latter allows for an interpretation in terms of how many times bigger one value is than another, from the point of view of statistical analyses, ratio scales are treated in the same way as interval scales, so we will not elaborate on them here.

Complications (6.2) – Physical scales and underlying psychological scales

The physical measurement scales, such as length, weight, time and temperature, are all at least interval scales. However, when one is used as a DV in a psychology experiment it may be *standing as* an indicator of the level of some other (psychological) variable. For example, temperature in a room might be employed as a measure of 'comfort'. Now, it may well be that over a fairly high range of temperatures, the higher the temperature the greater the discomfort of a person in the room, but there is no guarantee that increments of discomfort will be equal for equal changes in temperature at all parts of the scale. In other words, as a measurement of the psychological variable that we are actually interested in, we probably have an ordinal scale rather than an interval scale. Other examples might be time spent on a difficult problem as a measure of 'concentration' or 'persistence', or the distance people leave between themselves and other people when sitting on a bench as a measure of 'social closeness'. The point is that what determines the measurement status of the scale is how it relates to the *underlying variable* in which we are interested. Once again, though, the criterion for whether or not to use a parametric test is whether the resulting statistical inference of an effect on our DV is both *accurate* and *makes sense*.

Deciding Whether Your Data Are Parametric or Non-parametric

We need, at this point, to distinguish between **parametric** and **non-parametric tests**. There are two important differences. First, for a parametric test to be used, certain assumptions about the data need to be met. Second, if these assumptions are met, a parametric test will generally be more powerful than a non-parametric alternative; that is, the parametric test will have more chance of finding a significant effect if the null hypothesis is false (i.e., if the effect really exists). Recall that, for an independent groups design, two possible statistical tests were suggested; the independent groups *t*-test and the Mann–Whitney *U* test. The former is an example of a parametric test and the latter is an example of a non-parametric alternative that is available if the assumptions required for the parametric test are not met. Similarly, for a repeated measures (or matched pairs) design, the related *t*-test (a parametric test) and the Wilcoxon *T* test (a non-parametric alternative) were suggested.

What is a parametric test?

Parametric tests are those that involve assumptions about the estimation of specific **parameters** of the distribution of scores in the population(s) from which the data were sampled, and about the shape of that distribution. This probably sounds like gobbledegook, but the basic idea is not that difficult. Part of the initial difficulty concerns what exactly is meant by a 'parameter'. When we are describing a value (such as the mean, standard deviation or variance) that applies to a *sample* of data, the value is referred to as a *statistic*. This is really just an *estimate* of the value for the *population* from which our sample comes. A statistic is therefore variable, in that, if we obtained a different sample, we would expect the value of the statistic to change. When we are describing a value (mean, standard deviation, variance etc.) that applies to a population, on the other hand, there can only be one value and this is referred to as a parameter, not a statistic. So, a test is parametric if (i) it involves using a sample statistic, such as sample standard deviation, as an estimate of the population standard deviation – which is what we are really interested in of course – and (ii) a particular shape of the distribution of the population of scores is assumed.

What are the assumptions that must be met for a parametric test?

For the parametric tests we are dealing with, two special assumptions are required for these tests to yield good estimates of the probability of the means of the two samples coming from the same population. That is, of course, the probability that scores in the two samples could have arisen if the null hypothesis were true. The two assumptions are (i) **homogeneity of variance** of the two populations and (ii) **normal distribution** of scores in the two populations. In the case of homogeneity of variance, what this means is that the spread of scores in the two populations, as measured by the variance, should be equal. Of course, we do not know the population variances and have to rely on our sample variances to decide whether the homogeneity assumption is met. (We will see when we use SPSS to compute parametric statistics that statistical packages sometimes decide for us whether the equal variance assumption is met and, when it is not, go ahead anyway and compute a parametric statistic, with a correction built in to reduce the effects of the violation of the assumption.) In the case of normality of distributions, the distributions of the populations of scores should conform to the symmetrical, bell-shaped curves discussed in Chapter 4 and illustrated in Figure 4.5. Once again, we have to rely on the shapes of our sample distributions to help us decide whether the normality assumption is met.

How do we decide whether the parametric assumptions are met?

If the assumptions of homogeneity of variance and normality are not met, the probability value associated with the calculated value of the statistic used to test the null hypothesis will be an approximation rather than an exact value. Consequently, conclusions stating that the probability of the data arising when the null hypothesis is true is less than, say, .05 may be misleading. The probability of making a Type I error when concluding that the null hypothesis can be rejected may well be greater than .05. It is rather obvious that the assumptions of homogeneity of variance and normality are unlikely to be met precisely. However, it turns out that modest departures from these assumptions often have a very minor effect on the probability of making a Type I error. The technical way of describing this is to say that the probabilities associated with values of a statistic are **robust** under moderate departures from the assumptions of homogeneity of variance and normality.

So, how can you tell whether the parametric assumptions are met well enough to allow you to use a parametric test? Unfortunately, there is no hard and fast rule, but there are some rules of thumb that are helpful.

1. If the variance of the sample in one condition is more than four times greater or less than the variance in the other condition, you should think seriously about using a non-parametric statistic.
2. If, when you plot frequency distributions (histograms or frequency polygons) of scores in the two conditions, at least one distribution strongly resembles a different type of distribution more than it resembles a normal distribution, you should again think seriously about using a non-parametric statistic. Other types of distribution to look for include positively or negatively skewed distributions (see Figure 4.5), a rectangular distribution in which the frequencies of different scores are all very similar (thus, looking like a rectangle when plotted) and bimodal (or multimodal) distributions in which there are two or more clear humps in the distribution, instead of one, as in a normal distribution.

3. The smaller the sample size (i.e., number of participants), the more seriously you should take the violations of the two assumptions described above; the more ready you should be to go for a non-parametric statistic. A sample of less than 20 per condition is often offered as a rough guide to when you should be ready to act on violations of the parametric assumptions.

4. If you have an independent groups design, unequal group sizes should lead you to take violations of the parametric assumptions more seriously, particularly if the sample sizes are small. The greater the difference in sample sizes, the more problematic the use of a parametric test becomes, but the problem is much more serious when the samples are small. For example, one sample being half the size of the other may not be very worrying if samples sizes are 50 and 25, but sample sizes of 16 and 8 may be a cause for concern.

5. If sample distributions are non-normal, the situation is more serious if the shapes of the two distributions differ from one another. For example, it would be more serious if one was positively skewed and the other was negatively skewed or bimodal or normal, than if both were positively skewed.

6. A combination of different non-normal distributions, non-homogeneity of variance and small, unequal samples provides the strongest indication that a non-parametric test should be used.

Figure 6.2 shows a flow chart summarizing things to consider when deciding whether parametric assumptions have been violated sufficiently to warrant use of a non-parametric test. In the end, the researcher has to make a judgement about the degree of violations in combination with the presence of other warning signs. To use the flow chart in Figure 6.2, begin at the top. As you move down, the more descriptions that apply to your data, the more seriously you should consider using a non-parametric test. If all or most of the descriptions apply and you still use a parametric test, your statistical conclusion cannot be relied on and your analysis will rightly be criticized.

The Nature of the Specific Hypothesis to be Tested

Before conducting a statistical test, it is necessary to make a decision whether to specify a directional hypothesis (e.g., mean in experimental condition > mean in control condition) or to settle for a non-directional hypothesis (e.g., means in the two conditions will differ in either direction). This decision will determine whether a one-tailed or two-tailed test of the null hypothesis should be carried out. One- and two-tailed tests were discussed in Chapter 5.

Deciding what test to use

The final decision about which test to use will be depend on the considerations discussed above. These are summarized in the decision chart in Table 6.1. You should

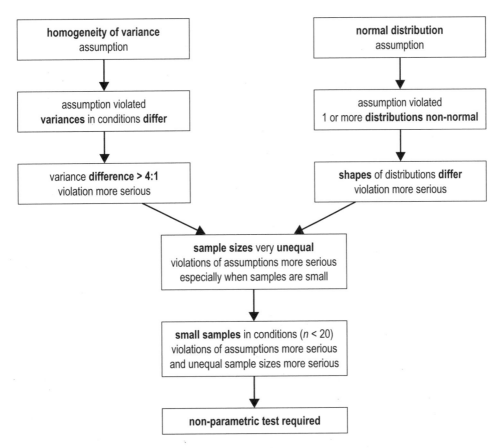

Figure 6.2 When should a non-parametric test be used?

begin at the top by deciding which kind of question your test is required to answer (condition effect, norm difference or association), and the associated design (repeated measures, independent groups, single sample or correlational). Next, you should look down the leftmost column and locate the level of measurement that applies to your data. If you have nominal or clearly ordinal data, the appropriate test will be entered at the intersection between the column and row you have selected. If, however, you decide that you have an interval or ratio scale, or a scale that is intermediate between ordinal and interval measurement, you will first need to decide whether parametric assumptions have been reasonably met. The appropriate test will be near the bottom of the chart below the 'yes' or 'no' that is your response to the parametric assumption question. It only remains (right at the bottom of the chart) to decide whether the test should be directional (hence one-tailed) or non-directional (hence two-tailed).

In the following chapters, we will focus on the specifics of carrying out the tests referred to in this chapter. Chapters 7, 8 and 9 will deal with **tests of differences** between scores obtained in the two conditions of an experiment, in which either nominal,

Table 6.1   Choosing a test from those included in this book

measurement scale	What are you testing for?							
	condition effect (difference between 2 means)				norm difference (difference between a sample mean and a population mean)		association between 2 variables (no manipulated variable)	
	What design are you using?							
	repeated measures (same participants in 2 conditions)		independent groups (different participants in 2 conditions)		one sample (single group of participants in 1 condition)		correlational (same participants measured on 2 dependent variables)	
NOMINAL	Sign test Ch 7, p 102		Chi Square Ch 7, p 106		no test provided		Chi Square Ch 7, p 106	
ORDINAL	Wilcoxon T non-parametric test Ch 8, p 118		Mann–Whitney U non-parametric test Ch 8, p 124		no test provided		Spearman rho non-parametric test Ch 10, p 170	
INTERVAL & RATIO & INTERMEDIATE (between ordinal and interval)*	Are parametric assumptions reasonably met?							
	yes related t-test	no Wilcoxon T test	yes independent groups t-test	no Mann–Whitney U test	yes one-sample t-test	no no test provided	yes Pearson r	no Spearman rho
	Ch 9, p 143	Ch 8, p 118	Ch 9, p 133	Ch 8, p 124	Ch 9, p 149		Ch 10, p 165	Ch 10, p 170

* Includes physical scales (e.g., time) when they are used as indicators of underlying psychological variables (e.g., persistence).

ordinal or interval data were used, respectively. In the case of interval data especially, it should be apparent from the chart in Table 6.1 that labelling the chapters
according to the level of measurement used is an 'organizational convenience' rather
than an acceptance that the measurement scale used strictly determines the choice
of test. For interval and ratio scales, and for scales intermediate between ordinal and
interval levels, the principal criterion underlying the choice of test is whether parametric assumptions are met to an acceptable degree. The final chapter will focus on
tests of association between DVs, distinguishing between those appropriate for different measurement scales and, in the case of interval and ratio scales and scales
intermediate between ordinal and interval levels, those suitable when parametric assumptions are or are not met.

SUMMARY OF CHAPTER

- The first consideration when selecting a statistical test is the nature of the
  research question being asked. Are you looking for a difference between
  means, a difference between the mean of a single sample and a known mean
  of a norm group or an association (correlation) between two DVs?
- If you are looking for a difference between means, you will be using an
  experimental (or quasi-experimental) design and will need to consider
  whether there will be different participants in each condition (independent
  groups design) or the same participants in each condition (repeated measures
  design) or matched pairs of participants in the two conditions (matched pairs
  design).
- The type of measurement scale used is a good indicator of which tests are
  likely to lead to statistical inferences that are readily interpretable. Measurement scales can be placed in a hierarchy (nominal, ordinal, interval, ratio)
  indicating increasing levels of information contained in the data.
- Statistical tests may be parametric or non-parametric. Parametric tests are
  more powerful than non-parametric ones. Parametric tests may be used with
  data measured either on interval scales or on scales intermediate between
  ordinal and interval levels, but only if the parametric assumptions necessary
  for a parametric test (homogeneity of variance and normal distributions) are
  reasonably met.
- Violations of the assumptions will increase the likelihood of making a Type
  I error. Violations are more serious (i) the smaller the overall sample size,
  (ii) the more unequal the sizes of samples in the two conditions, and (iii)
  the more different the shapes of the two distributions.
- The final decision to be made when selecting a statistical test is whether a
  directional (one-tailed) or non-directional (two-tailed) hypothesis is appropriate.

CHAPTER SEVEN

Tests of Significance for Nominal Data

Nominal Data

We will begin by reminding you what constitutes nominal data and how it might arise. Recall that nominal measurement involves assigning numbers to exclusive categories that differ from one another in some qualitative way. In our earlier discussion of measurement scales, the examples we gave were for variables that distinguished between existing characteristics of individuals, such as sex and nationality. These are, of course, IVs whose values are not determined by the researcher. In this chapter, however, we will be focusing on the use of nominal scales in experimental studies. These are studies in which levels of a nominal IV are manipulated by the researcher in order to observe a causal effect on a nominal DV. In experimental studies, numbers are assigned arbitrarily to the different categories, just as they were for sex (1, 2) and nationality (1, 2, 3).

Repeated Measures (or Matched Pairs) Experiment

As for other levels of measurement, experimental studies using nominal scales may use either (i) a repeated measures (or matched pairs) design or (ii) an independent groups design. We bracket repeated measures and matched pairs designs together because they are analysed in the same way. We will begin with an example of a repeated measures design using nominal scales.

Suppose we were interested in the population of people who do not generally take an interest in paintings (as indicated by their reported non-visiting of art galleries), and our research hypothesis was that such people would find representational paintings more attractive than abstract ones. Note that this is a directional hypothesis, so we could justify carrying out a one-tailed test. Our nominal IV would be *type of painting*, and it would include two levels, 'representational' and 'abstract'. To start with, we might collect prints of 15 pairs of paintings, with one representational and one abstract print in each pair (i.e., one print in each condition), ensuring that the two paintings in each pair are relatively similar in attractiveness to naïve viewers. Then, we could show one of the pairs to each of 15 people who do not visit art galleries, and ask them to say which of the pair they found most attractive. That would be our nominal DV. For each participant, we might label their judgement of the pair of paintings as '1' or '2' (or, more usually, '+' or '−'), depending on whether the representational or abstract member of the pair was considered more attractive. Remember, it doesn't really matter whether we use numbers or other symbols such as plus and minus signs because, in either case, they are just being used to identify categories (*representational preferred* or *abstract preferred*). Numbers are more convenient when we plan to do a statistical analysis on a computer, but in the present example the analysis is so simple that we would hardly be likely to use a computer and, in fact, plus and minus signs are usually used in these cases, which is why the test is referred to as a Sign test.

The data

To recapitulate, we have a repeated measures design because all participants respond to both conditions of the experiment, though the present design is unusual in that the two conditions may be presented simultaneously rather than one after another. If they were presented one after another, it would, as usual, be necessary to control order effects by counterbalancing; that is, half of the participants would see the representational painting first and half would see the abstract one first. We have nominal data because there are two qualitatively different categories of response (*representational preferred* and *abstract preferred*). Our interest lies in the frequencies of the two categories of response. Suppose the data obtained were as shown in Table 7.1.

If the null hypothesis were true (people who are not interested in art would be equally likely to prefer representational or abstract paintings), you would expect the number of participants showing a preference for a representational painting to be roughly similar to the number showing a preference for an abstract painting. On the other hand, if the null hypothesis were false (and the research hypothesis were true), you would expect more participants to express a preference for a representational painting. Now look at the data. Do you think that the data support the null hypothesis or the research hypothesis?

As always, we cannot come to a definite conclusion as to whether the null hypothesis is true or false. We can only come to a *probabilistic* conclusion. If the null hypothesis were true, we know there would be an equal chance of the preference going either way for each participant. On the other hand, if the null hypothesis were false, we would expect more participants to prefer representational paintings. But, how 'many more' would be enough to convince us that the data would have been unlikely to arise (by chance) if the null hypothesis were true? This is just like tossing

Table 7.1   Nominal data from a repeated measures design

Participant	Preference response	Coded response	
		numerical	sign (plus/minus)
1	representational	1	+
2	representational	1	+
3	abstract	2	−
4	representational	1	+
5	representational	1	+
6	representational	1	+
7	abstract	2	−
8	representational	1	+
9	abstract	2	−
10	representational	1	+
11	representational	1	+
12	representational	1	+
13	representational	1	+
14	representational	1	+
15	abstract	2	−

15 coins and asking how likely it would be for the split between heads and tails to be 15 : 0, 14 : 1, 13 : 2, 12 : 4, 11 : 5, and so on, if the coins were unbiased and there was no sleight of hand involved. Asking *how likely* each possible split between heads and tails might be just on the basis of chance is effectively asking what proportion of many thousands of repetitions of the coin-tossing (or the painting preference) experiment would yield each possible split. These proportions can be calculated from probability theory, but we do not need to do these calculations because they are summarized in statistical tables. If the proportion of times the *obtained split* (11 : 4 in Table 7.1) in our data, or a more extreme one, would occur when the null hypothesis is true is less than 1 in 20 (i.e., .05), we conclude that the null hypothesis can be rejected at the 5% level ($p < .05$) of probability. That is, in concluding that chance alone was not responsible for the preponderance of heads (or representational preferences), there is less than a .05 probability that we are mistaken (a Type I error) and it really was chance.

The Sign test

The test that we need to use to analyse our data is called the *Sign test*. We will refer to the statistic that we need to calculate to use this test as '*x*', which is simply the number of times the preference between the two conditions goes in the non-predicted direction. In other words, we simply need to count up the number of '2's

Statistical Table 7.1   Critical one- and two-tailed values of x for a Sign test, where x = the number of cases with the *less* frequent sign and N is the total number of positive and negative differences between pairs of scores, i.e., ties are not counted. x is significant if it is **less than or equal** to the table value (partial table – full table in Appendix 1)

	level of significance for a one-tailed test						
	.10	.05	.025	.01	.005	.001	.0005
	level of significance for a two-tailed test						
N	.20	.10	.05	.02	.01	.002	.001
4	0						
5	0	0					
6	0	0	0				
7	1	0	0	0			
8	1	1	0	0	0		
9	2	1	1	0	0		
10	2	1	1	0	0	0	
11	2	2	1	1	0	0	0
12	3	2	2	1	1	0	0
13	3	3	2	1	1	0	0
14	4	3	2	2	1	1	0
15	4	3	3	2	2	1	1
16	4	4	3	2	2	1	1
17	5	4	4	3	2	1	1
18	5	5	4	3	3	2	1

Source: The entries in this table were computed by Pat Dugard, a freelance statistician

(or number of minuses) in Table 7.1. The value of the statistic is therefore 4. All we have to do then is to refer to Statistical table 7.1 (a partial version of the table is shown here), which gives the *critical number of cases* (**critical value**) in the non-predicted direction that is required for significance at various levels of probability ($p < .05$, $p < .01$, etc).

Let's suppose that we want to test for one-tailed statistical significance at the 5% level (i.e., α is set at .05). We need to look in the .05 (1-tailed) column and in the row that corresponds to the number ($N = 15$) of participants in our experiment. The value given in the table at the intersection of the row and column is the largest number of participants for whom the representational–abstract preference can go in the *wrong* direction for us to be able to claim statistical significance at the 5% one-tailed level of probability. In our example, the value in the table is 3. As more than 3 preferences (4, in fact) went in the wrong direction, we have to conclude that the null hypothesis cannot be rejected at the stated level of probability.

As explained in Chapter 5, Complications (5.3), you should not make the error of talking about *accepting* the null hypothesis when it *cannot be rejected*.

Reporting results (7.1) – Sign test

The way this result would be described in a report of the experiment would be something like this:

> The frequencies of preferences for representational and abstract paintings were 11 and 4 respectively. In a one-tailed Sign test of the hypothesis that the frequency of preferences for representational paintings would exceed the frequency of preferences for abstract paintings, the difference in frequencies was not statistically significant. Thus, the null hypothesis could not be rejected ($N = 15$, $x = 4$, $p > .05$).

The decision just reported may seem rather arbitrary. Had there been just one more preference in the predicted direction, we would have made a different decision; that is, to reject the null hypothesis (see Complications (5.1) for a discussion of this issue).

Note that, if we had made a non-directional prediction (frequency of preferences would differ in either direction), we would have taken the frequency of the *least frequent preference* (coded 2 or minus in our example) as the value of the statistic. In this particular example, the two-tailed statistical decision would have been the same as the one-tailed decision (i.e., do not reject the null hypothesis) because the critical value in Statistical Table 7.1 is again 3.

Additional information (7.1) – Using a Sign test on ratings

Instead of asking participants which of two paintings they prefer, we might ask them to rate the two paintings, say, on a scale from 1 to 7. Suppose that one participant rated the representational painting (7) and the abstract painting (4) and another participant rated them (6) and (5) respectively. It would be risky to infer that the magnitude of the first participant's preference for a representational painting was greater than that of the second participant because it is quite likely that each participant uses the scale in his or her own way. So, because the difference scores cannot be reliably ranked, it would probably be unsafe to conclude that the differences between ratings of the two pictures represented an ordinal scale. It would be reasonable, however, to maintain that, for each participant, the direction of the difference between the two ratings implies at least a preference for the picture with the higher rating. So, we can use the directions of the differences to test the same hypothesis (preferences for representational paintings will be more frequent than preferences for abstract paintings). We simply indicate the direction of each difference with a plus or minus sign and count up the number of occurrences of the least frequent sign.

Independent Groups Experiment

Now we turn to an example of an independent groups design using nominal data. We will stay with the same hypothesis that motivated our repeated measures example in order to make the point that there are always alternative ways to design an experiment to test a given hypothesis. This time, we might recruit 30 participants and randomly allocate 15 to each of two conditions. The conditions are: *view representational paintings* or *view abstract paintings*. We would ask participants to look at some representational or some abstract paintings (depending on the condition to which participants have been allocated) that have been rated equal in 'attractiveness to naïve viewers' by an art expert. The participants would be asked to talk about their feelings about the paintings and their responses would be recorded. The recordings would then be classified by several judges as *predominantly positive* or *predominantly negative*. Only those on which the judges were in agreement would be used in the analysis. What we end up with will be a two-way classification of participants. They will be classified according to the type of paintings they saw (a manipulated IV) and according to whether their responses were predominantly positive or negative (a DV).

The data

The number of participants (excluding those for whom the judges disagreed) falling in each of the 4 possible categories (*representational/positive*, *representational/negative*, *abstract/positive* and *abstract/negative*) can be recorded in what is generally referred to as a **contingency table** (so called because we are often interested in whether the frequencies at the levels of one variable are *contingent* on the frequencies at the levels of the other). Suppose that judges disagreed over the classification of two participants in the representational condition and one participant in the abstract condition, and that the frequencies of the remaining 27 participants in each category were as shown in the contingency table (Table 7.2).

Table 7.2 Contingency table showing nominal data from an independent groups design

Response category	Type of paintings viewed		Marginal totals (rep. + abs.)
	representational	abstract	
predominantly positive	11	6	17
predominantly negative	2	8	10
marginal totals (pos. + neg.)	13	14	27

Looking at the data, you can see that the results went in the predicted direction. That is, participants shown representational paintings more frequently responded positively to them and participants shown abstract paintings more frequently responded negatively, though the difference was smaller in the latter case. In order to decide whether the pattern of frequencies is extreme enough to persuade us that the null hypothesis can be rejected at, say, the 5% level of probability, we need to know what pattern of frequencies could be expected if the null hypothesis were true. If the null hypothesis were true (i.e., frequencies of type of painting and category of response are independent of one another), we can calculate what the **expected frequencies** would be (i.e., on the basis of chance) in each of the four cells of the contingency table.

Calculation details (7.1) – Expected frequencies in a 2 × 2 contingency table

Look at the contingency table in Table 7.2. Now look at the marginal totals. You can see that 17/27 of the total group for whom judges were in agreement were predominantly positive. Note also that there are 13 participants in the representational condition. It follows that if *type of painting* and *response category* were independent (unrelated), 17/27 of the 13 participants should have been predominantly positive (i.e., 17/27 × 13 = 8.19). So, that is the expected frequency for the top left (representational painting/predominantly positive) cell in the contingency table. The other three expected frequencies can be obtained in the same way. That is:

$$\text{Expected cell frequency (E)} = \frac{\text{row total} \times \text{column total}}{\text{grand total}}$$

Alternatively, the other three expected frequencies can be obtained by subtraction because the expected frequencies have to add up to the marginal totals. For example, the expected frequency for the top right cell is (17 × 14)/27 = 8.81 (using the formula above) or 17 − 8.19 = 8.81 (by subtraction).

The Chi-Square test

Once the expected frequencies have been obtained, we can calculate the statistic, χ^2, which we will use to determine whether or not the observed (O) frequencies differ significantly from the expected (E) frequencies (i.e., under the null hypothesis).

Formulae (7.1) – The Chi-Square (χ^2) test

The formula for computing Chi-Square is:

$$\chi^2 = \sum \frac{(O - E)^2}{E}$$

So, for each of the four cells in the contingency table, you subtract the expected value from the observed value, square the result and divide that result by the expected value. Then you add up the results for the four cells. We are not going to provide a worked example of the calculation because our assumption is that you will use SPSS (or some similar statistical package) to compute the statistic. If you want to do the calculation by hand, it is simple enough and you can check your result against that provided by the statistical package.

Statistical Table 7.2 Critical two-tailed (i.e., non-directional) values of Chi-Square (χ^2). Chi-Square is significant if it is **greater than or equal** to the table value (partial table – full version in Appendix 1)

	level of significance for a two-tailed test						
df^1	0.20	0.10	0.05	0.02	0.01	0.002	0.0001
1^2	1.64	2.71	3.84	5.41	6.64	9.55	10.83
2	3.22	4.61	5.99	7.82	9.21	12.43	13.82
3	4.64	6.25	7.82	9.84	11.35	14.80	16.27

Source: The entries in this table were computed by Pat Dugard, a freelance statistician.
[1] df = (rows − 1) × (columns − 1)
[2] for a one-tailed test for 2 × 2 tables only (i.e., when df = 1), divide the probabilities at the top of the table by 2

SPSS operations and output (7.1) – Computing Chi-Square

In SPSS, the data in the contingency table are entered in three columns, one to indicate which type of painting is referred to, one to indicate which category of response was produced and the third to indicate the number (frequency) of participants in each of the four combinations of painting type and response category.

(i)   Select *Variable View* at the bottom of the SPSS Data Editor, and enter a name for each of the three variables (e.g., painting, response, freq).

(ii)   For the variable, 'painting', click in the *Values* column and then on the three dots that appear. In the dialogue box that appears, enter '1' in the *Value* space and 'representational' in the *Value Label* space, then select *Add*. In the same way, enter '2' and 'abstract' and click *Add* again, then *OK*.

(iii)   For the variable, 'response', follow the same procedure, entering '1' and 'positive', then '2' and 'negative'.

(iv)   Select *Data View* at the bottom of the Data Editor and enter the values '1, 1, 2, 2' in the 'painting' column, '1, 2, 1, 2' in the 'response' column and '11, 2, 6, 8' in the 'freq' column, as below:

painting	response	freq
1	1	11
1	2	2
2	1	6
2	2	8

(v)   Select *Data*, then *Weight Cases* from the top menu, click the radio button, *Weight cases by*, then enter 'freq' in the *Frequency Variable* slot, and click *OK*.

(vi)   From the top menu, select *Analyze*, *Descriptive Statistics* and *Crosstabs*, then move 'response' into *Rows* and 'painting' into *Columns*.

(vii)   Click *Statistics* and select *Chi-square*, then click *Continue*.

(viii)   Click *Cells* and select *Expected*, then click *Continue*, followed by *OK*.

The main output for the Chi-Square test follows:

RESPONSE * PICTURE Crosstabulation

			Painting		
			represent ational	abstract	Total
RESPONSE	positive	Count	11	6	17
		Expected Count	8.2	8.8	17.0
	negative	Count	2	8	10
		Expected Count	4.8	5.2	10.0
Total		Count	13	14	27
		Expected Count	13.0	14.0	27.0

Chi-Square Tests

	Value	df	Asymp. Sig. (2-sided)	Exact Sig. (2-sided)	Exact Sig. (1-sided)
Pearson Chi-Square	5.040[b]	1	.025		
Continuity Correction[a]	3.409	1	.065		
Likelihood Ratio	5.310	1	.021		
Fisher's Exact Test				.046	.031
Linear-by-Linear Association	4.854	1	.028		
N of Valid Cases	27				

a. Computed only for a 2x2 table

b. 1 cells (25.0%) have expected count less than 5. The minimum expected count is 4.81.

The value of Chi-Square (labelled 'Pearson Chi-Square') is 5.04 and the two-tailed level of significance is given as .025, which is of course less than .05. So, $p < .05$. There are several other features of the output that we need to discuss:

1. In the column headed 'df', the value entered in the 'Pearson Chi-Square' row is '1'. Recall that the concept of 'degrees of freedom' (df) was briefly introduced in Chapter 4 (Complications (4.2)). If you had computed Chi-Square by hand, you would need to look at Statistical Table 7.2 to find out whether your value of Chi-Square was statistically significant. (A partial version of the table is shown here.) In order to use the table, you need to know the df associated with your contingency table. We are only dealing with 2×2 contingency tables, for which the df is always '1'. You can see, therefore, that we are only concerned with the first row of critical values in Statistical Table 7.2. There, you can see that our value for Chi-Square (5.04) is significant in a two-tailed test at the 5% level (i.e., the obtained Chi-Square value is greater than the critical value of 3.84) but not at the 2% level (i.e., the obtained value is less than the critical value of 5.41). This concurs with the probability of .025 (i.e., between .05 and .02) given in the SPSS output.

2. There is some confusion over whether the critical values in Chi-Square tables should be described as one- or two-tailed. It depends on whether you focus on the single tail of the Chi-Square distribution that defines the rejection region for an obtained value of Chi-Square or on the non-directional nature of the hypothesis generally being tested with Chi-Square. If you find this confusing, Howell (2002, pp. 161–2, see reference in our 'brief list of recommended books') provides a more detailed explanation. We wish to focus on the nature of the hypothesis being evaluated, so we treat the critical values in the statistical table as being for two-tailed (i.e., in the sense of *non-directional*) tests. Directional (one-tailed) tests would not really make sense for contingency tables greater than 2×2 because the null hypothesis being tested is that the row and column variables are independent (unrelated) and they could be dependent in various different ways if Chi-Square were significant. So whether your *specific* (directional) research hypothesis is supported would remain unclear. In the 2×2 case, however, it may make sense to report one-tailed (directional) significance where, as in our example, it is clear that the relationship between the two variables was in the predicted direction, though many researchers would advise against one-tailed testing even in the 2×2 case. If you do want to report a one-tailed statistical result, the probability given in the statistical table (or the probability reported in the SPSS output) should be divided by 2 (i.e., critical values in the .05 column of the table are for $p = .05/2 = .025$ in a one-tailed test, and the SPSS significance value of .025 is equivalent to $.025/2 = .0125$ in a one-tailed test). Since neither of these probabilities is below the next level ($p < .01$) that is conventionally reported, we would still be reporting the same probability, $p < .05$, for a one-tailed test as for a two-tailed test.

3. The SPSS output concludes with the statement that '1 cells (sic) (25%) have expected count less than 5'. You can see in the output that the cell in question is the top

right one, with an expected frequency of 4.8. This is a warning to treat the statistical conclusion with caution. Many texts suggest that if any of the expected frequencies are low (< 5 is the most common critical value suggested), the analysis should not be attempted because the statistical decision cannot be relied upon. We agree with Howell (2002, pp. 158–9, see reference in our 'brief list of recommended books') that there is little need to be concerned in the 2×2 case unless the total sample size is less than about 8, at which point lack of power to find an effect is likely to be more of an issue than the possibility of finding too many significant results. In any case, SPSS will provide a 'Fisher Exact Probability Test' if expected frequencies are small. We will not discuss the so-called 'exact' tests in this book, but see Todman and Dugard's book (in our 'brief list of recommended books') if you want to find out more about this type of test.

4.   If you look at Note (a) in the SPSS output (just below the 'Chi-Square Tests' box) you will see that a **continuity correction** has been computed for the 2×2 case. This is important because, as you can see, the value of Chi-Square is reduced (to 3.41) when the correction is applied and this value is no longer significant in a two-tailed test ($p = .065$). The correction concerned is **Yates' correction for continuity**, which many texts suggest should be applied in the case of 2×2 contingency tables. We do not intend to explain the reasoning behind the correction or the arguments against using it. We accept the conclusion reached by Howell (2002), that the uncorrected Chi-Square provides a better approximation to the true probabilities than does Yates' correction. We recommend that you do not use the correction and, if you want the rationale behind this advice, it is given in Howell (2002, pp. 151–2, see reference in our 'brief list of recommended books').

Reporting results (7.2) – Chi-Square test

The way the result would be described in a report of the experiment would be something like:

> The frequencies of participants who responded positively or negatively to representational or abstract paintings is shown in Table X. In a one-tailed Chi-Square test of the hypothesis that participants with no particular interest in art would display more positive responses to representational paintings and more negative responses to abstract paintings, the differences in frequencies were in the predicted direction and were statistically significant. Thus, the null hypothesis could be rejected ($\chi^2 = 5.04$, $df = 1$, $p < .05$, one-tailed).

SUMMARY OF CHAPTER

- Nominal scales arise when numbers are assigned to mutually exclusive categories that differ in some qualitative way. It is 'frequencies' (counts) of cases in different categories that are analysed.
- It is possible to carry out experimental studies using nominal scales provided a nominal IV is manipulated by the researcher to observe an effect on a nominal DV.
- A repeated measures design in which the direction of differences constitutes the data can be analysed using a Sign test.
- Direction of difference data can be obtained directly (e.g., a preference between things in two categories) or indirectly from ratings of things in two categories.
- Ordinal or interval data can be converted to nominal scales, but this wastes information in the original data.
- An independent groups design that results in frequencies within cells in a two-way classification of participants, called a contingency table, can be analysed using a Chi-Square test.
- The Chi-Square test analyses the difference between observed and expected frequencies.
- For a 2×2 contingency table, the df is always 1. This corresponds to the first row of critical values in the statistical table for Chi-Square.
- For all contingency tables greater than 2×2, the Chi-Square test is always two-tailed. For 2×2 tables only, it is possible to carry out a one-tailed test.

CHAPTER EIGHT

Tests of Significance for Ordinal Data (and Interval/Ratio Data When Parametric Assumptions Are Not Met)

Ordinal data

Ordinal data have the same property of mutually exclusive categories as nominal data, plus the additional property that observations are meaningfully ranked in order of magnitude. Higher values in the scale always imply more of whatever is being measured, but equal differences between values do not imply equal differences in what is being measured. Thus, 10 may represent much more of something than 9, whereas 6 may represent just slightly more of that thing than 5.

Asking people to rank things – to place them in order of magnitude – is the simplest way of obtaining an ordinal scale. However, we saw in Chapter 6 that other procedures, such as rating things or using physical measurements to *stand for* psychological concepts (e.g., time on task standing for persistence), can also result in ordinal scales. Furthermore, many procedures, such as multiple-item rating scales, can produce data that are 'stronger' than ordinal but 'weaker' than interval. In such cases, many researchers, including us, would recommend using the non-parametric tests described in this chapter only if parametric assumptions are not reasonably well met. Finally, even with interval or ratio data, the tests in this chapter are appropriate if parametric assumptions are seriously violated. Remember: scale of measurement is a useful guide as to which tests to consider, but it is by no means the sole, or even the most important, criterion.

Non-parametric tests are sometimes described as **distribution-free tests** because they do not require any assumptions about the nature of the distributions of the populations in question. They are also sometimes described as **rank tests** because the analyses are carried out on the ranks of observations (ordinal numbers such as 1st,

2nd, 3rd etc.) rather than on cardinal numbers (scores) comprising the observations (i.e., 11, 9, 4, 7, 8 etc.). When a non-parametric test of the kind described in this chapter is called for, the first step is always to convert the raw observations into ranked data unless, of course, they started out as rankings.

Repeated Measures Experiment

As in the preceding chapter, we will begin with a repeated measures design. We will use an example in which the scores do not start out as ordinal data, in order to illustrate the initial step of converting the original data to ranks. We will use the example of a rating of computer anxiety from Chapter 6. Suppose we have reason to believe that qualitative aspects of early interactions that children have with computers, such as how relaxing these interactions were, affect the level of computer anxiety they feel when confronted with the prospect of having to use a computer again. Suppose, also, that there is evidence that girls in particular tend to be more relaxed when their learning is directed by a female teacher. We might then hypothesize that when girls without much prior experience with computers are instructed in a computing routine (like selecting and printing a picture, or moving pictures to different locations on a screen), they will show lower levels of computer anxiety when contemplating the next interaction if the one they have just had was with a female teacher.

First, we would recruit a number of girls (say, 12) who have had limited experience with computers (e.g., 'not more than a total of 5 hours' hands-on experience, whether supervised or not'). The girls would be divided randomly into two equal-sized (order of task) sub-groups and participants in each sub-group would be presented with two computing instruction routines (e.g., (A) *selecting and printing a picture*, and (B) *moving pictures to different locations on the monitor screen*). In order to control for order effects, one sub-group of girls would receive A followed by B and the other sub-group would receive B followed by A. Each participant would receive standardized individual training in the two routines, one week apart, with the order in which participants were treated being randomly determined across all participants, regardless of which sub-group they were in. One male teacher and one female teacher would provide the training. Within each task-order sub-group, a random half of the participants would first receive training from a female teacher, then from a male teacher, and the other half of each sub-group would first receive training from a male teacher, then from a female teacher. After each of the two training routines, participants would be asked, 'How nervous do you feel about learning to do another task on the computer?' They would be asked to choose between '*very nervous*', '*quite nervous*', '*slightly nervous*', '*hardly nervous at all*' and '*not a bit nervous*'. Their responses would be scored for computer anxiety from 5 (very nervous) to 1 (not a bit nervous). Thus, each participant would have two computer anxiety scores, one following training on one task with a female teacher and the other following training on the other task with a male teacher. The logic of the design is illustrated in Figure 8.1.

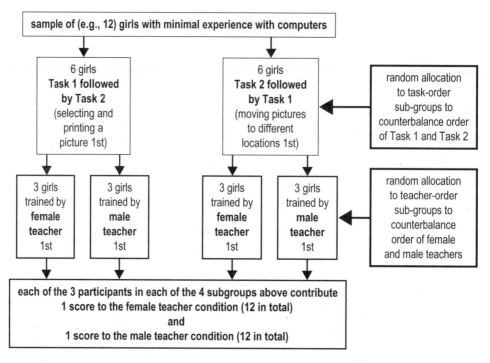

Figure 8.1   A repeated measures design with order effects controlled

Additional information (8.1) – Asymmetrical order effects

Counterbalancing effectively controls the order of task presentation and female/male training, provided any order effects are symmetrical; that is, scores on the DV are affected in the same way whichever condition comes first. For example, if there were a general effect of familiarity reducing computer anxiety, whichever condition (female or male teacher) came second for a given participant, it would tend to produce a lower computer anxiety score as a result of increased familiarity and this would tend to balance out over participants because equal numbers of them get the female and male conditions second. Similarly, Task A may be inherently easier than Task B, but effects of task difficulty on DV scores in the two conditions will tend to balance out because equal numbers of participants in the female teacher and male teacher conditions get Task A first and Task B first.

We cannot guarantee, however, that order effects will always be symmetrical. Sometimes the effects do not just depend on the order of the conditions, but also on the specifics of the conditions. For example, one condition, such as receiving a large reward for solving a problem, might result in participants interpreting a small reward (the other condition) as trivial when it follows the large reward, but their interpretation of a large reward when it follows a small reward may be less affected. Such kinds of asymmetrical order effects are sometimes described as **carry-over** or **sequential effects**. In our example, consider the possibility that there is a positive motivational effect of changing teachers that benefits the second training session, but only when the effect is from a male to a female teacher. This would produce a bias in favour of the female teacher condition (i.e., when it comes second) that would not be balanced out. This kind of asymmetrical effect is illustrated below:

First	Second	Asymmetrical effect
male ⟶	female	female > male
female ⟶	male	female = male

The data

To recapitulate, we have a repeated measures design because all participants have scores in both conditions of the experiment. We have ordinal data because we can rank the differences between the participants' ratings in the two conditions and it is reasonable to assume that higher ranks represent larger differences in computer anxiety. It is probably not safe, however, to assume that equal differences between ratings in the two conditions represent equal differences in computer anxiety. Therefore, we do not have anything approaching an interval scale and there is no point in asking whether parametric assumptions are met because a non-parametric test is called for. Suppose the data were as shown in Table 8.1.

Table 8.1 Ordinal computer anxiety data from a repeated measures design

Participant	Rating	
	female teacher	male teacher
1	2	4
2	1	4
3	1	5
4	3	5
5	2	2
6	3	2
7	1	4
8	3	3
9	2	5
10	3	5
11	4	1
12	4	4

Table 8.2   Ranks of differences between two ratings of computer anxiety

Participant	Female teacher	Male teacher	Difference (female–male)	Ranks of differences
1	2	4	−2	3
2	1	4	−3	6.5
3	1	5	−4	9
4	3	5	−2	3
5	2	2	0	omitted
6	3	2	1	1
7	1	4	−3	6.5
8	3	3	0	omitted
9	2	5	−3	6.5
10	3	5	−2	3
11	4	1	3	6.5
12	4	4	0	omitted

As we have a repeated measures design, we are dealing with differences between pairs of scores obtained by participants in the female teacher and male teacher conditions. As we are assuming that the data are at an ordinal level, but not an interval level, we analyse the ranks of the differences rather than the actual sizes of differences. The differences and the ranks of these differences are shown in Table 8.2.

Calculation details (8.1) – Obtaining ranks of differences

A statistical package such as SPSS will do the ranking for you automatically when you request the appropriate statistical analysis for a repeated measures design with two conditions and ordinal data. You may nonetheless want to see how the analysis is done. You can see in Table 8.2 that the differences in ratings between female and male teacher conditions have been entered in column 4. Differences in one direction (*female > male*) are entered as positive values and differences in the other direction (*female < male*) are entered as negative values. It does not matter which direction of differences you enter as positive and which as negative. Column 5 contains the ranks of the differences. There are 12 pairs of scores so the rankings should go from 1st (the smallest difference) to 12th (the largest difference), but it isn't quite that straightforward. In the first place, the ranks are obtained without regard to whether differences are positive or negative. Thus, a difference of '1' and a difference of '−1' would have the same rank. Differences that have the same rank (like '1' and '−1') are described as **ties**, and these complicate the ranking procedure. First, however, we need to deal with another kind of tie; that which arises when a pair of scores in the two conditions are equal, so that the difference is zero. As with the Sign test described in Chapter 7, when values in the two conditions are equal, that pair of scores is eliminated from the analysis; we focus exclusively on pairs of scores that differ in one direction or the other. Now we return to the ties that occur when two or more differences are equal, remembering that the direction of the difference is ignored. So, for example, the differences 2, 2, −2, 2, −2 are equal, and that means they must all be given the same rank.

Now look at Table 8.2 again. You can see that there are three ties in which the difference between conditions is zero and these are marked as 'omitted'. If you count up the number of differences of '1' or '−1' (i.e., the smallest difference, apart from zero differences, which are not counted), you will find there is just 1 of them. So that is given the rank 1. Now, considering the next smallest difference, there are 3 differences of plus or minus 2, so they occupy ranks 2 to 4, but must all be given the same rank. This is achieved by giving them all the rank that is the mean of the 3; that is, 3. Perhaps the simplest way to think of this is to write down the ranks from 2 to 4 and look for the midpoint, as below:

Midpoint = 3

The next smallest difference is plus or minus 3 and there are 4 of these, so they must occupy the ranks 5 to 8, of which the midpoint is 6.5, as illustrated below.

Midpoint = halfway between 6 and 7 = 6.5

Note that if there is an even number of ties, the shared rank will always be an integer (whole number) followed by a decimal point and the number 5, whereas, if there is an odd number of ties, the shared rank will always be an integer (the middle number in the ranks occupied by the ties). Finally, there is 1 difference of plus or minus 4, so it occupies rank 9. There are no ranks 10–12 because the three pairs of scores with zero difference are omitted from the analysis.

The Wilcoxon T test

The **Wilcoxon Matched-Pairs Signed-Ranks** test, to give it its full name, is used to decide whether the null hypothesis can be rejected. The statistic for this test is designated by a capital T. Having obtained the ranks of the differences between pairs of scores, the statistic, T, is easily obtained. Simply add up all of the ranks that represent differences in the positive direction and likewise for the ranks that represent differences in the negative direction. In our example, these come to 37.5 (sum of negative ranks) and 7.5 (sum of positive ranks). Now, if the null hypothesis were true, we would expect these two values to be fairly similar, but if the null hypothesis were false (and the research hypothesis were true), one condition would be expected to produce generally higher scores than the other, so that more of the high ranks would be in one direction and the two sums of rank values would differ greatly. As usual, we have to ask how *great* a difference is enough to persuade us that it is statistically significant at some level of probability (e.g., .05) and to decide to reject the null hypothesis. Again, as usual, a table giving critical values for the statistic, T, is available. The difference between the two sums of ranks will be greater as one value gets higher and the other gets lower. We could use the high value as our statistic and ask whether it is at least as high as some critical value, but it is the convention that the low value is taken as the statistic, T. Statistical Table 8.1 therefore gives critical values that T must be at least *as low as* for various sample sizes and levels

Statistical Table 8.1 Critical one- and two-tailed values of T for a Wilcoxon Matched-Pairs Signed-Ranks test, where T = the sum of differences with the least frequent sign and N = the total number of differences with either a positive or negative sign. T is significant if it is **less than or equal** to the table value (partial table – full version in Appendix 1)

	.10	.05	.025	.01	.005	.001
		level of significance for a one-tailed test				
N	.20	.10	.05	.02	.01	.002
		level of significance for a two-tailed test				
4	0					
5	2	0				
6	4	2	0			
7	6	3	2	0		
8	8	5	3	1	0	
9	11	8	5	3	1	
10	14	10	8	5	3	0
11	18	13	10	7	5	1
12	22	17	14	10	7	2

Source: The entries in this table were computed by Pat Dugard, a freelance statistician. N = number of non-equal pairs of scores

of probability, in order to claim statistical significance. A partial version of the table is shown here.

So, the value of our statistic is $T = 7.5$ (the sum of the positive ranks), and the number of participants whose scores in the two conditions differed is $N = 9$. As we made a directional prediction (that computer anxiety ratings would be higher in the male teacher condition), it is permissible to apply a one-tailed test. Assuming we have set the probability level for our statistical decision at $\alpha = .05$, we look down the one-tailed .05 column and across the row, $N = 9$ in Statistical Table 8.1. The value at the column/row intersection is 8. As our value for T is less than or equal to 8 (i.e., 7.5), we can decide to reject the null hypothesis in a one-tailed test at the 5% level.

Note that if we had carried out a two-tailed test, the critical value in the table would have been 5 and we could not have rejected the (non-directional) hypothesis. This makes it very clear that the decision to do a one-tailed test *must* be taken before the data have been collected, with the attendant risk that you could not claim statistical significance if the difference went in the non-predicted direction. If you decided to do a one-tailed test after seeing that a two-tailed test did not reach significance, that could be construed as 'cheating'.

You might like to know what is the smallest sample size with which it would be possible to find statistical significance. Well, if every difference went in the same direction, there would be no rank differences in one direction and the value of T would therefore be zero. You should be able to see from Statistical Table 8.1 that, if $T = 0$, it is possible to get statistical significance at the 5% level with five participants in a one-tailed test or with six participants in a two-tailed test.

One final point should be noted about the Wilcoxon test. You will be introduced to a parametric alternative to it in Chapter 9 and it is true that the parametric alternative is more powerful (less likely to miss a significant effect when the null hypothesis is indeed false), *provided* the parametric assumptions are reasonably met. However, although the Wilcoxon test does not require an interval scale of measurement, it certainly uses more than just the ordinal information in the data. In ranking the difference scores, we are making judgements about the relative *sizes* of the differences in the DV, which is quite close to interval measurement, where the only additional requirement is that the same difference (e.g., the difference between 2 and 4 and that between 3 and 5) represents an equal difference in the DV at all points along the scale. In other words, the Wilcoxon test is almost as powerful as its parametric alternative. The **power-efficiency** of the Wilcoxon test is close to 95% for small sample sizes, which means that *if* the necessary assumptions are met for the parametric alternative to the Wilcoxon test and the parametric test needs 10 participants to achieve a particular power, then the Wilcoxon test would need about $(10 \times 100)/95 = 10.53$ (i.e., 11 when rounded up to a whole number) participants with non-tied scores in the two conditions to achieve the same power. For small sample studies particularly, it should be apparent that, if there are serious doubts about the parametric assumptions, there would be little power lost when choosing the Wilcoxon test instead of its parametric alternative. (See Siegel and Castellan's book – referred to in the 'brief list of recommended books' – for arguments in favour of nonparametric statistics, together with a comprehensive coverage of nonparametric tests.)

SPSS operations and output (8.1) – Computing Wilcoxon *T*

In SPSS, data from repeated measures designs are entered in separate columns for each condition. Thus, each participant has data in one row (rows are called 'cases' in SPSS). So, two columns of data, as in Table 8.1, are entered under suitable labels.

(i)   Select *Variable View* at the bottom of the SPSS Data Editor, and enter a name for each condition (e.g., female, male).

(ii)   Select *Data View* at the bottom of the Data Editor and enter the two columns of data in the 'female' and 'male' columns.

(iii)   From the top menu, select *Analyze, Nonparametric Tests* and *2 Related Samples*, then click on 'female' and 'male' and move them into the *Test Pair(s) List.*

(iv)   Select *Options* and tick *Quartiles*, then click *Continue*, followed by *OK*.

Descriptive Statistics

		Percentiles		
	N	25th	50th (Median)	75th
MALE	9	1.0000	2.0000	3.0000
FEMALE	9	3.0000	4.0000	5.0000

Ranks

		N	Mean Rank	Sum of Ranks
FEMALE – MALE	Negative Ranks	2[a]	3.75	7.50
	Positive Ranks	7[b]	5.36	37.50
	Ties	3[c]		
	Total	12		

a. FEMALE < MALE
b. FEMALE > MALE
c. MALE = FEMALE

Test Statistics[b]

	FEMALE – MALE
Z	−1.799[a]
Asymp. Sig. (2-tailed)	.072

a. Based on negative ranks.
b. Wilcoxon Signed Ranks Test

The medians for the two conditions are given in the 'Descriptive Statistics' box. Note that it is not strictly meaningful to talk about the means for ordinal data, so it is the medians that you should present in a report of the experiment. If you want the means and standard deviations for any reason, after clicking on '*Options*' in SPSS, you should tick '*Descriptives*' as well as '*Quartiles*'. The two critical pieces of information to extract from the 'Ranks' box are the value of $T = 7.5$ (i.e., the smaller of the two 'Sum of Ranks') and $N = 12 - 3 = 9$ (i.e., Total − Ties). The values of T and N are then used in conjunction with Statistical Table 8.1, as previously described, to decide whether to reject (or fail to reject) the null hypothesis.

Reporting results (8.1) – Wilcoxon Matched-Pairs Signed-Ranks test

The way the result would be described in a report of the experiment would be something like:

> In a one-tailed Wilcoxon Signed-Ranks test, computer anxiety self-ratings by girls with minimal experience of using computers were, as predicted, significantly higher after performing a computing task with training provided by a female teacher (median = 2) than after performing a similar task with training provided by a male teacher (median = 4). Thus, the null hypothesis can be rejected ($T = 7.5$, $N = 9$, $p < .05$, one-tailed).

Complications (8.1) – Large sample statistics

The final SPSS output box, labelled 'Test Statistics', gives a value for a statistic, Z, and a probability value for the statistic. This is an approximation based on the normal distribution and it can be used on large samples because T is approximately normally distributed for such samples. 'Large samples' are often taken as above about $N = 25$, but there is no point in using the Z approximation for values of N that are given in the statistical table. The approximate (asymptotic) significance value given in the SPSS output is two-tailed. In our example, the value of the statistic is $Z = 1.799$ (ignore the negative sign) and the probability is $p = .072$. As this is not below .05, we conclude that the null hypothesis cannot be rejected in a two-tailed test ($Z = 1.80$, $p > .05$). This is consistent with our interpretation of T using the statistical table. The one-tailed probability is simply half of the two-tailed probability (i.e., .036), which is significant ($Z = 1.80$, $p < .05$, one-tailed). Again, this is consistent with our one-tailed decision using the statistical table.

Independent Groups Experiment

Now we present an example of an independent groups design using data that are ordinal but fall short of being on an interval scale. In order to illustrate that there is rarely just one possible design to test a given hypothesis, we will stay with the same hypothesis that motivated our repeated measures example. To remind you, the hypothesis is that when girls without much prior experience with computers are instructed in a computing routine (like selecting and printing a picture, or moving pictures to different locations on a screen), they will show lower levels of computer anxiety when contemplating the next interaction if the one they have just had was with a female teacher.

Let us suppose that we initially recruit 18 girls who meet our minimum computing experience criterion. For this design, we randomly allocate equal numbers of girls (i.e., 9) to the two conditions (*female teacher* and *male teacher*). Suppose, then, that two of the girls allocated to the *female teacher* group were absent due to illness on the day they were to be tested. It would be perfectly acceptable to continue with one group (*male teacher*) of 9 girls and the other group (*female teacher*) of 7 girls. We generally aim to have the same number of participants in each group, but it is not essential, provided that the imbalance is not due in any way to a variable under consideration. For example, if the two girls had dropped out because they hated using the computer, that would have biased the results.

In the independent groups design, each participant is trained in one condition only (either *female teacher* or *male teacher*), so all of the girls can be trained on the same task. Consequently, 'task' does not feature as a potential confounding variable, though it may of course still limit the general conclusions that can be drawn from the study. The particular task used might have characteristics that are not shared by other possible computing tasks, so that generalization of the results to other tasks is risky. This is an external validity issue. It would be possible to improve external validity by having more than one task, so that different *sub-groups* of participants could be given a different task. That would amount to making 'task' a second IV, which is beyond the scope of this book, in which we deal only with the basic experimental designs involving no more than two levels of a single IV. However, if you continue to study psychology, you will find that additional IVs are often built into the design in this way.

Although in the independent groups design we do not have to worry about *order* or *carry-over* effects, we do sacrifice the control over individual differences afforded by the repeated measures design. In the independent groups design, we rely on the random allocation of participants to conditions to prevent individual differences being a potential confound. The logic of the design is illustrated in Figure 8.2. In the event that individual differences have a big impact on the DV (computer anxiety), such differences will not affect one condition in a systematically different way than they will affect the other. Nonetheless, we will pay a price for having random individual differences. That price will be the lower power our statistical test will have to reject the null hypothesis even when it is in fact false. The pros and cons of alternative

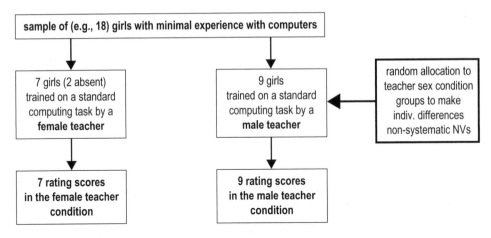

Figure 8.2 An independent groups design with unequal group sizes

designs have always to be weighed up in this way. There is not a single *correct* design.

As in the repeated measures design, it is highly desirable to train each child individually and in a random order, followed in this case by a single self-rating. If we were to train all of the girls in the same condition as a group, anything that happened in one group session (like one child getting very upset with the computer) might affect all of the members of the group in the same way, and this would offer a possible explanation for any statistically significant effect found. The design alternative of training *all* of the participants together is not an option because of the requirement to have a female teacher for some participants and a male teacher for the others.

The data

To recapitulate, we have an independent groups design because each participant is in only one condition of the experiment, and we have ordinal data because we can rank the ratings and it is reasonable to assume that higher ranks represent higher levels of computer anxiety. It is probably unsafe, however, to assume that equal differences in ratings, at different points in the scale, imply equal differences in computer anxiety. As we are not confident that we have something approaching an interval scale, there is no need to ask whether parametric assumptions are met because a non-parametric test is called for. Suppose that the data were as shown in Table 8.3.

As we have an independent groups design, we are interested in the differences between scores in the two conditions. As we are assuming that the data are at an ordinal level, but not at an interval level, we analyse the *ranks of ratings* rather than

Table 8.3 Ordinal computer anxiety data from an independent groups design

Participant	Male teacher	Participant	Female teacher
1	3	10	3
2	4	11	1
3	4	12	3
4	5	13	2
5	2	14	2
6	4	15	1
7	4	16	3
8	4		
9	5		

Table 8.4 Ranks of ratings of computer anxiety over both conditions

Male teacher ($n_1 = 9$)	ranks	Female teacher ($n_2 = 7$)	ranks
3	7.5	3	7.5
4	12	1	1.5
4	12	3	7.5
5	15.5	2	4
2	4	2	4
4	12	1	1.5
4	12	3	7.5
4	12		
5	15.5		
sum of male ranks	$R_1 = 102.5$	sum of female ranks	$R_2 = 33.5$

the actual ratings. In this case, we do a *single ranking* of the scores in both conditions (i.e., ranks 1 to 16). The procedure for dealing with tied scores is the same as was described for the ranking of difference scores (once pairs with zero difference had been discarded) in the repeated measures design. We will not, therefore, describe the procedure again, but will just show you the ranks in Table 8.4.

The Mann–Whitney U test

Rather confusingly, there is a test that is equivalent to the **Mann–Whitney** U test called Wilcoxon's Rank-Sum test, which uses a statistic W. However, we will use the

'Mann–Whitney U' test to avoid confusion with the Wilcoxon Matched-Pairs Signed-Ranks test that we used to analyse repeated measures data. It may be noted at the outset that our discussion of the power efficiency of the Wilcoxon T test applies equally to the Mann–Whitney U test.

The rationale underlying the Mann–Whitney test is very straightforward. If the null hypothesis is true, there should be a similar number of high scores (and therefore, scores with high ranks) in each condition. If the null hypothesis is false, there will tend to be a preponderance of high scores (and therefore, scores with high ranks) in one of the conditions. As usual, the statistical question is how great the preponderance in favour of one condition needs to be to persuade us that it was unlikely to have occurred if the null hypothesis were true. Now look at the bottom of Table 8.4, where the sums of ranks for the two conditions are given. We have to ask whether the probability of getting an imbalance between the sums of ranks as great as that between 102.5 and 33.5 is less than some conventional critical value, let's say $\alpha = .01$. If it is, we will conclude that the difference in ranks is statistically significant (i.e., $p < .01$) and we will decide to reject the null hypothesis. The Mann–Whitney test is used to decide whether the null hypothesis can be rejected. Precisely what aspect of the data the null hypothesis refers to in the case of this test is not straightforward (see Complications (8.2)), though if you just think of it as specifying that the medians of the groups do not differ, that will generally be adequate.

Complications (8.2) – The imprecision of the null hypothesis in a Mann–Whitney test

The Mann–Whitney test evaluates the null hypothesis that two sets of scores were randomly sampled from identical populations. This is a technical way of saying that the two sets of scores are indistinguishable. For parametric tests, we make assumptions about the nature of the distributions of populations (normal, with equal variances), so that we can focus on differences between the central tendencies (usually means) of our samples. In contrast, the Mann–Whitney test does not exclusively evaluate the difference between the central tendencies of two sets of scores. Though it is possible for the null hypothesis to be rejected because of differences in the shapes or dispersion (*spread-outness*) of the distributions of the two populations, the Mann–Whitney is particularly sensitive to differences in central tendency. Provided that the two populations have similar shapes and dispersion, the Mann–Whitney will effectively be dealing with differences between medians.

Formulae (8.1) – Mann–Whitney U

You are unlikely to need to calculate the statistic U by hand, because a statistical package like SPSS will readily do it for you, including the initial ranking of the data. We will give you the formulae for computing U, but we will not do the calculation for our example data. If you want to, you can check the SPSS result that we will provide by doing the computation by hand yourself. To compute U, you need three values: the two sample sizes (n_1 and n_2) and the sum of the ranks (R_1) for the group designated n_1. Whichever group is designated as n_1, the sum of ranks for that group must be designated as R_1.

There are two possible values of U, corresponding to the size of the larger and smaller sum of ranks, respectively. The convention is that we test the null hypothesis by focusing on the smaller sum of ranks and asking whether it is *small enough* to make it unlikely that it would have arisen if the null hypothesis were true. There are two formulae that you can use to compute the two values of U. Then you simply select the smaller of the two values to use when you look at the Statistical Table 8.2.

The first formula is:
$$U_1 = n_1 n_2 + \frac{n_1(n_1 + 1)}{2} - R_1$$

And the second is:
$$U_2 = n_1 n_2 - U_1$$

Using the designations of n_1, n_2 and R_1 shown in Table 8.4, the values of U_1 and U_2 from the above formulae are $U_1 = 5.5$ and $U_2 = 57.5$. Thus, we select the smaller of these values (5.5) as U to use with a Mann–Whitney statistical table. To use one of the set of Mann–Whitney statistical tables in Appendix 1, we need to select the one that gives critical values for the level of probability we have decided upon (.01 in our case) for either a one- or two-tailed test. Assuming we made a clear directional prediction before obtaining the data, we can choose to use the table giving one-tailed critical values for $\alpha = .01$. A partial version of this table is reproduced below as Statistical Table 8.2 (4). The full version of this table – as well as Statistical Tables 8.2 (1, 2, 3, 5 and 6) which give critical values for other alpha values – is in Appendix 1. Note that these tables have been constructed so that n_1 is always the larger of the two sample sizes if they differ.

To use the table, identify a row and column corresponding to $n_1 = 9$ and $n_2 = 7$. The critical value in the table at their intersection is 9. As our value of $U = 5.5$ is smaller than 9 (equal to 9 would have been small enough), we can conclude that the difference between ranks in the two conditions of our experiment is statistically significant and we can therefore decide to reject the null hypothesis.

Statistical Table 8.2(4) (one-tailed at .01; two tailed at .02) Critical one- and two-tailed values of U for a Mann–Whitney Independent Groups test, where U = the smaller of the two possible values and n_1 and n_2 = the numbers of participants in the two groups. Note that the table has been constructed so that n_1 is the larger of the two sample sizes if they differ. U is significant if it is **less than or equal** to the table value (partial table – full version in Appendix 1)

$n_2 \Rightarrow$ / $n_1 \Downarrow$	2	3	4	5	6	7	8	9	10	11	12	13	14	15	16	17	18	19	20
3																			
4																			
5			0	1															
6			1	2	3														
7		0	1	3	4	6													
8		0	2	4	6	8	10												
9		1	3	5	7	9	11	14											
10		1	3	6	8	11	13	16	19										
11		1	4	7	10	13	15	18	22	25									

Source: The entries in this table were computed by Pat Dugard, a freelance statistician.

SPSS operations and output (8.2) – Computing Mann–Whitney *U*

In SPSS, data from both conditions of an independent groups design are entered in a single column and another column is used to indicate which condition each score belongs to. Thus, just as for the repeated measures design, each participant has data in one row (remember that rows are called 'cases' in SPSS). So, the data in Table 8.3 are *not* entered in the way they are shown there, with a separate column for each condition.

1. Select *Variable View* at the bottom of the SPSS Data Editor. For the first variable, enter a name for the DV (e.g., rating) and, for the second variable, enter a name to stand for group membership (e.g., condit).
2. For the second variable, click under *Values* and again on the three dots that appear. In the Value Labels box, enter '1' in the *Value* space and 'male' in the *Value Label* space. Then click *Add*. In the same way enter '2' and 'female' and click *Add*, followed by *OK*.
3. Select *Data View* at the bottom of the Data Editor and enter the ratings in the 'Rating' column and '1's in the first 9 rows of the 'condit' column (corresponding to ratings in the male teacher condition), followed by '2's in the next 16 columns corresponding to ratings in the female teacher condition.

4. From the top menu, select *Analyze, Compare Means* and *Means*. In the *Means* dialogue box, move 'rating' into the *Dependent List* box and 'condit' into the *Independent List* box. Click *Options* and move *Median* from the *Statistics* box to the *Cell Statistics* box, then click *Continue* followed by *OK*.

5. Select *Analyse* again, followed by *Nonparametric Tests* and *2 Independent Samples*. Move *rating* into the *Test Variable List* and *condit* into the *Grouping Variable* space. Click *Define Groups* and enter '1' for *Group 1* and '2' for *Group 2*, then click *Continue* and *OK*.

Report

RATING

CONDIT	Mean	N	Std. Deviation	Median
male	3.8889	9	.9280	4.0000
female	2.1429	7	.8997	2.0000
Total	3.1250	16	1.2583	3.0000

Ranks

	CONDIT	N	Mean Rank	Sum of Ranks
RATING	male	9	11.39	102.50
	female	7	4.79	33.50
	Total	16		

Test Statistics[b]

	RATING
Mann-Whitney U	5.500
Wilcoxon W	33.500
Z	−2.828
Asymp. Sig. (2-tailed)	.005
Exact Sig. [2*(1-tailed Sig.)]	.003[a]

a. Not corrected for ties.
b. Grouping Variable: CONDIT

The medians for the two conditions are given in the 'Report' box. It is usual to report these in preference to the means. The two sums of ranks ($R_1 = 102.5$ and $R_2 = 33.5$) are given in the 'Ranks' box and the value of the Mann–Whitney statistic ($U = 5.5$) is given in the 'Test Statistics' box. Having obtained the statistic, you would look at the appropriate Mann–Whitney table of critical values for U to find out whether the obtained value is equal to or smaller than the critical value for the chosen probability level ($\alpha = .01$, in our case) in either a one- or two-tailed test, whichever was decided on before the data were collected (one-tailed, in our case). As we saw earlier, the table value is 9, therefore the difference between the two conditions is significant and the null hypothesis can be rejected.

Reporting results (8.2) – Mann–Whitney test

The way the result would be described in a report of the experiment would be something like:

> In a one-tailed Mann–Whitney test, self-ratings of computer anxiety by girls with minimal experience of using computers were, as predicted, significantly higher after performing a computing task when training on the task was provided by a male teacher (median = 4) than when training was provided by a female teacher (median = 2). Thus, the null hypothesis can be rejected ($U = 5.5$, $n_1 = 9$, $n_2 = 7$, $p < .01$, one-tailed).

Additional information (8.1) – Alternative Mann–Whitney statistics

Look again at the 'Test Statistics' box in SPSS Output 8.2. Some additional statistics are given there. First, the statistic called W is reported. As we mentioned earlier, this is an alternative statistic that is precisely equivalent to U. What that means is that, if you know U, you can always apply a formula to obtain W and vice versa. W has its own tables of critical values, but the statistical decision reached when using U with one of its tables and the decision reached when using W with its table will always be identical. The formula linking U and W is:

$$W = \frac{n_1(n_1 + 2n_2 + 1)}{2} - U$$

When calculating W, it *is* necessary to designate the smaller of the groups as n_1, and to use the U-value that is obtained when n_1 is designated as the smaller of the two groups in the formula for calculating U_1. So we would enter n_1 as 7, n_2 as 9 and U as 57.5 in the formula for W. You may like to check that, for our example, that gives $W = 33.5$, which is the value given in the SPSS 'Test Statistics' box and turns out to be nothing other than the sum of ranks for the smaller group (i.e., R_2 in Table 8.4). Some books give tables for U and others give tables for W. Just remember that, whichever you use, you will arrive at the same statistical decision.

The SPSS 'Test Statistics' box also gives a value for the statistic Z and a two-tailed probability associated with that value. Recall from our earlier discussion of large sample statistics in relation to the Wilcoxon test (Complications 8.1) that Z provides an approximation based on the normal distribution and its use is only recommended when sample sizes are larger than those provided in the appropriate non-parametric statistical table.

The final probability in the SPSS output is an 'exact' value that is based on all possible rearrangements of the data that has only become practical with the recent increase in computing power. The procedure is equivalent to the Mann–Whitney test, which makes use of the properties of ranks to achieve the same end. Exact tests (sometimes known as 'randomization' tests) really come into their own for the analysis of single-participant experiments, where the usual group statistics lack validity (see Todman and Dugard, 2001).

SUMMARY OF CHAPTER

- Ordinal scales arise as a result of ranking, either during data generation or subsequently as ranks are applied to raw data.
- Non-parametric tests based on ranks are frequently used to analyse ordinal data. They are also used to analyse interval data when the parametric assumptions are seriously violated.
- Because non-parametric tests require fewer assumptions about the distributions of populations, they are sometimes referred to as 'distribution-free' tests.
- Provided parametric assumptions are met, parametric tests are generally more powerful than non-parametric alternatives. However, the tests described in this chapter are only slightly less powerful than their parametric alternatives.
- The Wilcoxon Matched-Pairs Signed-Ranks test is a non-parametric test used to analyse data from repeated measures or matched pairs designs.
- In repeated measures designs, there is a risk of order effects and these have to be dealt with by means of counterbalancing.
- Asymmetrical order effects, often known as carry-over effects, are not removed by counterbalancing.
- In calculating the Wilcoxon statistic T, ranks are assigned to the differences between pairs of scores.
- The Mann–Whitney test is a non-parametric test used to analyse data from independent groups designs.
- In calculating the Mann–Whitney statistic U, a single ranking is applied to all scores regardless of which group they belong to.
- Medians, rather than means, are generally reported when the non-parametric tests described in this chapter are used.

CHAPTER NINE

Tests of Significance for Interval Data

In this chapter we discuss two important statistical tests that are used for testing hypotheses in an experimental design in which there are two conditions and the DV is measured on an interval scale. These tests are the **independent groups *t*-test**, which is appropriate when each condition of the experiment uses different participants, and the **related *t*-test**, which is suitable for an experiment in which the same participants are employed in both conditions (i.e., a repeated measures design) or there are matched pairs of participants. In addition, we will discuss the **one-sample *t*-test**, which is used when just one set of scores is obtained.

Remember that the fact that the DV has been measured by means of an interval scale is not in itself sufficient to warrant the use of a *t*-test. A *t*-test can be used only when parametric assumptions are met (see Chapter 6 for a detailed discussion on parametric and non-parametric data). More precisely, if a non-parametric test is called for and you have different participants in the conditions of the experiment, you should use the Mann–Whitney *U* test, while if the same participants or matched pairs of participants are used in the two conditions, then you should use the Wilcoxon Matched Pairs *T* test. These two non-parametric tests have been thoroughly discussed in Chapter 8.

Interval Data

We offered a detailed discussion of the nature of interval measurement in Chapter 6. However, we will briefly summarize this notion here. Basically, there are various ways of measuring a variable, and they vary in terms of the properties that the measurement scales possess. In an interval scale, not only do larger numbers mean more of whatever is being measured (which is a characteristic shared with ordinal scales) but, in addition, the intervals between numbers represent equal differences of the measured variable at all points of the scale. For instance, suppose that we are investigating the effect of noise on people's memory for words; we may set up an experiment in which we ask participants to read out 50 words either in a noisy environment or in a quiet one, and then we count the number of words that are remembered, expecting that participants who read the words out in the 'noise' condition would remember fewer words than participants in the 'quiet' condition. Clearly, the DV is the number of words remembered, and people can score from 0 (no words remembered at all) to 50 (all words remembered). In this case (provided that the words are all of comparable memorability), we may safely assume not only that, say, a score of 24 stands for a better memory than a score of 20, but also that the interval between 24 and 20 is broadly the same as that between 14 and 10 (or between 44 and 40, between 9 and 5, and so on).

The Independent-Groups *t*-test

Let us start by reminding you of the hypothetical experiment discussed in Chapter 2. This will allow us to introduce the first of the tests presented in this chapter, that is the 'independent groups *t*-test'.

Selecting a test for our 'mood' experiment

In the fictitious experiment used in Chapter 2, we wanted to test the following hypothesis: 'when people have a positive mood, their intellectual performance will be enhanced'. We therefore proposed to design an experiment involving two conditions. In the experimental condition a group of participants watch a movie excerpt with a funny content; in the control condition a different group of participants watch an excerpt with an emotionally neutral content. This should lead participants in the experimental condition to have a better mood than those in the control condition. To measure the level of intellectual performance we proposed to ask participants to solve 10 logical problems. (See Figure 2.1 for an overview of the experimental design.) Obviously, if our hypothesis is correct we should find that participants in the experimental condition (mood enhanced) tend to solve a higher number of logical problems (i.e., to have a better intellectual performance) than participants in the control condition (mood unaltered).

In Chapter 4 we presented a table (see Table 4.1) showing a hypothetical set of scores produced by respondents in both the experimental and the control conditions – remember that each score represents the number of logical problems solved by a specific participant. In that chapter we also calculated the mean score produced by respondents in each condition of the experiment. This was 6.8 in the experimental condition and 5.4 in the control condition. We can also tell you that the standard deviation was 1.3 in the experimental condition and 1.5 in the control condition. The means indicate that, as predicted, participants in the experimental condition did, overall, solve more problems than participants in the control condition. However, as we have often emphasized, the difference between means in itself cannot be used to infer that our hypothesis is correct: in order to make a proper inference we need to use a statistical test.

Which test should we use in order to see whether our hypothesis is correct or not? A careful look at Table 6.1 will help you to decide. We already know that, concerning the nature of the research question, we are looking for a causal effect of one variable (mood) on another (intellectual performance), which leads directly to the prediction of a difference between means. We also know that, concerning the type of experimental design that is used, we have allocated different participants to the two conditions and that, therefore, we have used an 'independent groups design'. (The reason why we used this type of design was discussed in Chapter 3, particularly in the section entitled '*Participant variables*'.) At this point the question we need to ask ourselves is concerned with the type of measurement scale that we have used. Did we use a nominal, ordinal, interval or ratio scale? Clearly, our scale was not a nominal one, because different scores do not refer only to different qualitative characteristics of the respondent, but refer to different degrees of our DV, that is 'intellectual perform-ance'. Next, we can ask whether our scale was limited to an ordinal level. The answer is that it was not, because we may confidently assume that intervals between numbers are broadly equivalent at all points of our scale. So, at this point we know that we have at least an interval scale.

So, regarding our experiment on mood and performance, we now know that we are looking for a difference between means, that our design is an independent groups one, and that our DV is measured on at least an interval scale. If you look at Table 6.1 you will realize that we have only two options in terms of the statistical test to be selected: either an independent groups t-test or a Mann–Whitney U test. To choose between these two tests we need to decide whether parametric assumptions are rea-sonably met or not. In Chapter 6 we offered some useful rules of thumb on how to decide whether the parametric assumptions are met (see Figure 6.2 for a schematic summary of these rules). On the basis of these rules we can be reasonably confident that in our experiment the parametric assumptions are met. This is because (i) the variance of the samples in the two conditions ($1.3^2 = 1.69$ and $1.5^2 = 2.25$) does not differ substantially, and because (ii) the frequency distribution of scores in each con-dition is reasonably close to a normal distribution (see Figure 4.1 for histograms and Figure 4.3 for frequency polygons for the data in the conditions of our experiment). So, the statistical test we should use to ascertain whether our hypothesis is correct is the independent groups t-test (consider that this specific test may also be defined as an 'unmatched t-test', a 't-test for two independent means', a 't-test for unrelated samples' and an 'independent samples t-test'; so, don't worry if other books use one of these labels: what they mean is always the same thing!).

The logic of the independent groups t-test

Once you know that what you need is the independent groups t-test, all you have to do is to enter your data into a computer package and use the appropriate procedure to run the test (see SPSS operations and output (9.1) for how to run this test using SPSS). The package will perform a series of calculations on your data, based on a specific mathematical formula. Here we will explain the rationale behind this formula, but we will not explain its mathematical details, as this is beyond the scope of this book. (See Formulae (9.1) if you want to see what one version of the formula for the *t*-test looks like.)

The independent *t*-test focuses on two things. First, it looks at the *difference between* the mean of the scores obtained by participants in the experimental condition and the mean of the scores obtained by participants in the control condition. Second, the *t*-test is interested in the variability of the scores obtained by participants *within* each condition. What the formula does is to contrast the difference between the means obtained in the two conditions with the general variability of the scores within each condition. The *t*-value represents an indicator of this contrast, which is summarized in the following verbal formula:

$$t = \frac{\text{difference between the mean scores in the two conditions}}{\text{general variability of scores within each condition}}$$

Technically, the 'general variability of scores within each condition' is defined as the 'standard error of the differences between means', but don't worry about that at this stage. Just remember that the denominator in the equation is an estimate of how 'spread out' scores are within the two conditions. Broadly speaking, the more different the two means and the less variable the scores within each condition, the higher the value of *t*. On the contrary, the less different the two means and the more variable the scores within each condition, the lower the *t*-value. Clearly, when the means in the two conditions are very different and the scores within each group have little variability, the difference between the two means is probably due to the fact that participants in the two conditions were exposed to different levels of the IV (i.e., that the difference is not due to chance). On the other hand, when the means are very similar and the scores within each group have high variability, it is quite likely that random variability would be sufficient to produce a small preponderance of higher scores in one condition, and we can be almost certain that the difference between the means is due to chance. That also implies that the higher the value of *t* the smaller the probability that the difference between the means is due to chance (i.e., random NVs).

Formulae (9.1) – The independent groups *t*-test

The formula for the independent groups *t*-test varies depending on whether the number of participants in the two groups is equal or not. The simplest version of the formula is the one that holds only when group sizes are equal, and that is the formula given below:

$$t = \frac{\bar{X}_1 - \bar{X}_2}{\sqrt{\dfrac{s_1^2 + s_2^2}{n}}}$$

where the symbols mean:

$\bar{X}_1$ = mean of scores in condition 1
$\bar{X}_2$ = mean of scores in condition 2
s_1^2 = sample variance of condition 1 (see Formulae (4.2))
s_2^2 = sample variance of condition 2
n = number of participants in each condition

So, the arithmetical operation that you see in the 'numerator' (i.e., the expression on the top) calculates the difference between the mean obtained by participants in the experimental condition and the mean obtained by those who were in the control condition. On the other hand, the arithmetical operations that you can see in the 'denominator' (i.e., the expression underneath) calculate the general degree of variability of the scores obtained by participants within each condition (broadly speaking, this is equivalent to the average standard deviation within the two conditions).

   If the number of participants in the two groups differs, the formula becomes a bit more complicated because the two sample variances in the denominator have to be weighted according to their sample sizes. The denominator in that formula will thus provide a **weighted average** of the two sample variances, usually referred to as a **pooled variance estimate**.

   As you are unlikely ever to need to do these calculations by hand, you do not need to worry about the details of the formulae for computing t, and we are not even going to show you the formula that applies when sample sizes are unequal. The formula that is used when sample sizes are equal will suffice as an illustration in case you are interested in how the calculations are done.

If you do ever calculate a t-statistic yourself, or you are given a t-value without being told anything about the probability of it having arisen by chance (i.e., its statistical significance), provided you know the sample sizes of the two groups, you can use a statistical table (as in Statistical Table 9.1, a partial version of which is shown here) to see whether the t-value is large enough to be statistically significant. The table gives the critical values of t (i.e., the minimum value needed for statistical significance at various levels of probability) for different sample sizes.

   To use the table, you need to know the calculated t-value (let's suppose it is $t = 2.62$) and the degrees of freedom (dfs) for your t-statistic. The concept of degrees of freedom was explained briefly in Chapter 4 (see Complications (4.2)). As two standard deviations are computed on the way to calculating t for an independent groups design (i.e., one for each group), two degrees of freedom are lost. So, instead of referring directly to the total sample size ($n_1 + n_2 = N$), the table specifies the df for the calculation of t (always $N - 2$ for an independent groups design, because one df is lost for each group). As an example of using the table, suppose you had carried out

Statistical Table 9.1   Critical values of *t*. *t* is significant when it **equals or exceeds** the table value (partial table – full version in Appendix 1)

df	level of significance for a one-tailed test						
	.10	.05	.025	.01	.005	.001	.0005
	level of significance for a two-tailed test						
	.20	.10	.05	.02	.01	.002	.001
1	3.08	6.31	12.71	31.82	63.66	318.31	636.62
2	1.89	2.92	4.30	6.96	9.92	22.33	31.60
3	1.64	2.35	3.18	4.54	5.84	10.22	12.92
28	1.31	1.70	2.05	2.47	2.76	3.41	3.67
29	1.31	1.70	2.05	2.46	2.76	3.40	3.66
30	1.31	1.70	2.04	2.46	2.75	3.39	3.65
40	1.30	1.68	2.02	2.42	2.70	3.31	3.55
60	1.30	1.67	2.00	2.39	2.66	3.23	3.46
120	1.29	1.66	1.98	2.36	2.62	3.16	3.37
2000	1.28	1.65	1.96	2.33	2.58	3.09	3.30

Source: The entries in this table were computed by Pat Dugard, a freelance statistician.
For an independent groups (between Ss) test, $df = N - 2$ (where N is the total number of scores in both groups)
For a related (within Ss or matched pairs) test, $df = N - 1$ (where N is the number of pairs of scores)

an experiment with 20 participants in an experimental condition and 15 participants in a control condition. Then $N = 20 + 15 = 35$ and the dfs are $35 - 2 = 33$. So, you look for 33 in the left-hand column of the table. If, as in this case, the required df value is not shown in the table, the cautious solution is to select the nearest *smaller* value ($df = 30$, in this example), and enter the table at that row. Next, you need to decide what alpha level (level of significance) you want to test for. Suppose you are interested in a two-tailed test at alpha = .01. You should look down that column third from the right and locate the critical value of t at its intersection with the row where $df = 30$. The critical value is 2.75. As the obtained t-value (2.62) is not as big as the critical value (2.75), you should conclude that the difference between the experimental and control means did not reach statistical significance at the 1% level (i.e., $p > .01$) in a two-tailed t-test.

Note that had you been testing a directional hypothesis (say, the experimental mean is greater than the control mean), you might have decided to use a one-tailed test and would have been looking down a different column (fourth from the right) and the critical value for t would have been 2.46. In that case, provided the experimental mean was indeed greater than the control mean, you would have concluded that the predicted difference in favour of the experimental condition was statistically significant at the 1% level ($p < .01$) in a one–tailed test.

We remind you (see Complications (5.1)) that, rather than just looking down the column containing critical values for a pre-selected alpha level, in practice, some researchers scan the columns to see what is the lowest level of significance that can be reported for the t-value they obtained. Thus, with 20 dfs and t-values of 2.12 and 3.12 for two related experiments, a researcher might refer to Statistical Table 9.1 and report that the effect in the first experiment was significant at the 5% level ($p < .05$) and that the effect in the second experiment was significant at the 1% level ($p < .01$), both in two-tailed tests. We also remind you (see Complications (5.4)) that no such exploratory strategy can be used to decide whether to report a one- or two-tailed level of significance. The decision to use a one- or two-tailed test must *always* be made in advance.

On the subject of one- and two-tailed tests, Statistical Table 9.1 (in common with several of the other statistical tables in this book) is particularly useful for the way it makes clear the relationship between critical values for the statistic and significance levels for one- and two-tailed tests. Looking at the top of the table, you can see, for example, that any value of t that is significant at the 10% level ($p < .10$) in a two-tailed test will be significant at the 5% level ($p < .05$) in a one-tailed test. The general rule is: whatever the probability that the obtained value of a statistic can be attributed to chance in a two-tailed test, the probability that it can be attributed to chance in a one-tailed test will be half of that (see 'One- and two-tailed tests' in Chapter 5 for an explanation of this rule). An example of an analysis using an independent groups t-test is given in 'SPSS Operations and Output (9.1)'.

SPSS operations and output (9.1) – Computing an independent groups *t*-test

The data we will use in this example analysis are those shown, albeit in a different layout, in Table 4.1. To perform an independent groups *t*-test in SPSS, you must devote one column to the IV and one to the DV. In the column concerning the IV (which, with reference to our fictitious experiment, we might label as 'mood') you specify which condition each participant in the experiment belongs to (usually coded as 1 and 2). In the column about the DV (which we could label as 'perform') you specify the scores produced by all participants in the experiment. Then proceed as follows:

(i)   Click on *Analyze*, from the menu at the top of the screen. Then click on *Compare means*, and then on *Independent Samples T-test*.
(ii)   Move the DV from the rectangular box on the left side of the window into the box called *Test variable*.
(iii)   Move the IV from the rectangular box on the left side of the window into the box called *Grouping variable*.
(iv)   Click on *Define groups* and then type in the numbers used in your data file to refer to each condition (i.e., each independent group of participants) in your experiment. For instance, regarding our fictitious experiment, if we had used 1 = good mood and 2 = neutral mood we would type 1 in the *Group 1* box and 2 in the *Group 2* box.

(v)   Click on *Continue* followed by *OK*.
(vi)   If you want to look at the shapes of the distributions of scores in the two conditions to see whether they are approximately normal, click on *Data*, then *Split File*. Click on the radio button *Organize output by groups* and move the IV into the *Groups Based on* box and click *OK*.
(vii) Click on *Graphs*, then *Histogram*. In the box on the left, select the DV and move it into the *Variable* slot, then click on *Display normal curve*, followed by OK.

The output includes the following (we have not reproduced the histograms because they can be seen in Figure 4.1):

Group Statistics

	MOOD	N	Mean	Std. Deviation	Std. Error Mean
PERFORM	good mood	20	6.8000	1.2814	.2865
	neutral mood	20	5.3500	1.4609	.3267

Independent Samples Test

		Levene's Test for Equality of Variances		t-test for Equality of Means						
									95% Confidence Interval of the Difference	
		F	Sig.	t	df	Sig. (2-tailed)	Mean Difference	Std. Error Difference	Lower	Upper
PERFORM	Equal variances assumed	.511	.479	3.337	38	.002	1.4500	.4345	.5703	2.3297
	Equal variances not assumed			3.337	37.365	.002	1.4500	.4345	.5699	2.3301

The SPSS output (9.1) refers to the data set (see Table 4.1) based on our imaginary 'mood and intellectual performance' experiment. The mean and standard deviation for each condition of the experiment can be seen in the '*Group Statistics*' table. In the table called '*Independent Samples Test*', you can see, among other things, the value of t (which in this case is 3.337), the df (38) and the probability of obtaining that specific value of t by chance in a two-tailed test of the hypothesis (which is .002) – see column labelled 'Sig. (2-tailed)'.

Note that the result of another test (using the statistic, F, which is not dealt with in this book) is presented towards the left of the 'Independent Samples Test' box. This is a test to see whether the parametric assumption of 'equality of variances' is met. If the variances differ significantly, you should look across the 'Equal variances not assumed' row of the table. Otherwise, as in this case, you should look across the 'Equal variances assumed' row. The probability (.002) is the same in both rows in this example because the variances in the two conditions are very similar (see squares

of SDs from the 'Group Statistics' box – i.e., $1.2814^2 = 1.64$ and $1.4609^2 = 2.13$).
Note that the df in the 'Equal variances not assumed' row is slightly reduced from
$df = 38$. This is how the program makes allowance for non-equality of variances,
though the reduction in df is too small in this case to affect the probability (.002).
If you ever need to report the df for an 'Equal variances not assumed' solution, you
should round the df down to a whole number, in this case from 37.365 to 37.

Finally, note that SPSS often produces additional output that exceeds your current needs (e.g., 'Std. Error Mean', ' Standard Error Difference' and '95% Confidence
Interval of the Difference' in the output above), and that at present you can safely
ignore.

Drawing inferences about our 'mood' experiment by using a t-test

As we explained in Chapter 5, experimental psychologists normally accept a value of
t that has less than a 5% probability of being obtained by chance, as an indication
that the experimental hypothesis is supported. So, if we submit the data collected in
our experiment on the effects of mood on performance to a t-test, we end up with
$t = 3.34$ (note that it is usually sensible to report statistical values to a maximum of
two decimal places). The probability of obtaining this specific t-value by chance, in a
study involving two groups of 20 participants (i.e., $df = 38$), are two in one-thousand,
or, if you prefer, 0.2% (experimental psychologists and statisticians express this idea
as $p = 0.002$, as explained in Chapter 5). Obviously, this probability is less than 5%
(and, indeed, less than 1%), and so, provided we had a valid experimental design,
we can infer that our manipulation probably had a strong effect, in the sense that
participants in the experimental condition (good mood) performed better than participants in the control condition (neutral mood). Therefore, we may conclude that
our experimental hypothesis – that 'when people have a positive mood, their intellectual performance will be enhanced' – was supported (or, technically speaking, the
null hypothesis can be rejected).

Remember that $t = 3.34$ is not necessarily associated with $p = 0.002$. This is so in
our experiment given the specific number of participants in each condition. However,
with a different number of participants per condition, this t-value would be associated with a different value of p. This is because in that case our experiment would
have different degrees of freedom (reported as 'df' in the SPSS output). Basically,
given the same value of t, the more the degrees of freedom, the smaller the value
of p. Putting it another way, the more degrees of freedom, the smaller will be the
value of t needed for a given level of statistical significance.

You should also remember another thing. We are assuming that our hypothesis is
correct on the basis of the values of t and p, but this is only because we know that
the mean score in the experimental condition was bigger than the mean score in the
control condition (thereby showing that intellectual performance was better under
good mood). But consider that, had the means been the other way around (i.e., 5.4
in the experimental condition and 6.8 in the control condition), you would have obtained

the same t-value (except that it would have been a negative value, i.e., $t = -3.337$) and the same p-value. However, in this case, the difference between the scores on intellectual performance in the two conditions would not, as indicated by the negative value of t, have been in the predicted direction! It goes without saying that, in this case, the hypothesis would have probably been wrong, and the null hypothesis could not have been rejected. In other words, our hypothesis was a directional hypothesis (i.e., we predicted not only that the two conditions would produce significantly different scores, but also the direction of this difference), therefore, only a difference in favour of the scores in the experimental condition will allow us to reject the null hypothesis. (See Chapter 5 for more information on the notion of directional hypotheses.) If we had decided, before collecting our data, to carry out a one-tailed test of the directional hypothesis, we would need to halve the two-tailed probability provided in the SPSS output, i.e., the one-tailed probability would be .001. If we had opted for a one-tailed test, therefore, even a p-value of .10 or less in the SPSS output would have been sufficient for us to report a significant one-tailed effect.

Additional information (9.1) – Effect size

If you use a great many participants, your experiment has a *high power*, and it is unlikely to miss a real effect even if it is very small (see Chapter 5, specifically in the section on 'Statistical decision errors' and in Additional information (5.6) for a discussion of 'power'). A very small effect that is picked up because the experiment has high power may be of limited theoretical or practical significance. Therefore, in addition to the usual information about statistical significance, it is useful to know whether the effect that was found is a large or small effect. Indeed, an increasing number of psychology journals now insist that information about **effect size** is reported along with the usual information about statistical significance. There are several measures of effect size in use. An intuitively meaningful one – in relation to the parametric analyses discussed in this chapter – is that defined as the difference between means in units of standard deviation. This is known as a standardized measure of the kind discussed in Chapter 4 in the section on 'z-scores'. The point about standardized measures is that they provide a stable interpretation of differences between measures regardless of the scale on which they are measured. For example, knowing that the mean number of problems solved in the two conditions of the mood experiment were 6.80 and 5.35 does not give us much idea of whether this is a 'big' or a 'small' difference. If we tell you, however, that the two means differ by 1.06 standard deviations and that an approximate guide to effect size (see Cohen in the 'brief list of recommended books') is that a difference of .2 of a SD is a small effect, a difference of .5 SD is a medium effect and a difference of .8 SD is a large effect, you can immediately conclude that the effect we found was quite large, as well as being statistically significant. The calculation of effect size (signified by 'd'), is straightforward:

$$d = \frac{\bar{X}_1 - \bar{X}_2}{SD}$$

where SD is the mean standard deviation of the two groups. Remember that equal variances (and of course SDs) in the populations from which the samples are drawn is a required assumption for parametric tests and the average of the two sample SDs is the best estimate we have of the joint population SD. (Note that if the numbers of participants in the two groups are not the same, a *weighted* average of the SDs has to be calculated – see Howell in the 'brief list of recommended books'.)

Reporting results (9.1) – The independent groups *t*-test

In a report of the experiment (assuming that a two-tailed test had been decided on) the result could be described as follows:

> In an independent groups *t*-test of the hypothesis that positive mood would result in higher intellectual performance than neutral mood, the difference in number of problems solved was in the predicted direction (positive mood mean = 6.80; neutral mood mean = 5.35) and was statistically significant (t (df = 38) = 3.34; $p < .05$; two-tailed). The effect size was given by $d = 1.06$.

Recall that some researchers would report the *lowest* conventional level of statistical probability reached (i.e., $p < .01$), rather than a predetermined alpha level (e.g., $p < .05$).

The Related (Repeated Measures) *t*-test

An imaginary experiment

Let us now consider another fictitious experiment. Suppose that we are studying 'spider phobia'. Then suppose that we have a theory according to which, because there are many venomous spiders, during evolution the human species has developed an 'adaptive' fear of spiders. This theory also holds that, because there are many more venomous spiders among the hairy than among the non-hairy ones, humans will find hairy spiders more scary than non-hairy ones. This theory sees phobia of spiders as just an exaggerated expression of this 'natural' fear, and therefore it predicts that, although spider-phobic people are afraid of all spiders, they tend to fear hairy spiders more than non-hairy ones. Now, in order to test this hypothesis, we can recruit 20 individuals who have been diagnosed as spider phobic, and show them a series of, say, 10 three-dimensional, very vivid pictures of different spiders, five of which belong to hairy species and five of which belong to non-hairy ones. While participants observe the different pictures, we can assess their level of anxiety by recording their pulse-rate. (Obviously, the order of presentation of pictures should be counterbalanced, as it is possible that the spiders observed later would elicit less anxiety than the ones observed earlier because of habituation.) Clearly, we expect that pulse-rate will be higher when participants see pictures of hairy spiders then when they see pictures of non-hairy ones. Finally, suppose that we find that, on average, participants' pulse-rate is 108.80 beats per minute (with a standard deviation of 9.10) when exposed to pictures of hairy spiders, and 105.40 beats per minute (with a standard deviation of 8.97) when exposed to pictures of non-hairy spiders.

Selecting a test for the 'spider phobia' experiment

Although the means indicate, as predicted, that viewing hairy spiders produces higher pulse-rates than viewing non-hairy ones, which statistical test should be used to test statistically the hypothesis that spider-phobic people find hairy spiders more scary than non-hairy ones? As usual we must start by deciding what we are testing for. We are clearly testing for a difference between conditions, as we want to know whether seeing different types of spiders produces different emotional responses. Second, we need to consider the type of research design we are using. Basically, we have two conditions, one in which participants are shown hairy spiders, and one in which the *same* participants are shown non-hairy spiders. Now, this is clearly a repeated measures design, as the same people are employed in both conditions of the experiment. Third, we must decide what kind of scale we have used to measure the DV, which is about the level of fear prompted by the view of spiders. We can consider our scale as an interval scale, as the intervals between the various levels of pulse-rate can be understood as being broadly the same. Finally, we need to know whether parametric assumptions are met. Given that the variability of the scores in the conditions is similar, as indicated by the standard deviations (9.10 and 8.97), and providing that the distribution of the pulse-rates for each type of spider was broadly similar to a normal distribution, we can say that parametric assumptions are reasonably met. At this point we can choose our statistical test; we are looking for a difference between conditions, we have a repeated measures design, we have used an interval measurement scale, and parametric assumptions are met: the test to be used is the related *t*-test! Had the parametric assumptions not been reasonably met, the test of choice would be the Wilcoxon Matched Pairs *T* test (see Table 6.1).

Additional information (9.2) – Control conditions

When we first introduced the notion of experimental and control conditions in Chapter 2, we explained that not all experiments include a control condition. This is the case in the spider phobia experiment. Here, the presentation of non-hairy spiders pictures is intended to produce an effect on participants (unlike the neutral condition in the mood experiment), and so it cannot be strictly defined as a 'control' condition. Therefore, conditions should not be labelled as experimental and control conditions; instead, they should be given descriptive names (e.g., *hairy* and *non-hairy*). Whether or not it is referred to as such, a control condition is one that involves a treatment that is the same as in the experimental condition in all respects except the critical one that is the subject of the hypothesis. A clear example of this is in treatment (e.g., drug) evaluation studies, where the control condition involves the giving of a *placebo* (something that appears the same as the treatment, but lacks the active ingredient).

At this point you should proceed as usual. That is, you enter your data into a data-file and analyse it using SPSS (see SPSS operations and output (9.2)). With alpha set at .05, a probability of $p < .05$ will allow you to reject the null hypothesis (see SPSS operations and output (9.2) to find the t-value and the two-tailed probability of obtaining that t-value by chance).

The logic of the related (repeated measures) t-test

As with the independent groups t-test, once you know that what you need is the related t-test, you only need to enter your data into a computer package and use the appropriate procedure to run the test (see SPSS operations and output (9.2) for how to run a related t-test using SPSS). The rationale behind the formula for a related t-test is basically the same as for the independent groups t-test. The principal difference is that the scores in the two conditions are converted to a single set of *difference* scores. For each participant, the score in one condition is subtracted from the score in the other condition. The analysis is then carried out on these difference scores. If the null hypothesis is true, we should expect the positive and negative differences to approximately balance out. So, under the null hypothesis, the mean of the differences is predicted to be zero. Technically, the mean of the hypothetical *population* of difference scores, of which our difference scores are a sample, is hypothesized to be zero.

Additional information (9.3) – Analysis of data from a matched pairs design

A matched pairs design is also analysed using a related t-test. Here there are different participants in the two conditions, but each participant in the 'hairy' condition has been matched with a participant in the 'non-hairy' condition. The variable on which they have been matched will be one, such as 'severity of phobia', which is likely to have a strong effect on the DV (pulse-rate) regardless of which condition the participant is in. Thus, a severe phobic is likely to have higher pulse-rates than a less severe phobic both in the hairy and non-hairy conditions. For this reason, each matched pair of participants can be treated as though they were the same participant being exposed to both conditions and the difference between their scores in the two conditions can be used in a related t-test, just as for a repeated measures design where it really is the same participant being exposed to both conditions. (See Additional information (6.1) for a discussion of the extent to which participant NVs are effectively controlled in a matched pairs design.)

As with the independent groups t-test, the related t-test contrasts two things. In this case, it contrasts the extent to which the mean of the sample of difference scores deviates from a population mean of zero with the variability within the sample of difference scores. Again, the t-value is an indicator of this contrast and may be summarized in the following verbal formula:

$$t = \frac{\text{difference between sample and population means of difference scores}}{\text{variability of difference scores within the sample}}$$

Technically, the 'variability of difference scores within the sample' is defined as the 'standard error of the mean' of the difference scores, but, once again, you do not need to be concerned about that at this stage. You just need to know that the denominator in the equation is an estimate of how 'spread out' the difference scores are. As with the independent groups t-test, the greater the difference in the numerator and the smaller the variability in the denominator, the higher the value of t. In this case, it can be inferred that the higher the value of t the smaller the probability that the deviation of the mean of difference scores from zero is due to chance (i.e., random NVs). The statistical formula can be seen in Formulae (9.2).

Formulae (9.2) – The related (repeated measures) *t*-test

$$t = \frac{\bar{D} - 0}{\dfrac{s_D}{\sqrt{n}}}$$

where the symbols mean:

$\bar{D}$ = mean of difference scores
s_D = standard deviation of difference scores (standard error of their mean)
n = number of difference scores (number of participants when repeated measures or number of matched pairs)

So, the arithmetical operation that you see in the numerator calculates the difference between the mean of the participants' difference scores and the hypothetical population mean of zero. On the other hand, the arithmetical operations that you can see in the denominator calculate the degree of variability of the sample of difference scores.

Once again, as you are unlikely ever to need to do these calculations by hand, you do not need to worry about the details of the formulae for computing *t*.

If you ever calculate a related *t*-statistic yourself, or you are given a related *t*-value without being told anything about the probability of it having arisen by chance (i.e., its statistical significance), provided you know the number of pairs of scores (usually, the total number of participants, but it would be the number of matched pairs of participants if you were using a matched pairs design), you can use the same statistical table (Statistical Table 9.1) to see whether the *t*-value is large enough to be statistically significant. The critical values of *t* given in the table are interpreted in the usual way (i.e., they are the minimum values needed for statistical significance at various levels of probability) for different sample sizes. Note, however, that the degrees of freedom for a related *t*-test are $N - 1$, where N is the number of pairs of scores (i.e., difference scores). This is because only one standard deviation has to be computed on the way to obtaining a related *t*-value (see Formulae (9.2)).

The SPSS output (9.2) refers to a data set (see Table 9.1) based on imaginary results that emerged from our hypothetical 'spider phobia' experiment. The mean and standard deviation for each condition of the experiment can be seen in the 'Paired Samples Statistics' table. In the table called 'Paired Samples Test', you can see, among other things, the value of *t*, which in this case is 2.311, the *df*, which is 19 and the probability of obtaining that specific value of *t* in a test of a two-tailed hypothesis, which is .032 (see column labelled 'Sig. (2-tailed)').

SPSS operations and output (9.2) – Computing a related *t*-test

To perform a related *t*-test in SPSS, you must create two columns, one for each condition of the experiment. That is, under one column you will include scores produced by each participant in one condition, and under the other column you will type scores produced by the same (or matched) participants in the other condition. For instance, concerning our 'spider phobia' experiment, you may create a column called 'hairy' (meaning 'hairy spiders') and a column called 'nonhairy' (meaning 'non-hairy' spiders) and enter participants' average pulse-rate when seeing each type of spider in the relevant column (by 'average' we mean that, given that participants' pulse-rate was taken five times for each type of spider, you need to calculate the mean of these five measures of pulse-rate). Then proceed as follows:

1. Click on *Analyze*, from the menu at the top of the screen. Then click on *Compare means*, and then on *Paired Samples T-test*.
2. Click on the two variables that you want to compare (e.g., hairy and nonhairy). As they are highlighted, move them into the box called *Paired variables* by clicking on the arrow button.
3. Click on *OK*.
4. In order to look at distributions of scores in the two conditions, click on *Graphs*, then *Histogram*. In the box on the left, select one of the conditions and move it into the *Variable* slot, then click on *Display normal curve*, followed by OK. Repeat with the other condition entered in the *Variable* slot.

Paired Samples Statistics

		Mean	N	Std. Deviation	Std. Error Mean
Pair 1	hairy spiders	108.8000	20	9.09945	2.03470
	non-hairy spiders	105.4000	20	8.97013	2.00578

Paired Samples Correlations

		N	Correlation	Sig.
Pair 1	hairy spiders & non-hairy spiders	20	.735	.000

Paired Samples Test

		Paired Differences							
					95% Confidence Interval of the Difference				
		Mean	Std. Deviation	Std. Error Mean	Lower	Upper	t	df	Sig. (2-tailed)
Pair 1	hairy spiders – non-hairy spiders	3.40000	6.58067	1.47148	.32015	6.47985	2.311	19	.032

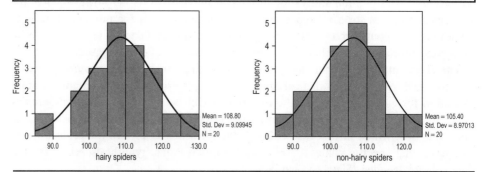

Table 9.1 Hypothetical data for a repeated measures design: pulse-rates (beats per minute) of spider phobics when viewing hairy and non-hairy spiders

Participant	IV: type of spider	
	hairy	non-hairy
1	110	113
2	115	111
3	110	103
4	111	104
5	103	98
6	111	107
7	130	125
8	89	91
9	116	110
10	121	117
11	112	112
12	104	87
13	119	108
14	100	99
15	104	110
16	104	100
17	98	113
18	115	110
19	110	103
20	88	94

The information in the 'Paired Samples Correlations' table simply tells you that there is a fairly strong positive relationship between scores in the two conditions. Measures of relationship (or *correlation*) between variables will be discussed in detail in Chapter 10. For the moment, just remember that a positive correlation implies that people who have relatively high pulse-rates in the 'hairy' condition tend also to have relatively high pulse-rates in the 'non-hairy' condition, and those with relatively low pulse-rates in the 'hairy' condition tend also to have relatively low pulse-rates in the 'non-hairy' condition. This suggests that a repeated measures design was a good choice because participant differences have a marked effect on the DV and are therefore well worth controlling (see Chapter 3 under the heading 'Controlling participant nuisance variables').

As the histograms indicate that both distributions of scores approximate to normal distributions and their variances do not differ greatly ($9.10^2 = 82.81$ and $8.97^2 = 80.46$), the assumptions required for a parametric test may be considered met. Note that for the related t-test, SPSS does not provide any adjustment for non-equal variances and it would be particularly unwise to use the parametric related t-test on data with substantially different variances in the two conditions. In that case, the alternative (non-parametric) Wilcoxon Matched Pairs T Test should certainly be preferred.

Recall that it is desirable to report *effect size* as well as statistical significance information. In this case, effect size (d) is given by the difference between the means for the two conditions divided by the standard deviation of the difference scores, which is given in the 'Paired Samples Test' table as 6.5807. So $d = (108.80 - 105.40)/6.58 = .52$. Using Cohen's convention, this is a small to medium effect.

Reporting results (9.2) – related *t*-test

The way the result would be described in a report of the experiment (assuming that alpha was set at .05 and a two-tailed test had been decided on) would be something like this:

> In a related t-test of the hypothesis that spider phobics would have higher pulse-rates when viewing hairy spiders than when viewing non-hairy spiders, the difference was statistically significant (hairy mean = 108.50; non-hairy mean = 105.75) in a two-tailed test (t ($df = 19$) = 2.31; $p < .05$). The effect size was $d = .52$.

Note that, even though a directional prediction was made, it is not 'wrong' to decide on a two-tailed test.

The One-Sample *t*-test

In some circumstances you may want to obtain scores on a DV in just one condition in order to compare the mean of those scores with some already known mean of another set of scores on that DV. As only one sample of scores is used in the analysis, the parametric test used is known as the 'one-sample *t*-test'. The usual parametric assumptions apply even though one of the means was obtained on a previous occasion, probably by a different researcher.

An example of an occasion when it might be appropriate to collect a single set of scores would be when you wanted to know whether the mean reading age of a group of 10-year-old children, who had been selected for participation in a remedial reading experiment, was significantly lower than that of the population of 10-year-old children in the schools from which the sample came. Provided that the reading test to be used had previously been administered to a representative sample of the population of 10-year-olds in the schools in question, the test could now be administered to the 'remedial' sample and a one-sample *t*-test could be used to test the difference between their mean reading age and that of the representative sample of 10-year-olds. Another example would be when it was required to establish that a group of people who were to take part in an experiment were 'typical' of the population from which the sample was drawn; that is, that the sample mean did not differ significantly from the known *population mean* on the DV (e.g., intelligence; reading age; reaction time). Another possibility would be that you intended to do an experiment similar to one you had seen reported and would like some assurance that the participants you had selected were similar to the participants in the reported experiment in some important respect. You might want the assurance so that you could make comparisons between the results of the reported experiment and the one that you would be carrying out.

The logic of the one-sample t-test

Essentially, the one-sample *t*-test is a more *general version* of the related *t*-test, because the known mean that the single set of scores is compared to can be any value. In the first example above, if the mean reading age of a representative sample of 10-year-olds in the relevant schools were 9.5 years, that would be the mean against which the scores of the 'remedial' sample would be tested. In another scenario, the mean IQ (intelligence quotient) of the UK population of 10-year-olds is often *set* at 100, with 'more intelligent' children having scores ranging above 100 and 'less intelligent' children having scores ranging below 100. If we wanted to establish whether a sample of 10-year-olds whom we intended to use in an experiment were *typical* of the UK population of 10-year-olds, we would test the IQs of our sample against the known mean of 100.

In the case of the related *t*-test, the situation is more constrained. Then, we are always working with a sample of *difference scores* and the hypothetical mean difference against which they are compared is always *zero*. In this sense the related *t*-test can be seen as a special case of the one-sample *t*-test, because the comparison mean for the related *t*-test is always the same – zero.

Another way of construing the relation between these two tests is to think of the sample of scores used in the one-sample *t*-tests as a set of *difference scores*, in which the second score to be subtracted from the first is zero. It is as though the first condition contained the single sample scores and the second condition contained a column of zeros. So, the formula for one-sample *t* (see Formulae (9.3)) is effectively the same as that for related *t*, the difference being that the value in the numerator that is subtracted does not have to be zero. This means that in SPSS it is necessary to specify the value of the population mean that is to be subtracted from the sample mean.

Formulae (9.3) – The one-sample *t*-test

$$t = \frac{\bar{X} - \mu}{\frac{s}{\sqrt{n}}}$$

where the symbols mean:

$\bar{X}$ = mean of scores in the single sample
μ = known mean of population from which the sample is drawn
s = standard deviation of scores in the single sample
n = number of scores (i.e., participants) in the single sample

---

Remember that the related *t*-test and the one-sample *t*-test are effectively doing the same job. In fact, if you wished, you could compute related *t* using the SPSS procedure for a one-sample *t*-test (the procedure for a one-sample *t*-test is shown in SPSS operations and output (9.3)). All you would need to do would be to specify the value of the 'Test Value' (i.e., the population mean) as zero. Conversely, you could compute one-sample *t* using the SPSS procedure for a related *t*-test (see SPSS operations and output (9.2)). In this case, all you would need to do would be to enter the sample scores under the first condition and a column of zeros under the second condition.

An illustrative set of IQ scores is provided for a sample of 15 10-year-olds in Table 9.2. In this example, the reason for calculating a one-sample *t*-value might be to establish whether the mean of the sample scores differs significantly from the known 10-year-old population mean of 100.

Table 9.2 Hypothetical data for a one sample design: IQ scores of a sample of 10-year-old children

Participant	IQ score
1	95
2	87
3	101
4	96
5	105
6	116
7	102
8	81
9	97
10	90
11	123
12	86
13	95
14	104
15	83

SPSS operations and output (9.3) – Computing a one-sample *t*-test

To perform a one-sample *t*-test, you must enter the sample scores in one column and then proceed as follows:

(i)   Click on *Analyze*, from the menu at the top of the screen. Then click on *Compare Means*, and then on *One-Sample T test*.
(ii) Move the DV scores for the sample into the *Test Variable(s)* box.
(iii) Enter '100' in the *Test Value* box and click OK.

One-Sample Statistics

	N	Mean	Std. Deviation	Std. Error Mean
IQSCORE	15	97.4000	11.7096	3.0234

One-Sample Test

	Test Value = 100					
					95% Confidence Interval of the Difference	
	t	df	Sig. (2-tailed)	Mean Difference	Lower	Upper
IQSCORE	−.860	14	.404	−2.6000	−9.0845	3.8845

The SPSS output (9.3) refers to the imaginary IQ data set in Table 9.2. The mean (97.40) and standard deviation (11.71) of the sample of DV scores are shown in the table called 'One-Sample Statistics'. The 'One-Sample Test' table shows the value of t (−.860). This is a negative value because the sample mean is lower than the population mean of 100. That table also shows the df ($N − 1 = 14$) and the two-tailed probability of obtaining the specific value of t when the null hypothesis is true.

Once again, we should report effect size as well as statistical significance information. In this case, effect size (d) is given by the difference between the mean of the sample and the population mean divided by the standard deviation of the population (which is set at 15 by the IQ test constructors). So $d = (97.4 − 100)/15 = −.17$ (the minus sign can be ignored). Using Cohen's convention, this is a very small effect.

Reporting results (9.3) – One-sample *t*-test

The way the result would be described in a report of the study (assuming that alpha was set at .05 and a two-tailed test had been decided on) would be something like this:

In a one-sample t-test of the hypothesis that the mean IQ of a sample of 10-year-olds would differ from the population mean of 100, the sample mean of 97.40 did not differ significantly from the population mean (t ($df = 14$) = .86; $p > .05$; two-tailed). It is therefore reasonable to treat the sample as representative of the population with respect to IQ. The effect size was given by $d = .17$.

SUMMARY OF CHAPTER

- In an experiment, when the DV has been measured on an interval scale (or a scale intermediate between ordinal and interval) and parametric assumptions are met, the statistical test to be used is a t-test.
- With an independent groups design the specific t-test to use is the independent groups t-test. This contrasts the difference between the mean scores in the two conditions of the experiment with the general variability of the scores within each condition. The t-value represents an indicator of this contrast. The higher the value of t, the lower the probability that the observed difference between means emerged by chance. If the probability of obtaining a specific value of t is less than 5%, and the difference between means is in the right direction, the null hypothesis can be rejected.
- When the experiment is based on a repeated measures design, the t-test to be used is the related t-test. This contrasts the mean difference between participants' scores in two conditions with a difference of zero assumed for a hypothetical population of difference scores when the null hypothesis is true.
- When the experiment is based on a matched pairs design, we use the related t-test again. This test contrasts the mean difference between matched pairs of participants' scores in two conditions with a population difference of zero.
- When a single sample design is used, the t-test to be used is the one-sample t-test. This is similar to the related t-test, but in this case the mean of the single sample of scores is contrasted with the known mean of the population of scores from which the sample was drawn.

CHAPTER TEN

Correlational Studies

Experiments and Correlational Studies

Let us start this chapter by reminding you of the essence of experiments. In an experiment the researcher tests the hypothesis that a change in one thing will *cause* a change in another thing (e.g., changing mood will *cause* a change in intellectual performance). To test such a hypothesis, the researcher manipulates the IV (i.e., creates different situations in which participants are exposed to different levels of the IV), holds all other variables constant, and then observes how the DV changes from one situation to another. When changes in the DV are observed, the researcher can infer a cause–effect relationship between the IV and the DV (providing that you have a 'true' experiment, that the experiment is well conducted, and that changes in the DV are not actually caused by other – nuisance – variables).

As emphasized several times throughout this book, not all hypotheses in psychology are concerned with causal effects (i.e., with things causing changes in other things). In some cases, psychologists may wish to test the hypothesis that two things change together, without making any claim about which one causes which. For instance, we might want to test the hypothesis that people with higher salaries have higher self-esteem. In this case we would be 'simply' claiming that self-esteem and salary change together: when self-esteem is low salary will also be low, and if self-esteem is high salary will also be high. We would be 'agnostic' concerning which produces which; that is, we would not wish to state either that higher self-esteem leads people to earn more money, or that earning more money produces an increase in self-esteem. We would accept that it could be either way, or neither (in fact, it might be that a third thing, say the 'level of education', influences both self-esteem and salary, and that is why they change together).

Is there any difference in the way we test a hypothesis that a change in one thing will cause a change in another thing, and the way we test a hypothesis that two things change together? The answer to this question is a straightforward 'yes'; there is a big difference! When we hypothesize that two things change together we do not need to manipulate (deliberately change) the levels of one thing (the IV) to see how this manipulation affects another thing (the DV). This is because we are not hypo-thesizing that changes in one thing will cause changes in another. That means that we do *not* need to conduct an experiment to test this kind of hypothesis. All we need to do is to measure both things that, in our view, change together (i.e., are **correlated**), and then test the hypothesis statistically to see if there is evidence that they do really change together. This type of study is known as a **correlational study**.

In the next sections we will discuss how data collected by means of a correlational study are usually analysed. We will deal with two broad and relatively distinct issues. First, we will deal with **correlational analysis**; that is, we will discuss how to see whether two variables are correlated, and how to explore the nature of the correlation. Second, we will discuss **linear regression analysis**. This will involve showing you how to estimate how much one variable will change as the other variable changes by a given amount, and how to use our knowledge of a specific participant's score on one variable to make predictions about that participant's score on the other variable.

Correlational Analysis

How can we explore the relationship between two variables in depth? We can use a set of procedures that are normally subsumed under the heading of 'correlational analysis'. These procedures involve describing the relationship visually and numeric-ally, and testing its statistical significance.

Obtaining a visual description of a relationship: the scattergram

Let us use again the example above about the hypothesized relationship between salary and self-esteem. In order to test this hypothesis we could select a sample of participants (say 20) and then measure the two variables that we are interested in. That is, we could provide participants with a questionnaire in which they are asked to inform us about their salary, and to respond to some items that are meant to assess their level of self-esteem.

How can we obtain an informative description of the data we have collected? To start with, we may simply display the row data by putting the salary (expressed in pounds per year) and the level of self-esteem (expressed as, say, a number ranging from 1 = low self-esteem to 20 = high self-esteem) of each participant in different columns within a table. Suppose that this table looks like Table 10.1.

From a cursory inspection of Table 10.1, we can see that, in general, people earning more money tend to have higher self-esteem. However, there is a better way to describe and visualize data about the relationship between two variables: we can create a scattergram (also known as a scatterplot). A scattergram is a specific type of graph showing the position of each participant – represented by a dot – in a two-dimensional space representing the two variables. The specific position of each participant depends on his/her score on each variable. Since this definition may sound

Table 10.1   Annual salary and self-esteem score (0–20) of 20 participants

Participant	Salary(£/yr)	Self-esteem
1	14,000	7
2	25,000	11
3	23,000	10
4	37,000	15
5	30,000	12
6	12,000	5
7	32,000	14
8	22,000	10
9	19,000	7
10	41,000	17
11	22,000	9
12	12,000	4
13	29,000	13
14	35,000	12
15	22,000	9
16	43,000	16
17	16,000	5
18	22,000	10
19	31,000	14
20	30,000	13

rather abstract, let's have a look at a scattergram of the data in Table 10.1, and explain it. The SPSS operations required to produce a scattergram of the data are shown in SPSS operations and output (10.1). We have modified the output graph in several ways to make it as we wish it to appear and the modified graph is presented in Figure 10.1. SPSS allows you to modify its output in this way and that is something you can readily learn to do for yourself.

We will now focus on our modified graph (see Figure 10.1) to explain the various features of the scattergram. As you can see, in this graph there are two axes – a horizontal one (the X-axis) and a vertical one (the Y-axis) – joined at the bottom left corner. The X-axis is subdivided in units of measurement representing the different scores that can be obtained on the self-esteem scale and the Y-axis is subdivided in units representing the different salaries that participants in our study can earn. The point at which the two axes touch one another, in the bottom left-hand corner, is the point of lowest possible score for both self-esteem and salary. Now, the dots represent the position of each participant in the two-dimensional space within the two axes. A participant's position is defined by the point at which two imaginary lines meet each other, one starting from the point on the X-axis representing the

SPSS operations and output (10.1) – The scattergram

To obtain a scattergram you should proceed as follows:

(i)   Go to the menu at the top of the screen and click on *Graphs* and then on *Scatter.*
(ii) Click on *Simple*; then click on the button labelled as *Define.*
(iii) Click on one of the two variables and move it into the box labelled as *Y-axis*. Then click on the other variable and move it into the box labelled as *X-axis*. (For current purposes it does not matter which one is the *X* variable and which one is the *Y* variable.)
(iv) Click on *OK.*

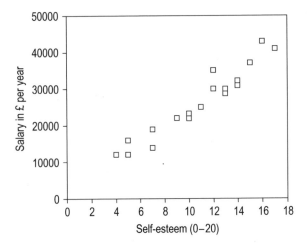

Figure 10.1   Scattergram showing a positive relationship between annual salary and self-esteem

participant's score on one variable, and one starting from the point on the *Y*-axis representing the participant's score on the other variable. For instance, let us focus for a moment on participant number 1. As you can see in Table 10.1, this participant earns £14,000 per year, and has a score of 7 on self-esteem. The dot representing this participant is the point at which an imaginary vertical line starting from the point on the *X*-axis corresponding to self-esteem = 7, and an imaginary horizontal line starting from the point on the *Y*-axis corresponding to a salary of £14,000, meet. Note that the reason there are 18 rather than 20 points on the graph is because there are two pairs of identical points (8 and 18; 11 and 15).

By looking at the pattern of the dots in the scattergram you can form a rather accurate idea of whether the two variables are indeed related, and, in the event that the variables are related, of the nature of the relationship. In our example, you will immediately notice that the dots are clustered around an imaginary straight line. This is an indication that there exists a relationship between the two variables. At this point, you may start considering the *nature* of the relationship. Let us be specific about the observations you can make when looking at a scattergram.

THE DIRECTION OF THE RELATIONSHIP

By looking at a scattergram you can see the *direction of the relationship* between the two variables under investigation. There are two possible types of direction that an imaginary straight line can take when the variables are related.

Positive relationship – When high scores on one variable tend to be associated with high scores on the other variable, and therefore low scores on one variable tend to be associated with low scores on the other variable, the direction of the relationship between the variables is described as *positive*. When this is the case, the imaginary line around which the dots are bunched will point upward from bottom left to top right). Note that this is exactly the case in our fictitious study on salary and self-esteem; what you see in Figure 10.1 is that higher scores on the variable 'salary' tend to correspond to higher scores on the variable 'self-esteem', and that the line points upward from left to right.

Negative relationship – When high scores on one variable tend to be associated with low scores on the other variable, the direction of the relationship between the variables is described as *negative*. When this is the case, the imaginary straight line will point downward from top left to bottom right. This would have been the case if we had found that, as the salary increases, the level of self-esteem decreases. In Figure 10.2 you can see a scattergram showing data that we could have obtained in our study on salary and self-esteem if there had been a negative relationship between these two variables.

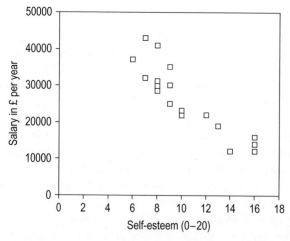

Figure 10.2   Scattergram showing a negative relationship between annual salary and self-esteem

THE STRENGTH OF THE RELATIONSHIP

How closely the dots are bunched around the imaginary line may vary. The important thing about the pattern of the dots is that the more tightly bunched around the line they are, the stronger the relationship between the two variables. In other words, a scattergram will reveal the *strength (or magnitude) of the relationship*: it will tell us the degree to which the two variables change together. Concerning the scattergrams in Figure 10.1 and 10.2, we can certainly say that the relationship is relatively strong. However, our data could have easily indicated a weaker relationship. For instance, we could have obtained data that produced either the scattergram in Figure 10.3a or that in Figure 10.3b. Both scattergrams would indicate that there is a relationship

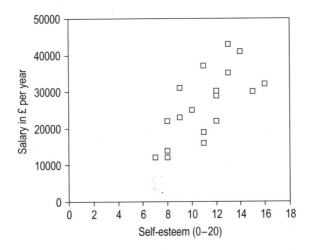

Figure 10.3a   Scattergram showing a *weak* positive relationship between annual salary and self-esteem

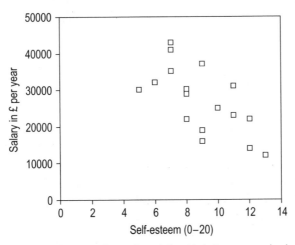

Figure 10.3b   Scattergram showing a *weak* negative relationship between annual salary and self-esteem

between the variables (a positive one in the scattergram in Figure 10.3a, and a negative one in the scattergram in Figure 10.3b). In each case, however, the relationship would have been considerably weaker than those shown in Figures 10.1 and 10.2.

It is useful to note that had the dots perfectly fitted the imaginary line, we would have a *perfect relationship*, which, of course, can be either positive (as in the scattergram in Figure 10.4a) or negative (as in the scattergram in Figure 10.4b). This is, of course, the strongest relationship that you can observe. On the other hand, had the dots had no pattern (as in the scattergram in Figure 10.4c), we cannot even speak of a relationship because, as a matter of fact, in this case there would be no relationship at all.

THE FORM OF THE RELATIONSHIP

A relationship between two variables measured with either an ordinal or interval scale can be linear or non-linear. A **linear relationship** is one where the imaginary line around which the dots are clustered tends to be straight (this is true regardless of the direction of the relationship). So, the relationships illustrated in Figures 10.1, 10.2, 10.3a and b, 10.4a and b (but not Figure 10.4c!) are all linear. Obviously, the relationships in Figure 10.4 a and b are *perfect* linear relationships. A **non-linear relationship** is one where two variables are related, but in a way that does not give rise to a simple straight line. Figure 10.5a shows a non-linear relationship where there is no linear component to the relationship, and Figure 10.5b shows a non-linear relationship between variables that do also have a (albeit weaker) linear component (i.e., it would still be possible to draw an imaginary straight line that the points roughly cluster around).

In the remaining part of this chapter we will deal exclusively with linear relationships between variables. If you come across variables for which a scattergram indicates (as in Figures 10.5a and 10.5b) that they have a non-linear relationship, it would generally be very misleading to carry out linear correlational analyses of the kind we will be describing. Non-linear (curvilinear) correlational analyses are possible, but they are beyond the scope of this book.

Obtaining a numerical description of the strength of a relationship: The correlation coefficient

Inspecting a scattergram will help you to form a fairly good idea of the strength of the relationship between two variables. However, it is possible to quantify this strength in a more precise, rigorous fashion, by calculating a descriptive statistic called the **coefficient of correlation**. The most commonly used coefficient is represented by r, though, as we shall see, an alternative coefficient represented by r_s (or **rho**, which is the Greek letter ρ) is sometimes more appropriate. We will begin by discussing the general interpretation of a coefficient of correlation, using r as our example, but recognizing that the interpretation applies equally to r_s. We will then go on to consider when each of these coefficients should be used, how they are calculated and their statistical interpretation.

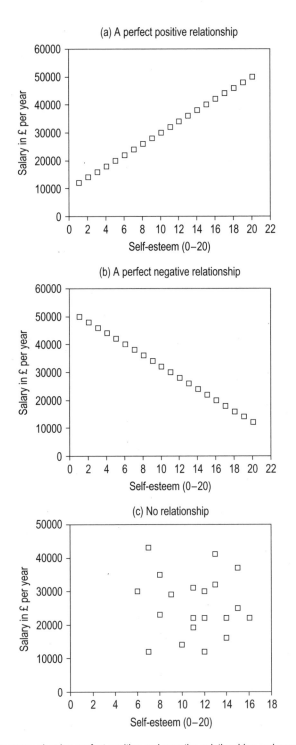

Figure 10.4 Scattergrams showing perfect positive and negative relationships and no relationship

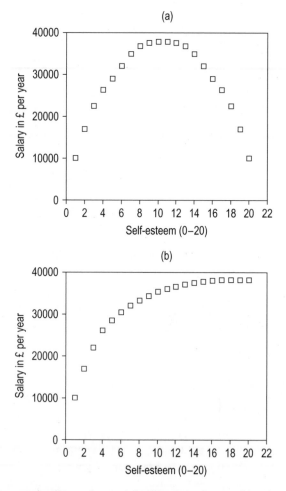

Figure 10.5 Scattergrams showing non-linear relationships. In scattergram (a), at low levels of self-esteem there is a positive relationship, which is 'cancelled out' by a negative relationship at high levels of self-esteem. In scattergram (b), when self-esteem is low, a given increase in self-esteem (say, one point on the scale) is associated with a large increase in income but, as the level of self-esteem gets higher, the increase in income associated with each extra point on the self-esteem scale gets progressively smaller.

When a value for r (or r_s) is calculated, it is always in the range from −1 to +1. While the sign of this value represents the direction of the relationship (which will be positive if the sign is +, and negative if the sign is −), the absolute value of the coefficient (i.e., the number that follows the sign) represents the strength of relationship. An r of +1 represents a perfect, positive correlation (as in Figure 10.4a), while an r of −1 represents a perfect negative correlation (as in Figure 10.4b). Clearly, values between 0 and +1 and between 0 and −1 represent intermediate degrees of either positive or negative correlation. So, the nearer to +1 or to −1 a correlation is, the stronger the relationship. However, if a non-linear relationship is apparent from examination of a scattergram of the variables (as, for instance, in Figure 10.5a and b), considerable caution should be exercised in the interpretation of any linear correlation coefficient that you calculate. If an r of 0 is obtained, then that means that there is no linear relationship between the two variables (as in 10.4c) – but remember, an r of zero invariably means that there is no *linear* relationship between two variables, but it does not necessarily mean that there is *no* relationship at all.

At this point you might wonder how strong a relationship should be in order to be considered as a strong relationship. This is somewhat arbitrary, and different researchers may have different views on this. However, many researchers broadly agree that a correlation ranging from +0.7 to +0.9 (or from −0.7 to −0.9) can be seen as a 'strong' relationship, that a correlation ranging from +0.4 to +0.6 (or from −0.4 to −0.6) indicates a 'moderate' relationship, and that a correlation between +0.1 to +0.3 (or between −0.1 to −0.3) is a 'weak' relationship.

Additional information (10.1) – Outliers

Another reason for inspecting scattergrams, apart from discerning the *nature* of the relationship between variables, is to identify possible **outliers** that might distort the numerical value of the correlation. Just one data point that is completely out of line with the pattern of the rest of the data points might produce a spuriously high value for r (as in Figure 10.6a) or, on the other hand, might result in a misleadingly low value for the coefficient (as in Figure 10.6b). When one or more outliers are apparent, it is worth considering whether there is any obvious explanation for it (or them), such as a participant leaving a zero off the end of his or her salary, or obtaining a self-esteem rating that is 'off the scale' (i.e., greater than the maximum possible). In such cases, it is sensible to re-do the correlational analysis with the outlier(s) omitted. If there is no obvious explanation, however, there is a problem with removing apparent outliers. It may look as though you are just removing 'inconvenient' data points in order to get a value for r in the range that you predicted!

Given that there exist several ways of calculating the correlation coefficient, you may wonder which procedure you should use. The answer is that it depends on the way in which the variables were measured. If the variables were measured with interval scales (or scales intermediate between ordinal and interval scales – see Complications (6.2)),

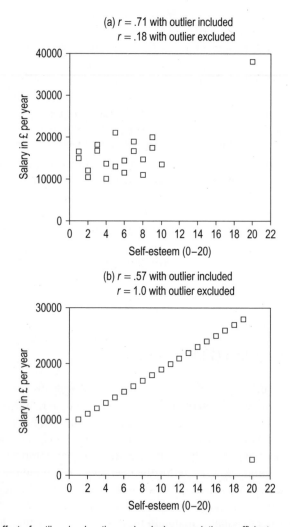

Figure 10.6 The effect of outliers in elevating and reducing correlation coefficients

you should use **Pearson's product–moment correlation coefficient** (abbreviated as *r*), provided the usual parametric assumptions are reasonably met (see Table 6.1). If the parametric assumptions are not satisfied or the variables were measured on an ordinal scale, then you should use a procedure known as **Spearman's rank order correlation coefficient** (abbreviated as r_s or *rho*). Below, we briefly discuss the logic underlying these two correlation coefficients and explain how to assess the statistical significance of a correlation coefficient.

PEARSON'S PRODUCT–MOMENT CORRELATION COEFFICIENT *(R)*

Suppose that you hypothesize a positive relationship between children's age and the number of countries they can correctly name. In order to test this hypothesis, you recruit 10 children, whose age ranges from 5 to 14 years, and ask them to name as many countries as they can. That means that we have two variables that are both measured on an interval scale (see Table 10.2). In this case the presumption would be that the Pearson product–moment correlation coefficient (*r*) should be used. (Obviously, this procedure should be used also when the two variables are measured on a ratio scale, or when one is measured on a ratio scale and the other is measured on an interval scale.) We need to qualify the presumption that Pearson's *r* should be used by reminding you that this is a parametric statistic and that, therefore, you should use it only when data reasonably meet parametric assumptions. If this is not the case, you should use Spearman's r_s. Finally, remember that Pearson's *r* must be used only when the relationship between the two variables under investigation is linear; therefore, before using it you should look at the scattergram and make sure that the relationship is linear.

Formulae (10.1) – The Pearson product–moment correlation coefficient (*r*)

A formula for Pearson's *r* is as follows:

$$r = \frac{\dfrac{\Sigma(X - \bar{X})(Y - \bar{Y})}{N - 1}}{s_X s_Y}$$

Generally speaking, this formula compares the extent to which participants' scores on the two variables vary together (i.e., the degree to which high scores on one variable correspond to high scores on the other variable), also known as **covariance**, with the variability of scores obtained by participants in each variable (i.e., the degree to which scores on each variable are dispersed around the mean). The covariance is measured in the numerator (note how similar it is to variance – if the Ys were changed to Xs, we would have $\Sigma(X - \bar{X})^2/(N - 1)$, which is the formula for the variance – see Formulae (4.2)), and the dispersion (standard deviations) is represented in the denominator. The more covariance and the less dispersion, the higher (i.e., closer to either −1 or +1) the value of *r*. On the contrary, the less covariance and the more dispersion, the smaller (i.e., closer to zero) the value of *r*.

Table 10.2   Children's ages and the number of nations they could name

Participant	Age	Nations named
1	5	1
2	6	2
3	7	2
4	8	5
5	9	7
6	10	6
7	11	6
8	12	9
9	13	8
10	14	10

SPSS operations and output (10.2) – Computing Pearson's *r*

To compute Pearson's *r* you need to proceed as follows:

(i)   Go to the menu at the top of the screen and click on *Analyze*, then on *Correlate*, and finally on *Bivariate*.
(ii)   Click on each of the two variables of interest, and move them into the box labelled as *Variables*.
(iii) In the section labelled as *Correlation Coefficients* click on the option labelled *Pearson*, and then click on *OK*.

Below you can see an example (based on our imaginary study investigating the relationship between age and the number of countries known) of an output generated by this procedure (see Table 10.2 for the data set used to produce this output).

Correlations

		AGE	NATIONS
AGE	Pearson Correlation	1	.948**
	Sig. (2-tailed)	.	.000
	N	10	10
NATIONS	Pearson Correlation	.948**	1
	Sig. (2-tailed)	.000	.
	N	10	10

**Correlation is significant at the 0.01 level (2-tailed).

THE STATISTICAL SIGNIFICANCE OF A CORRELATION COEFFICIENT

The correlation coefficient constitutes a single figure that gives a precise idea of the degree to which two variables comprising a sample of pairs of scores are related to one another. However, normally we want to use our data to draw inferences about the general population from which our sample has been drawn. Specifically, we want to test the null hypothesis that the correlation between the two variables in the population is zero.

We will use the SPSS output for the correlational analysis of the age/nation data to see how statistical significance is determined. So, suppose that, although we can see in the table labelled 'Correlations' that age and nations named by the 10 children in our sample are strongly related ($r = .95$), we want to know the extent to which these results apply to the general population. That is, does this strong relationship largely reflect the situation within the population, or is it something that we have obtained by chance? To answer this question we simply have to know the probability of obtaining an r of 0.95 in a sample of 10 participants when there is really no relationship between the two variables. This information can be found in the appropriate statistical table (see Statistical Table 10.1, of which a partial version is shown here) and also in the SPSS output. As usual, if the probability of obtaining an r of 0.95 – or any other value – is less than 5% (or 0.05) we say that a correlation coefficient is statistically significant at the 5% level, and conclude that our hypothesis is supported (i.e., we reject the null hypothesis).

Separate from the issue of the statistical significance of r, the square of r (i.e., r^2) gives you useful additional information. It is known as the **coefficient of determination** and is a measure of the proportion of variability in one of the correlated variables that can be predicted from variability in the other. This is discussed further when we go on to look at linear regression analysis, in the section on 'The accuracy of a prediction'.

Remember that hypotheses about a correlation can be either directional or non-directional. A directional hypothesis is like our hypothesis above about age and nations named; that is, it predicts a correlation in a specific direction. In our case the direction predicted is positive (i.e., higher age will go with a higher number of nations named); however, a directional hypothesis may predict a negative direction (e.g., the higher a person's level of extraversion, the lower the time he/she will spend at home). A non-directional hypothesis predicts a correlation between two variables that might be either positive or negative. For example, we might expect a person's level of neuroticism to be related to creativity, but we are unsure whether high neuroticism will go with high creativity (a positive correlation) or with low creativity (a negative correlation). It is never 'wrong' to do a two-tailed test of a hypothesis, even if you have a directional prediction. You just need to realize that if the result is in the opposite direction to your prediction you can't claim support for your hypothesis, even if the correlation reaches the critical value for significance in a two-tailed test. (Reasons why some researchers prefer *never* to do one-tailed tests were discussed in Complications (5.4)).

Statistical Table 10.1   Pearson's product–moment correlation coefficient: Critical values
of *r* for one- and two-tailed tests. *r* is significant if it **equals or exceeds** the table value
(partial table – full version in Appendix 1)

	level of significance for a one-tailed test						
	.10	.05	.025	.01	.005	.001	.0005
df	level of significance for a two-tailed test						
(*N*–2)	.20	.10	.05	.02	.01	.002	.001
1	0.9511	0.9877	0.9969	0.9995	0.9999	1.0000	1.0000
2	0.8000	0.9000	0.9500	0.9800	0.9900	0.9980	0.9990
3	0.6870	0.8054	0.8783	0.9343	0.9587	0.9859	0.9911
4	0.6084	0.7293	0.8114	0.8822	0.9172	0.9633	0.9741
5	0.5509	0.6694	0.7545	0.8329	0.8745	0.9350	0.9509
6	0.5067	0.6215	0.7067	0.7887	0.8343	0.9049	0.9249
7	0.4716	0.5822	0.6664	0.7498	0.7977	0.8751	0.8983
8	0.4428	0.5494	0.6319	0.7155	0.7646	0.8467	0.8721
9	0.4187	0.5214	0.6021	0.6851	0.7348	0.8199	0.8470
10	0.3981	0.4973	0.5760	0.6581	0.7079	0.7950	0.8233
11	0.3802	0.4762	0.5529	0.6339	0.6835	0.7717	0.8010

Source: The entries in this table were computed by D.R. McDonald at the University of
Dundee.

Suppose that we wanted to carry out a two-tailed test of our hypothesis, with
$\alpha = .001$ (two-tailed because we want to avoid the accusation that some researchers
might be inclined to make: that we are trying to 'squeeze significance out of our
data' by using the lower probability associated with a one-tailed test). Referring to
Statistical Table 10.1 (of which a partial version is shown here), we look down the
furthest right column and across the row with $10 - 2 = 8$ *df*. The critical value for
r given in the table is .87. As our correlation was greater than that ($r = .95$), we can
conclude that the null hypothesis can be rejected. The correlation between age and
nations named is statistically significant at $p < .001$ in a two-tailed test.

Referring again to the SPSS output for the Pearson *r* analysis, we see that the
value of *r* is followed by the symbol ** which, as specified at the bottom of the table,
means that this value is significant at the 0.01 level. Therefore, the probability of
obtaining this value by chance is less than 1%, and so this value is statistically
significant. Again, keep in mind that this level of significance refers to a two-tailed
hypothesis, that is, one stating that the two variables are related without specifying
whether they are positive or negatively related. However, we predicted that the variables would be *positively* related, and so we had a directional hypothesis and could
decide to use a one-tailed test (provided that we were prepared to conclude that the
hypothesis was not supported in the event that a negative correlation coefficient was

found, no matter how large it might be). If we chose to do a one-tailed test, we could halve the probability (i.e., $.01/2 = .005$), though it is usual to report significance at $p < .05$, $p < .01$ or $p < .001$, rather than other intermediate values. Incidentally, you can see that the two-tailed significance level given in the table is .000. That means that the lowest significance level that could be reported is $p < .001$ (since $p = .000$, given to three decimal places, is less than .001). Perhaps you will agree that the information given in the statistical table is rather more specific than that given in the SPSS output.

Reporting results (10.1) – Correlation

When reporting results of a correlation, you should specify whether the relationship explored was statistically significant, and include information about the type of correlation coefficient used and its calculated value, the sample size, the probability level, and whether the test used was one- or two-tailed. For instance, your statement might look as follows:

> A Pearson correlation was computed for the relationship between age and number of nations named by children. This revealed that these variables were, as predicted, positively related and that the correlation was statistically significant ($r = +.95$, $n = 10$, $p < .001$, two-tailed).

SPEARMAN'S RANK ORDER CORRELATION (R_S OR *RHO*)

When the usual parametric assumptions are not met, an alternative to the Pearson r correlation coefficient is provided by Spearman's rank order correlation, which is usually referred to either as r_s or *rho*. We will use the symbol r_s so that the correlation indices we discuss are consistently represented by the letter r. Spearman's correlation coefficient is a non-parametric statistic and, as such, operates on ranked (i.e., ordinal) data. To be specific, Spearman's r_s *should* be used instead of Pearson's r in the following circumstances:

1. When both variables are measured on clear ordinal scales, as when the original data are collected in the form of rankings of participants on the variables.
2. When one variable is measured on an interval scale and the other is measured on an ordinal scale (this is because r_s is indicated for the less powerful type of measurement, that is the ordinal one).
3. When both variables are measured on an interval scale (or a scale intermediate between an ordinal and interval scale) but data do not meet parametric assumptions (see Chapter 6 for a detailed discussion of parametric and non-parametric tests and, in particular, Table 6.1 on how to choose a test).

As an example, we will return to the fictitious study we used earlier, where we predict a relationship between salary and self-esteem (see Table 10.1 for the data). In order to decide which correlation coefficient to use we need to focus on the nature of the measurement. What type of scale was used to measure the two variables? Concerning the measurement of salary, we used an interval scale. This is because not only does a higher value indicate more of the thing that is measured (income in this case), but the intervals between values can be seen as representing *equal* differences in the variable being measured at all points on the scale. That is, the difference between a salary of, say, £36,000 and £32,000 is the same as the difference between £21,000 and £17,000 (or between £23,000 and £19,000, and so on). On the other hand, the measure of self-esteem is based on ordinal data; a higher number indicates more self-esteem, but we cannot assume that the self-esteem of a participant scoring 18 and that of a participant scoring 12 is exactly the same as the difference between the self-esteem of a participant scoring 9 and that of a participant scoring 3. Although the measurement could be intermediate between ordinal and interval, the 'safe' decision is to use the non-parametric statistic r_s (this is also the decision we make for the sake of providing an example of the computation of r_s).

As you can see in the 'Correlations' table in SPSS operations and output (10.3), the Spearman r_s for the relationship between salary and self-esteem is 0.965. This figure is followed by the symbol ** which, as explained at the bottom of the table, means that this value is significant at the 0.01 level. That means that the probability of obtaining this value by chance is less than 1%, and that therefore this value is statistically significant. As with the Pearson correlation coefficient, you should also keep in mind that this level of significance refers to a two-tailed hypothesis, that is, to a hypothesis stating that the two variables are related without specifying whether they are positively or negatively related. The discussion about one- and two-tailed tests in the earlier section under the heading *'The statistical significance of a correlation coefficient'*, which referred to the Pearson coefficient, applies equally to the Spearman coefficient of correlation. Similarly, the way in which a statistical table was used to interpret the Pearson coefficient applies equally to the use of a statistical table for interpreting the Spearman coefficient, but a different statistical table is used – Statistical Table 10.2, in place of Statistical Table 10.1. A partial version of Statistical Table 10.2 is shown here, with the row and column indicated for a two-tailed test with $\alpha = .09$. As the entry at the intersection of the row and column (.57) is less than the obtained value of $r_s = .97$, it can be concluded that the correlation was significant ($r_s = .97$, $n = 20$, $p < .01$, two-tailed).

Linear Regression Analysis

Correlational analysis allows us to investigate the strength, the direction and the form of the relationship between two variables. So, going back to our fictitious study on age and knowledge of nations example, correlational analysis is telling us that there is a strong positive linear relationship between age and number of known nations. That

Formulae (10.2) – The Spearman rank order correlation coefficient (r_s)

A formula for Spearman's r_s coefficient of correlation is often provided in statistics books. This formula was useful before computing power made it simple to calculate r_s without resort to a calculator (or pen and paper). It is really only of historical interest now, and we show it to you in that spirit. We do not expect that you would ever choose to use it. The formula is applied to the ranks of the scores for the two variables (if they are not already in the form of ranks). The formula is as follows:

$$r_s = 1 - \frac{6\sum D^2}{N(N^2 - 1)}$$

where D = the difference between each pair of ranks (the procedure for assigning ranks was described in detail in 'Calculation details 8.1') and N = number of pairs of scores (i.e., number of participants)

Broadly speaking, the calculations involved in the formula above are based on the following logic. For each variable, the Spearman r_s assigns a rank to each score, and then it compares the rank on one variable with the rank on the other variable, for each participant. When the rank difference between each pair of scores tends to be low – meaning that, in general, high scores on one variable correspond to high scores on the other variable – r_s will be close to 1. On the contrary, when the rank difference tends to be high – indicating that high scores on one variable generally correspond to low scores on the other variable – r_s will be close to −1 (r_s is +1 when all differences are zero, and −1 when differences tend to be very large).

At this point we should add that, if there are ties in the data (i.e., two or more participants have the same score on a variable), using the formula will result in the wrong answer! The more ties there are, the greater the error, and the error is always in the direction of making r_s bigger than it should be. This is another reason for not using the formula above for calculating r_s. The correct formula to use is that for Pearson's r, but applied to ranks rather than raw scores. When that is done, the correct value for r_s is always obtained, regardless of how many ties there are in the data. This is how SPSS calculates the Spearman coefficient.

SPSS operations and output (10.3) – Computing Spearman's r_s

To compute Spearman's r_s you need to proceed as follows:

(i)   Go to the menu at the top of the screen and click on *Analyze*, then on *Correlate*, and finally on *Bivariate*.
(ii)   Click on each of the two variables of interest, and move them into the box labelled *Variables*.
(iii) In the section labelled as *Correlation Coefficients* click on the option labelled *Spearman*, and then click on *OK*.

Alternatively, you could convert the scores to ranks yourself and then do a Pearson *r* correlation, as shown below:

(i)   Go to the menu at the top of the screen and click on *Transform*, then on *Rank Cases*.
(ii)   Click on each of the two new rank order variables, and move them into the box labelled *Variables*. Click on *OK*.
(iii) Click on *Analyse*, then on *Correlate*, then on *Bivariate*. In the section labelled as *Correlation Coefficients* click on the option labelled *Pearson*, and then click on *OK*.

You might like to check that these two procedures result in the same value for r_s (i.e., .965). Below you can see the output generated by the first procedure.

Correlations

			SELF-ESTEEM	SALARY
Spearman's rho	SELF-ESTEEM	Correlation Coefficient	1.000	.965**
		Sig. (2-tailed)	.	.000
		N	20	20
	SALARY	Correlation Coefficient	.965**	1.000
		Sig. (2-tailed)	.000	.
		N	20	20

**Correlation is significant at the .01 level (2-tailed).

is, age and known nations increase together in a linear way. However, correlational analysis has some limitations, in that it is unable to deal with two important issues.

First of all, correlational analysis tells us nothing about *how much* one variable will change if the other variable changes by a certain amount. For instance, knowing that age and known nations increase together says nothing about how many more nations children will be able to name as they grow older by, say, 6 months. Second, correlational analysis does not allow us to predict how a person with a specific score on one variable will score on the other variable. That is, knowing that age and known nations increase together cannot predict how many nations a child of, say, 9 years and 6 months of age is typically able to name.

Statistical Table 10.2 Spearman's rank-order correlation coefficient (r_s): Critical values of r_s for one- and two-tailed tests. r_s is significant if it equals or exceeds the table value (partial table – full version in Appendix 1)

N (num of pairs)	level of significance for a one-tailed test					
	.10	.05	.025	.01	.005	.001
	level of significance for a two-tailed test					
	.20	.10	.05	.02	.01	.002
4	1.0000	1.0000				
5	0.8000	0.9000	1.0000	1.0000		
6	0.6571	0.8286	0.8857	0.9429	1.0000	
18	0.3189	0.4014	0.4758	0.5542	0.6037	0.6925
19	0.3088	0.3912	0.4579	0.5351	0.5842	0.6737
20	0.2993	0.3805	0.4466	0.5203	0.5684	0.6602

Source: The entries in this table were computed by Pat Dugard, a freelance statistician.

Now, provided that the relationship between the variables that we are exploring is linear, it is possible to address the issue mentioned above. That is, it is possible to make two kind of *predictions*, namely (i) how much one variable will change on the basis of known changes on another variable, and (ii) how a particular individual with a given score on one variable will score on another variable. This can be done through a procedure called *linear regression analysis*.

The regression line

In order to carry out linear regression analysis, you need to understand the **regression line**. Suppose, for instance, that our fictitious study on age and named nations produced the data reported in Table 10.2. Once we have obtained a scattergram based on these data, it is also possible to draw a line that provides the best estimate of number of named nations from the age of a participant for each point in this scattergram (see Figure 10.7). Such a line is what we call a 'regression line', and is also known as the **line of best fit**, because no other possible line drawn through the dots would have a better fit with the dots (i.e., would be a better estimate of the number of named nations for each individual represented by a dot).

If this idea does not sound clear enough, have a look at the three scattergrams represented in Figure 10.8a, b, and c. The three scattergrams are the same (they all represent data obtained from the study on age and named nations). However, we have drawn a different line for each scattergram. In two cases, the line does not fit the cases well at all, whilst in one case we have the line of best fit. Now, which one of these

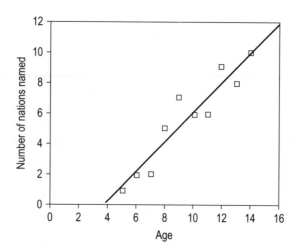

Figure 10.7 Scattergram showing the relationship between children's age and number of nations they were able to name

lines is the line of best fit? As you probably discern, it is the one in Figure 10.8b. This is because, in both the line in Figure 10.8a and the line in Figure 10.8c, only few cases are near the line (i.e., fit the line well), while many cases are very distant from the line. On the contrary, the line in Figure 10.8b fits almost all cases reasonably well.

As you move along the X-axis by one unit of measurement, the regression line will move up (if the relationship between the variables is positive) or down (if the relationship is negative) by a given number of units along the Y-axis. Now, the number of units that the regression line moves on the Y-axis for each unit it moves along the X-axis is called the **slope**, and is denoted by the letter *b*. Consider, for instance, the scattergram in Figure 10.7b, representing data from our fictitious 'age and nations' study. For each unit on the X-axis (i.e., 1 year), the regression line moves up a bit less than 1 unit on the Y-axis, and so the value of the slope must be slightly below 1. It is also the case that the regression line cuts (intercepts) the Y-axis at a specific point; this point is known as **intercept**, or as point *a*. In fact, the intercept is not shown in Figure 10.7b, but you can see that if the Y-axis and the regression line were both extended downwards they would meet at a point below zero on the Y-axis. That is, the intercept is a negative value. Together, the slope and the intercept completely define the location of a straight line in relation to the two axes.

Now that you are familiar with the regression line, we are ready to explain how to predict (i) how one variable will change given a specific change on another variable, and (ii) how a particular individual with a given score on one variable will score on another variable. To explain this, it is necessary to refer to the SPSS output of a linear regression analysis. Therefore, we will show you how to do linear regression analysis with SPSS, and then we will use the SPSS output to explain how to make predictions. We will use the study on age and nations named as an example.

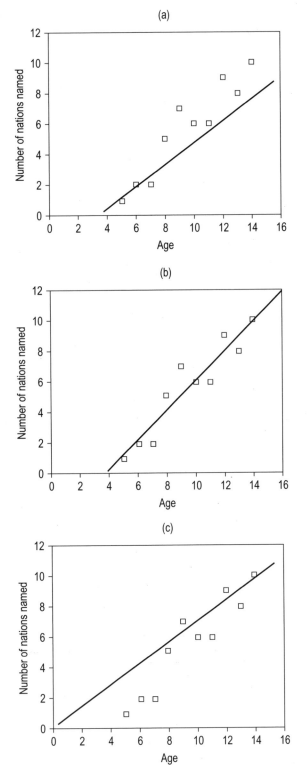

Figure 10.8 Scattergrams showing lines fitted to points, one of them being the 'line of best fit'

SPSS operations and output (10.4) – Linear regression analysis

To start with, you can obtain the regression line. You need to proceed as follows:

(i)   Go to the menu at the top of the screen and click on *Graphs* and then on *Scatter*.
(ii) Click on *Simple*; then click on the button labelled as *Define*.
(iii) Click on the predictor variable and move it into the box labelled as *X-axis*. Then click on the criterion variable and move it into the box labelled as *Y-axis*.
(iv) Click on *OK*. This will give you a simple scattergram.
(v)   Double-click on the graph, then double click on one of the points. Close the *Properties* box and select *Chart* from the top menu, then select *Add Chart Element*, then *Fit Line at Total*.

You can now compute linear regression by proceeding as follows:

(i)   Go to the menu at the top of the screen and click on *Analyze*, then on *Regression*, then on *Linear*.
(ii) Move the predictor variable to the box labelled as *Independent*, and the criterion variable to the box called *Dependent*.
(iii) Click on the *Statistics* button, and make sure that the boxes next to *Estimates*, *Confidence intervals*, and *Model fit* are checked; then click on *Continue*.
(iv) Click on *OK*.

Below we include parts of an output obtained with data from the age and nations study.

Model Summary

Model	R	R Square	Adjusted R Square	Std. Error of the Estimate
1	.948[a]	.898	.885	1.05025

a. Predictors: (Constant), AGE

Coefficients[a]

Model		Unstandardized Coefficients		Standardized Coefficients	t	Sig.
		B	Std. Error	Beta		
1	(Constant)	–3.612	1.148		–3.148	.014
	AGE	.970	.116	.948	8.386	.000

a. Dependent Variable: NATIONS

Predicting changes in one variable when values of another variable are known

How can we predict how much one variable will change on the basis of known changes on another variable? With specific reference to our example, how can we predict how many more nations children will be able to name as they grow one year older?

Before we deal with this question, you need to become familiar with some terminology. When we take one variable and we use changes in this variable to predict changes in another variable, the former variable is known as a **predictor variable** (or **explanatory variable**), and the latter is defined as a **criterion variable** (or **outcome variable**). When doing a scattergram, the values of the predictor variable are normally put on the X-axis and the values of the criterion variable on the Y-axis. Therefore, researchers conventionally call the predictor variable X and the criterion variable Y, and they talk about the '**regression of Y on X**'. From now on we will be using the same convention. So, concerning our interest in predicting how many more nations children can name as they grow one year older, we will consider the variable 'age' as the predictor variable, that is X, and the variable 'nations named' as the criterion variable, that is Y.

Additional information (10.1) – Predictor and criterion, or IV and DV?

Sometimes researchers use the term 'independent variable' (IV) and 'dependent variable' (DV) instead of 'predictor' and 'criterion' variable. However, there are good reasons for not doing so. The problem is that, if we use the terms IV and DV, there is an implication that we are dealing with a causal relationship between two variables (i.e., a situation in which changes in one variable *cause* changes in another). However, psychologists cannot pretend to explore causal relationships between two variables when using a correlational design. This is why using the terms IV and DV could be misleading.

We can now answer the question of how many more nations children can name as they grow one year older. What we need to do is to look at the value of b in the SPSS output. This tells you about the value of the **regression coefficient** (*slope* and *regression coefficient* are interchangeable terms for the same notion). To find this value look at the 'Coefficients' table. This value is indicated by the letter B, which is placed below the value of the Constant (this refers to the 'intercept', or a, which in our example is −3.612) under the 'Unstandardized Coefficients' column. As you can see, the regression coefficient is 0.970. This indicates that as age increases by one unit (i.e., one year), the number of nations named increases by 0.97, that is, almost one. So, every year children learn the name of one more country (the number 0.970 can be rounded to 1). The value of the regression coefficient is also expressed in standard deviations; this is under 'Standardized Coefficients', and is expressed as 'Beta'. So, Beta represents a standardized regression coefficient, and is very useful for forming an idea of the amount of change that takes place in the criterion variable as the value of the predictor variable changes. In our case, the value of Beta is 0.948 (i.e., almost one standard deviation), indicating that as the value of the predictor variable (age) goes up by 1 standard deviation, the value of the criterion variable (nations named) will go up by almost one standard deviation (quite a big change!).

THE SIGNIFICANCE OF THE REGRESSION COEFFICIENT

Once you have made predictions about the values that the criterion variable will take as the predictor variable takes given values, it is possible to find the statistical significance of b. That is, you can find out the probability that a given value of b might emerge by chance. All you need to do is to look under the column labelled as 'Sig.', also in the 'Coefficients' table. You will see that the probability of obtaining that specific value of b (or the corresponding value of Beta) by chance is given as 0.000 (i.e., $p < .001$). As always, if the probability that the obtained value of b could emerge by chance is less than 5% (expressed as $p < 0.05$), we can conclude that it is unlikely that that value of b was obtained by chance. It will, in fact, be significant if and only if the correlation is significant.

THE ACCURACY OF A PREDICTION

The fact that the value of Beta is relatively high (and therefore statistically significant) does not necessarily mean that your prediction is accurate. In fact, it is possible to obtain a very high value of Beta and, nonetheless, to make a prediction that is far from accurate. This will happen when an increase in the predictor variable corresponds to a substantial increase in the criterion variable but the correlation between the two variables is weak. This is because the regression line is not a good representation of the position of the cases when the dots are widely scattered around it, and so predictions based on this line will not be very accurate.

For instance, let us go back to our fictitious study on salary and self-esteem, and suppose that the data were not as shown in Table 10.1, but were such as to give the relationship illustrated in the scattergram in Figure 10.3a. Here you can see that an increase in the salary is related to a substantial increase in self-esteem. Clearly, in this case Beta is certainly going to have a high value. On the other hand, you can be sure that, because the correlation between salary and self-esteem is low (as indicated by the way in which dots are scattered widely around the regression line), Beta will not allow you to make accurate predictions of the values of self-esteem.

So, how do we assess the accuracy of a prediction? As mentioned in the earlier section on 'The statistical significance of a correlation coefficient', the square of the Pearson correlation coefficient (expressed as r^2), known as the 'coefficient of determination', provides useful information. The coefficient of determination tells you the degree to which the variability in one measure (e.g., nations named) is attributable to variability in the other measure (e.g., age). By doing so, r^2 basically quantifies the accuracy of a prediction based on the regression line. The value of r^2 will range from 0 to 1 (unlike a correlation coefficient, which ranges from −1 to +1) and the higher the value the more accurate the prediction. To assess the value of r^2 just look at the 'Model Summary' table. Here you can see the Pearson's coefficient of correlation (r) between the two variables, reported as 'R', which is very high, that is 0.948. You can also see the coefficient of determination (r^2), reported as 'R Square' (you can safely ignore the adjusted value of r^2 at this stage), which is 0.885, indicating that the variability of the predictor variable (in this case 'age') can predict .89 of the variability of the criterion variable (the number of nations named by participants), which is a highly accurate level of estimation of the number of nations named.

Predicting how an individual with a given score on the predictor variable will score on the criterion variable

You might want to predict how an individual with a given score on the predictor variable will score on the criterion variable. For instance, suppose you are having a chat with a friend of yours who has a 12-year-old child, and suppose that this friend is wondering how many countries her child would be likely to be able to list if asked. Based on the regression line generated by your data-set (see SPSS operations and output (10.4)), you will be able to satisfy your friend's curiosity. All you need to do is to locate the 12-year point on the X-axis (the predictor variable; that is, 'age'), and move vertically from this point until you meet the regression line; then you have to move horizontally toward the Y-axis (the criterion variable, that is the 'number of countries named') until you meet the Y-axis. The value corresponding to the point in which you meet the Y-axis indicates the best guess of the number of countries that your friend's child would be able to list. In our case this value is something very close to 8, only a tiny bit above it.

Obviously, making this type of prediction by using the regression line does not always allow you to be precise. A more precise and efficient procedure is to use a specific algebraic equation, known as a **linear regression equation**, which is an equation that specifies the location of a straight line by reference to two axes. This equation can be used to calculate how someone, whose score on the predictor variable (X-axis) is known, is likely to score on the outcome variable (Y-axis). This is what the equation looks like:

$$Y = a + bX$$

So, how can this formula help me to predict how many countries a 12-year-old should be able to name? First, you need to find out the values for a (the intercept) and for b (the slope). This entails either calculating these values by using formulae, which are beyond the scope of this book, or, much more easily, finding them by using SPSS (see SPSS operations and output (10.4)). Then, all you have to do with the equation is to replace the letters a and b with the values you have found, and X with the relevant value of the predictor variable. So, by looking at the output included in SPSS operations and output (10.4), you can see that the value for a is -3.612 (as specified above, to find this value look at value of the Constant in the 'Coefficients' table), and the value for b is 0.970. Since the value of the predictor variable you are interested in is 12, your equation will now look like this: $Y = -3.612 + 0.970 * 12$. The result of this calculation is 8.028. That means that we predict that a 12-year-old child will be able to name approximately 8 countries. (Obviously, the number 8.028 is an abstraction, as you cannot name 8 countries plus a fraction of a country! That's why we can round it down to 8. If the number had been something like, say, 8.476, then we could have concluded that a 12-year-old child will be able to name approximately 8 to 9 countries.)

Finally, remember that predictions can be more or less accurate depending on the strength of the correlation between the two variables under consideration. The prediction of an individual's value on the criterion variable based on our knowledge of this individual's value on the predictor variable will be more accurate when the correlation between the two variables is strong than when the correlation is weak.

Reporting results (10.2) – Regression analysis

When reporting the results from a regression analysis, exactly what should be included depends on the purpose behind the analysis. However, a report of the example analysis we have discussed might look something like this:

A simple (i.e., only one predictor variable) regression analysis of *nations named* (Y) *on age* (X) was carried out. This resulted in the regression equation: $Y = -3.612 + 0.970X$. The regression coefficient was statistically significant ($b = .97$, $t = 8.39$, $p < .001$) and the value of the standardized coefficient (*beta* $= .95$) indicated that a change in the predictor variable (age) corresponds to a substantial change in the outcome variable (nations named). The value of r^2 was .89, indicating that the variability of the predictor variable (age) can predict .89 of the variability of the criterion variable (nations named), which is a highly accurate level of estimation. Finally, the solution of the equation for $X = 12$ years indicated that a 12-year-old child might be expected to be able to name approximately 8 nations.

Complications (10.1) – Correlational and regression analysis in experiments

Occasionally, you may find experiments in which data are analysed by means of correlational and regression analyses, such as are normally used in correlational studies. Also, occasionally researchers analyse data collected through correlational studies by means of analytic procedures that are normally used in experiments. Although we are not offering a detailed treatment of this issue in this book, you should be aware of it. The important point is that the design of a study is conceptually distinct from the methods of statistical analysis used, or, if you like, that statistics address questions of difference, association and so on, *regardless of* the design. Having said that, it is certainly true that experimental designs are most often analysed using statistics that test for differences between conditions and that correlational studies are most often analysed using statistics that test for relationships among conditions.

Additional information 10.2 – Correlational studies with more than two variables

Correlational studies may involve the investigation of the relationships between more than just two variables. For instance, you might want to explore the possibility that self-esteem and salary are correlated with one another, and that they are both correlated with 'years of education'. Also, you might want to measure which one among several variables is the best predictor of a given criterion variable. In this case you need to measure all the variables you want to investigate, and apply some advanced procedures (e.g., partial correlation, or multiple regression) that are beyond the scope of this book. (See the books by Howell and Allison in the 'brief list of recommended books'.)

SUMMARY OF CHAPTER

- Sometimes researchers hypothesize that two variables are related (i.e., change together), without making claims about which variable influences which. These types of hypotheses are tested by means of 'correlational studies'.
- A relationship between two variables can be explored by means of either correlational analysis or regression analysis.
- Correlational analysis is used to (i) describe the relationship between two variables in a visual and numerical fashion, and to (ii) test the statistical significance of the relationship.
- To give a visual description of a relationship, researchers use the 'scattergram', which helps to form an idea of (i) the direction (whether it is positive or negative), (ii) the strength (magnitude) and (iii) the form (whether it is linear or non-linear), of the relationship under investigation.
- The strength of a relationship can be expressed numerically by calculating a descriptive statistic called the 'coefficient of correlation' (or r), whose value ranges from -1 to $+1$. This can be calculated in several ways. Normally, the 'Pearson's product–moment correlation coefficient' (or r) is used when parametric assumptions are met (usually when there is an interval scale), while the 'Spearman rank order correlation' (r_s or rho) is used when parametric assumptions are not met (typically, when there is an ordinal scale). As usual, if the probability of obtaining a given r is less than 5% (expressed as $p < 0.05$), we say that it is statistically significant.
- Linear regression analysis can be used to predict (i) how much one variable will change on the basis of known changes on another variable, and (ii) how

a particular individual with a given score on one variable will score on another variable.

- Linear regression analysis is based on the 'regression line'. This is the line providing the best estimate of the criterion variable from the predictor for each point in the scattergram.

- As you move one unit of measurement along the X-axis, the regression line will move up (if the relationship between the variables is positive) or down (if the relationship is negative) by a given number of units along the Y-axis. The number of units that the regression line moves up the Y-axis for each unit it moves along the X-axis is called the 'slope' (or b). The point at which the regression line cuts the Y-axis is known as the 'intercept' (or a).

- When we use changes in one variable to make predictions about changes in another variable, the former is known as the 'predictor variable' and the latter as the 'criterion variable'.

- The extent to which the criterion variable will change if the predictor variable changes by a certain amount is called the 'regression coefficient' (which is equivalent to the slope). If the probability that the obtained value of b could emerge by chance is less than 5%, then it is unlikely that that value of b was obtained by chance.

- A prediction can be more or less accurate, regardless of whether the predicted changes in the outcome variable are substantial or not. The accuracy of a prediction can be numerically expressed by the square of the Pearson correlation coefficient, known as the 'coefficient of determination' (r^2). Its value ranges from 0 to 1, and the higher the value the more accurate the prediction.

- To make predictions about how an individual with a given score on the predictor variable would score on the criterion variable, we use the regression line. However, a more precise procedure is to use a 'linear regression equation'.

- Predictions can be more or less accurate depending on the strength of the correlation between the two variables under consideration. The prediction of an individual's score on the criterion variable based on our knowledge of this individual's value on the predictor variable will be more accurate when the correlation between the two variables is strong.

APPENDIX 1

Statistical Tables

Statistical Table 4.1 Probabilities associated with values as extreme as observed values of z in the normal distribution.

Statistical Table 7.1 Critical one- and two-tailed values of x for a Sign test.

Statistical Table 7.2 Critical two-tailed (i.e., non-directional) values of Chi-Square (χ^2).

Statistical Table 8.1 Critical one- and two-tailed values of T for a Wilcoxon Matched-Pairs Signed-Ranks test.

Statistical Table 8.2(1) (one-tailed at .10; two-tailed at .20) Critical one- and two-tailed values of U for a Mann–Whitney Independent Groups test.

Statistical Table 8.2(2) (one-tailed at .05; two-tailed at .1) Critical one- and two-tailed values of U for a Mann–Whitney Independent Groups test.

Statistical Table 8.2(3) (one-tailed at .025; two-tailed at .05) Critical one- and two-tailed values of U for a Mann–Whitney Independent Groups test.

Statistical Table 8.2(4) (one-tailed at .01; two-tailed at .02) Critical one- and two-tailed values of U for a Mann–Whitney Independent Groups test.

Statistical Table 8.2(5) (one-tailed at .005; two-tailed at .01) Critical one- and two-tailed values of U for a Mann–Whitney Independent Groups test.

Statistical Table 8.2(6) (one-tailed at .001; two-tailed at .002) Critical one- and two-tailed values of U for a Mann–Whitney Independent Groups test.

Statistical Table 9.1 Critical values of t.

Statistical Table 10.1 Pearson's product–moment correlation coefficient: Critical values of r for one- and two-tailed tests.

Statistical Table 10.2 Spearman's rank-order correlation coefficient (r_s): Critical values of r_s for one- and two-tailed tests.

Statistical Table 4.1 Probabilities associated with values as extreme as observed values of z in the normal distribution

z-value	2nd decimal place of observed z-value									
	0.00	0.01	0.02	0.03	0.04	0.05	0.06	0.07	0.08	0.09
0.0	0.5000	0.4960	0.4920	0.4880	0.4840	0.4801	0.4761	0.4721	0.4681	0.4641
0.1	0.4602	0.4562	0.4522	0.4483	0.4443	0.4404	0.4364	0.4325	0.4286	0.4247
0.2	0.4207	0.4168	0.4129	0.4090	0.4052	0.4013	0.3974	0.3936	0.3897	0.3859
0.3	0.3821	0.3783	0.3745	0.3707	0.3669	0.3632	0.3594	0.3557	0.3520	0.3483
0.4	0.3446	0.3409	0.3372	0.3336	0.3300	0.3264	0.3228	0.3192	0.3156	0.3121
0.5	0.3085	0.3050	0.3015	0.2981	0.2946	0.2912	0.2877	0.2843	0.2810	0.2776
0.6	0.2743	0.2709	0.2676	0.2643	0.2611	0.2578	0.2546	0.2514	0.2483	0.2451
0.7	0.2420	0.2389	0.2358	0.2327	0.2296	0.2266	0.2236	0.2206	0.2177	0.2148
0.8	0.2119	0.2090	0.2061	0.2033	0.2005	0.1977	0.1949	0.1922	0.1894	0.1867
0.9	0.1841	0.1814	0.1788	0.1762	0.1736	0.1711	0.1685	0.1660	0.1635	0.1611
1.0	0.1587	0.1562	0.1539	0.1515	0.1492	0.1469	0.1446	0.1423	0.1401	0.1379
1.1	0.1357	0.1335	0.1314	0.1292	0.1271	0.1251	0.1230	0.1210	0.1190	0.1170
1.2	0.1151	0.1131	0.1112	0.1093	0.1075	0.1056	0.1038	0.1020	0.1003	0.0985
1.3	0.0968	0.0951	0.0934	0.0918	0.0901	0.0885	0.0869	0.0853	0.0838	0.0823
1.4	0.0808	0.0793	0.0778	0.0764	0.0749	0.0735	0.0721	0.0708	0.0694	0.0681
1.5	0.0668	0.0655	0.0643	0.0630	0.0618	0.0606	0.0594	0.0582	0.0571	0.0559
1.6	0.0548	0.0537	0.0526	0.0516	0.0505	0.0495	0.0485	0.0475	0.0465	0.0455
1.7	0.0446	0.0436	0.0427	0.0418	0.0409	0.0401	0.0392	0.0384	0.0375	0.0367
1.8	0.0359	0.0351	0.0344	0.0336	0.0329	0.0322	0.0314	0.0307	0.0301	0.0294
1.9	0.0287	0.0281	0.0274	0.0268	0.0262	0.0256	0.0250	0.0244	0.0239	0.0233
2.0	0.0228	0.0222	0.0217	0.0212	0.0207	0.0202	0.0197	0.0192	0.0188	0.0183
2.1	0.0179	0.0174	0.0170	0.0166	0.0162	0.0158	0.0154	0.0150	0.0146	0.0143
2.2	0.0139	0.0136	0.0132	0.0129	0.0125	0.0122	0.0119	0.0116	0.0113	0.0110
2.3	0.0107	0.0104	0.0102	0.0099	0.0096	0.0094	0.0091	0.0089	0.0087	0.0084
2.4	0.0082	0.0080	0.0078	0.0075	0.0073	0.0071	0.0069	0.0068	0.0066	0.0064
2.5	0.0062	0.0060	0.0059	0.0057	0.0055	0.0054	0.0052	0.0051	0.0049	0.0048
2.6	0.0047	0.0045	0.0044	0.0043	0.0041	0.0040	0.0039	0.0038	0.0037	0.0036
2.7	0.0035	0.0034	0.0033	0.0032	0.0031	0.0030	0.0029	0.0028	0.0027	0.0026
2.8	0.0026	0.0025	0.0024	0.0023	0.0023	0.0022	0.0021	0.0021	0.0020	0.0019
2.9	0.0019	0.0018	0.0018	0.0017	0.0016	0.0016	0.0015	0.0015	0.0014	0.0014
3.0	0.0013	0.0013	0.0013	0.0012	0.0012	0.0011	0.0011	0.0011	0.0010	0.0010
3.1	0.0010	0.0009	0.0009	0.0009	0.0008	0.0008	0.0008	0.0008	0.0007	0.0007
3.2	0.0007									
3.3	0.0005									
3.4	0.0003									
3.5	0.00023									
3.6	0.00016									
3.7	0.00011									
3.8	0.00007									
3.9	0.00005									

Source: The entries in this table were computed by D.R. McDonald at the University of Dundee.

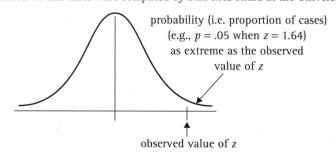

probability (i.e. proportion of cases)
(e.g., p = .05 when z = 1.64)
as extreme as the observed
value of z

observed value of z

Statistical Table 7.1 Critical one- and two-tailed values of x for a Sign test, where x = the number of cases with the *less* frequent sign and N is the total number of positive and negative differences between pairs of scores, i.e., ties are not counted. (x is significant if it is **less than or equal** to the table value)

	level of significance for a one-tailed test						
	.10	.05	.025	.01	.005	.001	.0005
	level of significance for a two-tailed test						
N	.20	.10	.05	.02	.01	.002	.001
4	0						
5	0	0					
6	0	0	0				
7	1	0	0	0			
8	1	1	0	0	0		
9	2	1	1	0	0		
10	2	1	1	0	0	0	
11	2	2	1	1	0	0	0
12	3	2	2	1	1	0	0
13	3	3	2	1	1	0	0
14	4	3	2	2	1	1	0
15	4	3	3	2	2	1	1
16	4	4	3	2	2	1	1
17	5	4	4	3	2	1	1
18	5	5	4	3	3	2	1
19	6	5	4	4	3	2	2
20	6	5	5	4	3	2	2
21	7	6	5	4	4	3	2
22	7	6	5	5	4	3	3
23	7	7	6	5	4	3	3
24	8	7	6	5	5	4	3
25	8	7	7	6	5	4	4
26	9	8	7	6	6	4	4
27	9	8	7	7	6	5	4
28	10	9	8	7	6	5	5
29	10	9	8	7	7	5	5
30	10	10	9	8	7	6	5

Source: The entries in this table were computed by Pat Dugard, a freelance statistician.

Statistical Table 7.2   Critical two-tailed (i.e., non-directional) values of Chi-Square (χ^2) (Chi-Square is significant if it is **greater than or equal** to the table value)

df^1	\multicolumn{7}{c}{level of significance for a two-tailed test}
	0.20	0.10	0.05	0.02	0.01	0.002	0.0001
1^2	1.64	2.71	3.84	5.41	6.64	9.55	10.83
2	3.22	4.61	5.99	7.82	9.21	12.43	13.82
3	4.64	6.25	7.82	9.84	11.35	14.80	16.27
4	5.99	7.78	9.49	11.67	13.28	16.92	18.47
5	7.29	9.24	11.07	13.39	15.09	18.91	20.52
6	8.56	10.65	12.59	15.03	16.81	20.79	22.46
7	9.80	12.02	14.07	16.62	18.48	22.60	24.32
8	11.03	13.36	15.51	18.17	20.09	24.35	26.12
9	12.24	14.68	16.92	19.68	21.67	26.06	27.88
10	13.44	15.99	18.31	21.16	23.21	27.72	29.59
12	15.81	18.55	21.03	24.05	26.22	30.96	32.91
14	18.15	21.06	23.69	26.87	29.14	34.09	36.12
16	20.47	23.54	26.30	29.63	32.00	37.15	39.25
18	22.76	25.99	28.87	32.35	34.81	40.14	42.31
20	25.04	28.41	31.41	35.02	37.57	43.07	45.32
25	30.68	34.38	37.65	41.57	44.31	50.22	52.62
30	36.25	40.26	43.77	47.96	50.89	57.17	59.70
35	41.78	46.06	49.80	54.24	57.34	63.96	66.62
40	47.27	51.81	55.76	60.44	63.69	70.62	73.40
45	52.73	57.51	61.66	66.56	69.96	77.18	80.08
50	58.16	63.17	67.51	72.61	76.15	83.66	86.66
55	63.58	68.80	73.31	78.62	82.29	90.06	93.17
60	68.97	74.40	79.08	84.58	88.38	96.40	99.61
65	74.35	79.97	84.82	90.50	94.42	102.69	105.99
70	79.72	85.53	90.53	96.39	100.43	108.93	112.32
80	90.41	96.58	101.88	108.07	112.33	121.28	124.84
100	111.67	118.50	124.34	131.14	135.81	145.58	149.45

Source: The entries in this table were computed by Pat Dugard, a freelance statistician.
[1] df = (rows − 1) × (columns − 1)
[2] for a one-tailed test for 2 × 2 tables only (i.e., when df = 1), divide the probabilities at the top of the table by 2

Statistical Table 8.1 Critical one- and two-tailed values of T for a Wilcoxon Matched-Pairs Signed-Ranks test, where T = the sum of differences with the least frequent sign and N = the total number of differences with either a positive or negative sign. (T is significant if it is **less than or equal** to the table value)

N	level of significance for a one-tailed test					
	.10	.05	.025	.01	.005	.001
	level of significance for a two-tailed test					
	.20	.10	.05	.02	.01	.002
4	0					
5	2	0				
6	4	2	0			
7	6	3	2	0		
8	8	5	3	1	0	
9	11	8	5	3	1	
10	14	10	8	5	3	0
11	18	13	10	7	5	1
12	22	17	14	10	7	2
13	26	21	17	12	9	4
14	31	25	21	15	12	6
15	37	30	25	19	16	8
16	42	35	29	23	19	11
17	49	41	35	28	23	14
18	55	47	40	32	27	18
19	62	53	46	37	32	21
20	70	60	52	43	37	23
21	78	67	58	50	44	32
22	86	75	65	55	47	34
23	95	83	73	62	54	40
24	104	91	81	69	61	46
25	115	101	89	76	68	51
26	124	110	98	84	75	58
27	135	119	107	93	83	63
28	146	130	116	101	91	71
29	157	141	126	111	101	80
30	169	152	136	119	106	85
31	181	163	147	129	118	95
32	195	175	159	140	127	102
33	208	187	170	151	137	111
34	221	200	183	163	149	123
35	236	213	195	175	159	130
36	250	227	208	185	171	139
37	266	241	221	198	182	153
38	281	256	234	211	194	163
39	297	271	249	224	209	176
40	314	286	264	238	219	186

Source: The entries in this table were computed by Pat Dugard, a freelance statistician.
N = number of non-equal pairs of scores

Statistical Table 8.2(1) (one-tailed at .10; two-tailed at .20) Critical one- and two-tailed values of U for a Mann–Whitney Independent Groups test, where U = the smaller of the two possible values and n_1 and n_2 = the numbers of participants in the two groups. (U is significant if it is **less than or equal** to the table value)

$n_1 \Rightarrow$ $n_2 \Downarrow$	2	3	4	5	6	7	8	9	10	11	12	13	14	15	16	17	18	19	20
3		0																	
4		1	3																
5	1	2	4	5															
6	1	3	5	7	9														
7	1	4	6	9	11	13													
8	2	5	7	10	13	16	19												
9	2	5	8	12	15	18	21	25											
10	3	6	10	13	17	21	24	28	32										
11	3	7	11	15	19	23	27	31	36	40									
12	4	8	12	17	21	26	30	35	39	44	49								
13	4	9	14	18	23	28	33	38	43	48	53	58							
14	5	9	15	20	25	30	36	42	47	52	57	64	69						
15	5	10	16	22	27	33	39	45	51	57	63	68	74	81					
16	5	11	17	23	29	35	42	48	54	61	67	74	80	86	92				
17	5	12	18	25	32	38	45	52	58	65	72	79	85	92	99	105			
18	6	13	20	27	34	41	48	55	63	69	76	84	91	98	105	113	120		
19	6	14	21	28	36	43	50	59	65	74	81	89	96	104	112	120	128	120	
20	7	15	22	30	38	46	54	62	70	78	85	94	102	110	119	127	135	128	152

Source: The entries in this table were computed by Pat Dugard, a freelance statistician.

Statistical Table 8.2(2) (one-tailed at .05; two-tailed at .1)   Critical one- and two-tailed values of U for a Mann–Whitney Independent Groups test, where U = the smaller of the two possible values and n_1 and n_2 = the numbers of participants in the two groups. (U is significant if it is **less than or equal** to the table value)

$n_1 \Rightarrow$ $n_2 \Downarrow$	2	3	4	5	6	7	8	9	10	11	12	13	14	15	16	17	18	19	20
3		0																	
4		0	1																
5	0	1	2	4															
6	0	2	3	5	7														
7	0	2	4	6	8	11													
8	1	3	5	8	10	13	15												
9	1	4	6	9	12	15	18	21											
10	1	4	7	10	14	17	20	24	27										
11	1	5	8	12	16	19	23	27	31	34									
12	2	5	9	13	17	22	26	30	34	38	42								
13	2	6	11	15	19	24	28	33	38	42	47	51							
14	3	7	12	16	21	26	31	37	41	46	51	56	61						
15	3	7	13	18	23	28	33	39	44	50	55	60	66	72					
16	3	8	13	19	24	30	36	42	48	54	60	65	71	77	83				
17	3	9	15	20	26	32	39	45	51	57	64	70	76	83	89	95			
18	3	9	16	22	28	35	41	48	55	61	68	75	82	88	95	102	109		
19	4	10	17	23	30	37	44	51	58	65	72	79	87	94	101	109	116	123	
20	4	11	18	25	32	39	47	54	62	69	76	84	92	100	107	114	123	130	138

Source: The entries in this table were computed by Pat Dugard, a freelance statistician.

Statistical Table 8.2(3) (one-tailed at .025; two-tailed at .05)   Critical one- and two-tailed values of U for a Mann–Whitney Independent Groups test, where U = the smaller of the two possible values and n_1 and n_2 = the numbers of participants in the two groups. (U is significant if it is **less than or equal** to the table value)

$n_1 \Rightarrow$ $n_2 \Downarrow$	2	3	4	5	6	7	8	9	10	11	12	13	14	15	16	17	18	19	20
3																			
4			0																
5		0	1	2															
6		1	2	3	5														
7		1	3	5	6	8													
8	0	2	3	6	8	10	13												
9	0	2	4	7	9	12	15	17											
10	0	3	5	8	11	14	17	20	23										
11	0	3	6	9	13	16	19	23	26	30									
12	1	3	7	11	14	18	22	26	29	33	37								
13	1	4	8	12	16	20	24	28	33	37	41	45							
14	1	5	9	13	17	22	26	31	36	40	45	50	54						
15	1	5	10	14	19	24	29	34	38	44	49	54	59	64					
16	1	6	11	16	21	26	31	36	42	48	53	59	64	69	74				
17	2	6	12	17	22	28	34	39	45	51	57	63	69	75	80	86			
18	2	6	13	18	24	30	36	42	49	55	61	67	73	80	86	93	99		
19	2	7	13	19	26	31	39	45	52	58	65	72	78	85	92	99	106	112	
20	2	8	14	20	27	34	41	48	55	62	68	76	83	90	98	104	112	119	127

Source: The entries in this table were computed by Pat Dugard, a freelance statistician.

Statistical Table 8.2(4) (one-tailed at .01; two-tailed at .02) Critical one- and two-tailed values of U for a Mann–Whitney Independent Groups test, where U = the smaller of the two possible values and n_1 and n_2 = the numbers of participants in the two groups. (U is significant if it is **less than or equal** to the table value)

$n_1 \Rightarrow$ / $n_2 \Downarrow$	2	3	4	5	6	7	8	9	10	11	12	13	14	15	16	17	18	19	20
3																			
4																			
5			0	1															
6			1	2	3														
7		0	1	3	4	6													
8		0	2	4	6	8	10												
9		1	3	5	7	9	11	14											
10		1	3	6	8	11	13	16	19										
11		1	4	7	10	13	15	18	22	25									
12		2	5	8	11	14	18	21	24	28	31								
13	0	2	5	8	12	15	20	23	27	31	35	38							
14	0	2	6	10	13	18	22	26	30	34	38	43	47						
15	0	3	7	11	15	19	24	28	32	38	42	46	52	57					
16	0	3	7	12	16	21	26	30	36	40	46	50	56	61	65				
17	0	4	8	12	17	23	28	33	39	44	49	54	60	66	71	76			
18	1	4	9	14	19	24	30	35	41	47	53	59	65	71	76	82	88		
19	1	4	9	15	20	26	33	38	44	50	56	62	69	75	82	88	94	101	
20	1	5	11	16	22	28	35	40	47	53	60	67	73	80	87	93	100	107	115

Source: The entries in this table were computed by Pat Dugard, a freelance statistician.

Statistical Table 8.2(5) (one–tailed at .005; two–tailed at .01) Critical one- and two-tailed values of U for a Mann–Whitney Independent Groups test, where U = the smaller of the two possible values and n_1 and n_2 = the numbers of participants in the two groups. (U is significant if it is **less than or equal** to the table value)

$n_1 \Rightarrow$ $n_2 \Downarrow$	2	3	4	5	6	7	8	9	10	11	12	13	14	15	16	17	18	19	20
3																			
4																			
5				0															
6		0	1	1															
7		0	1	3	4														
8		1	2	4	6	8													
9	0	1	3	5	7	9	11												
10	0	2	4	6	9	11	13	16											
11	0	2	5	7	10	13	16	18	21										
12	1	3	6	9	12	15	18	21	24	28									
13	1	3	7	10	13	17	20	23	27	31	34								
14	1	4	8	11	15	19	23	26	30	34	39	41							
15	1	5	8	12	16	20	24	28	33	37	41	47	52						
16		2	5	10	13	17	23	26	32	36	42	45	51	55	59				
17		2	6	10	14	19	24	29	35	39	44	49	54	59	64	70			
18		2	6	11	16	20	25	31	37	43	47	52	59	63	70	75	81		
19	0	3	7	12	17	22	28	34	39	45	51	57	63	69	75	81	87	93	
20	0	3	8	13	18	24	31	36	42	48	54	61	67	74	78	85	92	95	106

Source: The entries in this table were computed by Pat Dugard, a freelance statistician.

Statistical Table 8.2(6) (one-tailed at .001; two-tailed at .002) Critical one- and two-tailed values of U for a Mann-Whitney Independent Groups test, where U = the smaller of the two possible values and n_1 and n_2 = the numbers of participants in the two groups. (U is significant if it is **less than or equal** to the table value)

$n_1 \Rightarrow$ / $n_2 \Downarrow$	2	3	4	5	6	7	8	9	10	11	12	13	14	15	16	17	18	19	20
3																			
4																			
5																			
6																			
7					0	1													
8				0	1	3	4												
9				1	2	3	5	7											
10			0	1	3	4	6	8	10										
11			0	2	3	6	7	9	12	14									
12			0	2	3	6	9	12	14	17	20								
13			1	2	4	7	11	12	17	20	23	26							
14			1	4	6	9	12	15	19	22	25	31	32						
15			2	4	7	10	14	17	22	24	28	31	36	40					
16			2	5	8	11	15	19	23	27	31	35	39	43	48				
17		0	2	5	7	12	17	22	25	29	34	37	43	47	52	57			
18		0	3	6	10	14	17	23	25	33	36	41	45	52	56	61	66		
19		0	3	7	12	15	20	26	29	34	39	44	52	55	62	67	72	76	
20		0	3	7	12	17	21	25	32	36	41	48	54	59	66	69	75	78	87

Source: The entries in this table were computed by Pat Dugard, a freelance statistician.

Statistical Table 9.1 Critical values of t (t is significant when it **equals or exceeds** the table value)

df	level of significance for a one-tailed test						
	.10	.05	.025	.01	.005	.001	.0005
	level of significance for a two-tailed test						
	.20	.10	.05	.02	.01	.002	.001
1	3.08	6.31	12.71	31.82	63.66	318.31	636.62
2	1.89	2.92	4.30	6.96	9.92	22.33	31.60
3	1.64	2.35	3.18	4.54	5.84	10.22	12.92
4	1.53	2.13	2.78	3.75	4.60	7.17	8.61
5	1.48	2.02	2.57	3.36	4.03	5.89	6.87
6	1.44	1.94	2.45	3.14	3.71	5.21	5.96
7	1.41	1.89	2.36	3.00	3.50	4.79	5.41
8	1.40	1.86	2.31	2.90	3.36	4.50	5.04
9	1.38	1.83	2.26	2.82	3.25	4.30	4.78
10	1.37	1.81	2.23	2.76	3.17	4.14	4.59
11	1.36	1.80	2.20	2.72	3.11	4.03	4.44
12	1.36	1.78	2.18	2.68	3.05	3.93	4.32
13	1.35	1.77	2.16	2.65	3.01	3.85	4.22
14	1.35	1.76	2.14	2.62	2.98	3.79	4.14
15	1.34	1.75	2.13	2.60	2.95	3.73	4.07
16	1.34	1.75	2.12	2.58	2.92	3.69	4.02
17	1.33	1.74	2.11	2.57	2.90	3.65	3.97
18	1.33	1.73	2.10	2.55	2.88	3.61	3.92
19	1.33	1.73	2.09	2.54	2.86	3.58	3.88
20	1.33	1.72	2.09	2.53	2.85	3.55	3.85
21	1.32	1.72	2.08	2.52	2.83	3.53	3.82
22	1.32	1.72	2.07	2.51	2.82	3.51	3.79
23	1.32	1.71	2.07	2.50	2.81	3.49	3.77
24	1.32	1.71	2.06	2.49	2.80	3.47	3.75
25	1.32	1.71	2.06	2.49	2.79	3.45	3.73
26	1.31	1.71	2.06	2.48	2.78	3.44	3.71
27	1.31	1.70	2.05	2.47	2.77	3.42	3.69
28	1.31	1.70	2.05	2.47	2.76	3.41	3.67
29	1.31	1.70	2.05	2.46	2.76	3.40	3.66
30	1.31	1.70	2.04	2.46	2.75	3.39	3.65
40	1.30	1.68	2.02	2.42	2.70	3.31	3.55
60	1.30	1.67	2.00	2.39	2.66	3.23	3.46
120	1.29	1.66	1.98	2.36	2.62	3.16	3.37
2000	1.28	1.65	1.96	2.33	2.58	3.09	3.30

Source: The entries in this table were computed by Pat Dugard, a freelance statistician.
For an independent groups (between Ss) test, $df = N - 2$ (where N is the total number of scores in both groups)
For a related (within Ss or matched pairs) test, $df = N - 1$ (where N is the number of pairs of scores)

Statistical Table 10.1 Pearson's product–moment correlation coefficient: Critical values of r for one- and two-tailed tests (r is significant if it **equals or exceeds** the table value)

df (N-2)	level of significance for a one-tailed test						
	.10	.05	.025	.01	.005	.001	.0005
	level of significance for a two-tailed test						
	.20	.10	.05	.02	.01	.002	.001
1	0.9511	0.9877	0.9969	0.9995	0.9999	1.0000	1.0000
2	0.8000	0.9000	0.9500	0.9800	0.9900	0.9980	0.9990
3	0.6870	0.8054	0.8783	0.9343	0.9587	0.9859	0.9911
4	0.6084	0.7293	0.8114	0.8822	0.9172	0.9633	0.9741
5	0.5509	0.6694	0.7545	0.8329	0.8745	0.9350	0.9509
6	0.5067	0.6215	0.7067	0.7887	0.8343	0.9049	0.9249
7	0.4716	0.5822	0.6664	0.7498	0.7977	0.8751	0.8983
8	0.4428	0.5494	0.6319	0.7155	0.7646	0.8467	0.8721
9	0.4187	0.5214	0.6021	0.6851	0.7348	0.8199	0.8470
10	0.3981	0.4973	0.5760	0.6581	0.7079	0.7950	0.8233
11	0.3802	0.4762	0.5529	0.6339	0.6835	0.7717	0.8010
12	0.3646	0.4575	0.5324	0.6120	0.6614	0.7501	0.7800
13	0.3507	0.4409	0.5140	0.5923	0.6411	0.7301	0.7604
14	0.3383	0.4259	0.4973	0.5742	0.6226	0.7114	0.7419
15	0.3271	0.4124	0.4821	0.5577	0.6055	0.6940	0.7247
16	0.3170	0.4000	0.4683	0.5425	0.5897	0.6777	0.7084
17	0.3077	0.3887	0.4555	0.5285	0.5751	0.6624	0.6932
18	0.2992	0.3783	0.4438	0.5155	0.5614	0.6481	0.6788
19	0.2914	0.3687	0.4329	0.5034	0.5487	0.6346	0.6652
20	0.2841	0.3598	0.4227	0.4921	0.5368	0.6219	0.6524
25	0.2546	0.3233	0.3809	0.4451	0.4869	0.5679	0.5974
30	0.2327	0.2960	0.3494	0.4093	0.4487	0.5257	0.5541
35	0.2156	0.2746	0.3246	0.3810	0.4182	0.4916	0.5189
40	0.2018	0.2573	0.3044	0.3578	0.3932	0.4633	0.4896
45	0.1903	0.2429	0.2876	0.3384	0.3721	0.4394	0.4647
50	0.1806	0.2306	0.2732	0.3218	0.3542	0.4188	0.4432
60	0.1650	0.2108	0.2500	0.2948	0.3248	0.3850	0.4079
70	0.1528	0.1954	0.2319	0.2737	0.3017	0.3583	0.3798
80	0.1430	0.1829	0.2172	0.2565	0.2830	0.3364	0.3568
90	0.1348	0.1726	0.2050	0.2422	0.2673	0.3181	0.3375
100	0.1279	0.1638	0.1946	0.2301	0.2540	0.3025	0.3211

Source: The entries in this table were computed by D.R. McDonald at the University of Dundee.

Statistical Table 10.2 Spearman's rank-order correlation coefficient (r_s): Critical values of r_s for one- and two-tailed tests (r_s is significant if it equals or exceeds the table value)

N	level of significance for a one-tailed test					
	.10	.05	.025	.01	.005	.001
(num of	level of significance for a two-tailed test					
pairs)	.20	.10	.05	.02	.01	.002
4	1.0000	1.0000				
5	0.8000	0.9000	1.0000	1.0000		
6	0.6571	0.8286	0.8857	0.9429	1.0000	
7	0.6071	0.7143	0.7857	0.8929	0.9286	1.0000
8	0.5238	0.6429	0.7381	0.8333	0.8810	0.9524
9	0.4833	0.6000	0.6833	0.7667	0.8167	0.9167
10	0.4546	0.5636	0.6485	0.7455	0.7939	0.8788
11	0.4182	0.5273	0.6182	0.7091	0.7546	0.8364
12	0.3986	0.5035	0.5874	0.6713	0.7273	0.8252
13	0.3791	0.4780	0.5604	0.6484	0.7033	0.7967
14	0.3670	0.4637	0.5429	0.6308	0.6791	0.7670
15	0.3500	0.4429	0.5179	0.6036	0.6536	0.7464
16	0.3412	0.4265	0.5000	0.5765	0.6206	0.7294
17	0.3284	0.4167	0.4853	0.5662	0.6177	0.7132
18	0.3189	0.4014	0.4758	0.5542	0.6037	0.6925
19	0.3088	0.3912	0.4579	0.5351	0.5842	0.6737
20	0.2993	0.3805	0.4466	0.5203	0.5684	0.6602

Source: The entries in this table were computed by Pat Dugard, a freelance statistician.

GLOSSARY

Alpha (α) level
Level of confidence (probability of being mistaken in rejecting the null hypothesis) that you are willing to accept as evidence of statistical significance (e.g., $p < .05$; $p < .01$).

Asymmetrical order effects
An order effect is asymmetrical if, in a repeated measures experiment, the effect on the second condition of having previously been presented with the other condition is different if the order of presentation of the conditions is reversed.

Between-subjects design
An alternative label often used instead of 'Independent groups design'. See 'Independent groups design'.

Carry-over effects
Asymmetrical order effects that occur when order effects depend on the specifics of experimental conditions as well as on the order of the conditions. These effects are not controlled by counterbalancing the order of conditions.

Categorical variable
A discrete variable that doesn't take numerical values at all (e.g., sex) – when numbers are assigned (e.g., male – 1, female – 2), they are only codes for categories.

Central tendency, measures of
An average, most representative value of a set of scores. The most commonly used are the mean and the median.

Chi-Square test (χ^2)
A test of the association between (or, conversely, the independence of) frequencies in exclusive categories of two or more variables (e.g., sex: male/female, age: young/old). Frequency data are obtained using a nominal (or categoric) scale.

Classification variable
See 'Categorical variable'.

Coefficient of correlation
A statistic that indicates the strength of relationship between variables.

Coefficient of determination (symbolized by r^2)
A measure of the proportion of variability in one variable that can be predicted from the variability in another (correlated) variable.

Computational formula
A formula that is equivalent to a defining formula, but is easier to use for calculations done by hand or with a computer.

Conditions
When there is only one independent variable in an experiment, each 'level' of the IV may be referred to as a condition of the experiment – note that 'level of IV' and 'condition' are not synonymous when there is more than one IV (which designs are beyond the scope of this book).

Confounding variable
This is a systematic nuisance variable, whose effects on the dependent variable are inextricably mixed up with (cannot be distinguished from) the effects of the independent variable.

Constant
To say that a variable is kept constant means that it can take only one value in an experiment (e.g., stimulus exposure time = 5 seconds). It will therefore have been eliminated as a potential nuisance variable.

Construct validity
The extent to which a variable used in an experiment actually reflects the theoretical construct (concept, 'thing') that we intend to measure.

Contingency table
A table of frequencies of cases (e.g., people or events) falling into mutually exclusive categories. It can be in one or more dimensions. This is how nominal data are usually represented.

Continuity correction
See 'Yates' correction for continuity'.

Continuous variable
A variable that can take values over a continuous range (e.g., mood – from very bad to very good, or temperature – from very cold to very hot, with no restriction in principle to whole number values.

Control condition
A condition in which the experimenter does not attempt to alter the normal level of an independent variable, sometimes referred to as a baseline condition (e.g., normal mood).

Correlated
Variables are said to be positively correlated if high values on one tend to occur with high values on the other, and low values likewise tend to occur together (e.g., height and weight; tall people tend to be heavier and short people tend to be lighter on average). Variables are negatively correlated if high values of one tend to occur with low values of the other.

Correlational analysis
A statistical analysis carried out to test hypotheses about (non-causal) relationships among variables.

Correlational study
This is a non-experimental study that does not involve the manipulation of an independent variable and from which it is not possible to infer a causal effect. Rather, it will be a study concerned with the strength of relationship between variables.

Counterbalancing
To reduce order effects in a repeated measures experiment, the conditions of the experiment are given in different orders to two randomly selected halves of the participants.

Covariance
Extent to which high scores on one variable correspond to high scores on another variable, and similarly with low scores.

Cover story
A plausible rationale for the experimental procedure designed to prevent participants from guessing the experimental hypothesis – a mild deception, which now needs to receive ethical approval.

Criterion variable
A variable in which changes are predicted from changes in the values of another (predictor) variable.

Critical value
The table value that a calculated statistic must equal or exceed (or sometimes, equal or be less than) for the result to be judged statistically significant at a given level of probability.

Data
Scores or measurements of participants or other systematic observations made during a research study.

Degrees of freedom
The number of values that are free to vary when calculating a statistic. For example, if a mean has been calculated and its value is to remain fixed, $n - 1$ deviations from the mean could be changed (would be free to vary) but the last remaining deviation would be 'fixed' by the need for the deviations around the mean to sum to zero.

Demand characteristics
A threat to the validity of an experiment, whereby cues convey the hypothesis to participants so that they behave in ways that will confirm the hypothesis in order to please the experimenter.

Dependent variable
A variable in an experiment, the level of which it is hypothesized will change when levels of an independent variable are varied – a variable in an experiment on which participants will obtain scores or be measured.

Descriptive statistics
Graphical or numerical summaries of data (e.g., histogram, mean, standard deviation).

Directional prediction
A prediction that the means for the conditions of an experiment will differ in a specified direction. In this case, a significant difference in the 'wrong' direction would not lead to rejection of the null hypothesis.

Discrete variable
A variable that can only take whole number values (e.g., number of problems solved), or no numerical values – see 'Categorical variables'.

Dispersion, measures of
The extent to which scores are spread on either side of the average value of a set of scores (e.g., standard deviation).

Distribution-free tests
See 'Non-parametric tests'.

Ecological validity
The extent to which findings from an experiment can be generalized to settings other than the one that has been constructed for the purpose of the experiment.

Effect size
The size of an effect as distinct from its statistical significance. One measure of effect size is the difference between means in units of standard deviation.

Empirical evidence
Observations that can be replicated by others.

Error of measurement
This is said occur in the measurement of a dependent variable when there is an effect of a nuisance variable on the DV.

Expected frequencies
In a contingency table, the frequencies that would be expected if the null hypothesis were true (i.e., the frequencies in the table are independent of one another).

Experiment
A procedure for investigating causal links between different things, which involves changing one thing and observing the effect on another thing, while keeping everything else unchanged.

Experimental condition
A condition in which the experimenter alters the normal level of an independent variable (e.g., mood enhancement).

Experimental control
Prevention of the effects of systematic nuisance variables (i.e., systematic errors) in the measurement of a dependent variable.

Experimental hypothesis
A prediction about a causal effect of modifying the level of one variable (the independent variable) on another (the dependent variable).

Experimenter expectancy
A threat to the validity of an experiment, arising from a tendency for an experimenter to construct or conduct an experiment in such a way that it is more likely to support the hypothesis.

Explanatory variable
See 'Predictor variable'.

External validity
The extent to which any relationship that is observed between variables in an experiment can be generalized to different contexts and different individuals.

Extraneous variables
See 'Nuisance variables'.

Frequency distribution
A count of how many times each value of a variable occurs in a set of data.

Frequency polygon
A graphical display of a frequency distribution, in which the vertical columns used in a histogram are replaced by a dot at the midpoint of the top of each column to represent how often each score occurs in a data set, and the dots are joined up with straight lines.

Histogram
The simplest histogram is a graphical display of a frequency distribution that uses vertical columns to represent how often each score occurs in a set of data.

Homogeneity of variance
Equality of the extent to which scores are spread out (as measured by 'variance') in two or more distributions of scores.

Hypothesis
A formal statement of a prediction that a specific change in one thing will *produce* a specific change in another thing (see 'Experimental hypothesis'), or a prediction that a specific change in one thing will be *associated* with a specific change in another thing.

Hypothetical distribution of the differences between means
A plot of the frequency of various sizes of differences between two means that would be expected if an experiment were repeated (in our imagination) many times when the null hypothesis is true (i.e., only random effects are operating).

Imaginary distribution
A hypothetical frequency distribution of the entire population of possible scores on a variable.

Independent groups design
An experimental study in which different groups of participants each receive only one level (condition) of an independent variable.

Independent groups *t*-test
A parametric test of the difference between means of participants allocated to two different conditions of an experiment.

Independent variable
A variable in an experiment that is manipulated in order to see how different levels of it affect some other (dependent) variable.

Indicator
A score on a dependent variable that is based on a means of assessment that is a plausible, adequate exemplification of whatever is represented by the DV.

Intercept (denoted by *a*)
Point at which a regression line cuts the *Y*-axis.

Internal validity
The extent to which it can be inferred that any difference in the dependent variable between conditions of an experiment is due to the manipulation of levels of the independent variable. This depends on the extent to which the presence of systematic nuisance variables is avoided.

Interval (or equal interval) scale
Observations are ranked in order of magnitude and, in addition, the intervals between numbers are equal at all parts of the scale (e.g., temperature).

Irrelevant variables
See 'Nuisance variables'.

Levels of measurement
A hierarchy of measurement scales ranging from nominal to ordinal to interval to ratio scales. The numbers used within scales have additional properties as you move from nominal through ratio scales. This means that additional operations can be performed on numbers as the level of measurement gets higher.

Levels of treatment
Refers to the different ways, resulting from a researcher's manipulations of an independent variable, in which participants are treated in different conditions in an experiment.

Line of best fit
See 'Regression line'.

Linear regression analysis
A statistical analyses carried out to estimate changes in a (criterion) variable when another (predictor) variable changes by a given amount.

Linear regression equation
Gives the location of a straight line with reference to two axes (X and Y), by specifying the intercept of the line on the Y axis (a) and the slope of the line Y/X (b).

Linear relationship
When equal changes in one variable go with equal changes in another variable at all levels of the first variable. When plotted in a scattergram, the points cluster around a straight line.

Manipulation
When an experimenter varies (changes) the levels of an independent variable to create the different conditions in an experiment.

Manipulation check
This is a measurement that is taken for the purpose of confirming that an independent variable actually took the intended levels in the different conditions of an experiment.

Mann–Whitney U test
A non-parametric (rank order) test of the difference between means of participants allocated to two different conditions of an experiment.

Matched subjects design
A modification of the independent groups design, in which pairs of participants who are matched on some relevant variable(s) are randomly allocated to levels of the independent variable in order to achieve some control over participant differences.

Mean
A measure of central tendency (average), which is the sum of a set of scores divided by the number of scores.

Mean deviation
The average deviation of a set of scores from their mean, ignoring direction.

Measure
A measure is the means of assessment of a variable – it must be precise and rigorous.

Measurement scales
See 'Levels of measurement'.

Median
A measure of central tendency (average), which is the value of a set of scores that has an equal number of scores above and below it.

Mode
A measure of central tendency (average), which is the value that occurs most frequently in a set of scores.

Negatively skewed distribution
The tail on the left side of the peak, where the smaller values lie, is longer than the tail on the right side, where there are the bigger values.

Nominal scale
The lowest level of measurement – numbers are simply labels for mutually exclusive categories, such as gender or nationality.

Non-directional prediction
A prediction that means for the conditions of an experiment will differ, without specifying the direction of the difference.

Non-linear relationship
When equal changes in one variable go with different changes in another variable at different levels of the first variable. When plotted in a scattergram, the points cluster around a curve.

Non-parametric tests
Tests that do not require assumptions of homogeneity (equality) of variance or normal (bell-shaped) distributions of scores. They also do not require interval or ratio level of measurement and include rank tests.

Non-specific hypothesis
A prediction that a statistic (e.g., the difference between means) will fall within some range (e.g., above or below zero for the research hypothesis).

Normal distribution
A bell-shaped frequency distribution that is mathematically defined. Approximations to the 'ideal' normal distribution are often obtained when a variable being measured is affected by numerous random nuisance variables (chance effects). Most values are close to the mean of the measurements, with fewer and fewer showing large positive or negative differences from the mean (i.e., as the tails of the distribution are approached). This ideal normal distribution is useful because known proportions of cases fall within specified areas under the curve (most obviously, 50% are above the mean).

Nuisance variables
Variables other than the independent variable that may affect scores on the dependent variable in an experiment.

Null hypothesis
Contrary to an experimental hypothesis, a prediction that modifying the level of one variable (the independent variable) will not cause changes in another variable (the dependent variable) – it is predicted that any observed changes in the dependent variable can be accounted for by the effects of uncontrolled random nuisance variables (i.e., chance).

One-sample *t*-test
A parametric test of the difference between the mean of a single sample of participants and a known mean of another sample (typically, a normative or representative sample of a population, obtained on a previous occasion.

One-tailed test
Only the tail of the distribution in the predicted direction is considered. If α is set at .05 and the value for the statistic falls among the 5% most extreme values in the predicted direction, the decision will be to reject the null hypothesis ($p < .05$, one-tailed). If the statistic falls anywhere else (including in the other tail), the decision will be to fail to reject the null hypothesis ($p > .05$, one-tailed).

Operational definition
This is the process of specifying clearly and explicitly the methods (i.e., the operations) used to measure a dependent variable.

Opportunity sample
A sample that is selected because it is readily available rather than because it is strictly representative of the population of interest (e.g., students in a laboratory class).

Order effect
In a repeated measures design, scores in each condition of the dependent variable may depend on which condition comes first. For example, if there is a practice effect, scores would tend to be raised in the condition that came second.

Ordinal scale
Observations are ranked in order of magnitude (i.e., 1st, 2nd, 3rd etc), but the intervals (difference) between numbers may differ at different parts of the scale (e.g., a preference order).

Outcome variable
See 'Criterion variable'.

Outlier
A highly deviant or extreme score that is likely to distort statistics such as the mean and standard deviation.

Parameter
A value that applies to a population, and is therefore 'fixed'. This differs from a statistic, which is an estimate of a population value based on a sample drawn from the population, which can vary from sample to sample.

Parametric tests
Tests that require assumptions about the distribution of scores in the population(s) from which data were sampled. Two special assumptions required for parametric tests are (i) homogeneity of variance (equal spread of scores) and (ii) normal (bell-shaped) distributions of scores.

Participant variables
Nuisance variables associated with characteristics of participants in an experiment (e.g., personality, intelligence, etc.).

Participants
People who take part in an experiment or other research study – see also 'subjects'.

Pearson's (product–moment) correlation coefficient (r)

Calculates strength of linear relationship between variables. It is generally used when parametric assumptions are met, typically with interval data. It ranges between 1 (perfect positive correlation) and −1 (perfect negative correlation).

Philosophy of science

The study of how science should work and how it does, in fact, work.

Pooled variance estimate

See 'Weighted average'.

Population

A wide (possibly infinite) well-defined set of something. All of the possible objects of a particular kind. It does not necessarily refer to people (e.g. the population of first year university students in the UK) or even to tangible entities of any kind (e.g., trees in Scotland, stars in the Milky Way). It can refer to an entirely imaginary set of all possible scores that could have been obtained by an infinite number of participants in an experiment.

Population validity

The extent to which findings from an experiment can be generalized to people who differ in some important respects from those who participated in the experiment.

Positively skewed distribution

The tail on the right side of the peak, where the bigger values lie, is longer than the tail on the left side, where there are the smaller values.

Power

The probability of finding a statistically significant effect when the null hypothesis is in fact untrue. The probability is $1 - \beta$ (i.e., if $\beta = 0.2$, then the power = $1 - 0.2$ = 0.8 or 80%). A power of around 0.8 is generally considered acceptable.

Power-efficiency

Concerns the increase in sample size that is necessary for a non-parametric test to have the same power as an alternative parametric test – e.g., if a non-parametric test requires $n = 25$ to achieve the same power a parametric test with $n = 20$, the power-efficiency of the non-parametric test = $100 \times 20/25 = 80\%$.

Predictor variable

A variable in which changes are used in regression analysis to predict values on another (criterion) variable.

Probabilistic

A conclusion is probabilistic when it is not definite – there is some possibility (usually small) that the conclusion is mistaken, as when it is concluded that there is a 5% probability that an apparent effect of one variable on another may have been due to the random (chance) effects of uncontrolled (nuisance) variables.

Qualitative variable
See 'Categorical variable'.

Quantitative variable
A variable for which we have good quantitative measurements (e.g., temperature, reaction time, counts of people arriving at a queue).

Quasi-experiment
This is an experiment in which participants are assigned to levels of an independent variable on the basis of their pre-existing status on the variable (e.g., when sex is the IV, the conditions are 'male' and 'female' are pre-existing). An inference that levels of the IV cause differences in the DV between conditions is not justified, even if the differences are statistically significant.

r
See 'Pearson's (product–moment) correlation coefficient (r)'.

r^2
See 'Coefficient of determination'.

r_s
Symbol representing the Spearman rank order coefficient of correlation, which is generally used when parametric assumptions are not met, typically with ordinal data.

Random allocation
The assignment of participants or observation times to experimental conditions in such a way that each one has an equal chance of being assigned to each condition.

Random error
This is the type of error produced by a non-systematic nuisance variable, where the effect is to increase variability in the measurement of a dependent variable, with an equal probability of raising or lowering scores in either condition of an experiment.

Random nuisance variable
A variable, other than the independent variable, that has effects on the dependent variable in an experiment, with an equal probability of affecting participants in either condition of the experiment.

Random procedure
A means that is adopted for assigning participants or test occasions to experimental conditions, such that each participant or test occasion has an equal probability of being assigned to each condition.

Random sample of a population of scores
The scores on a variable obtained in an experiment may be regarded as a random sample of an imaginary distribution (i.e., the imaginary population) of all possible scores on the variable.

Random sampling
A procedure for selecting people (or things) in such a way that every member of the population of interest has an equal chance of being selected.

Range
The difference between the highest and lowest score in a set of scores.

Rank tests
See 'Non-parametric tests'.

Ratio scales
As well as the intervals between numbers being equal at different parts of the scale, there is a point on the scale that represents a true zero in terms of whatever is being measured (e.g., 'not fired' for distance covered by a bullet). This means that ratios between measurements are meaningful (e.g., 100 metres covered is twice the distance of 50 metres covered).

Raw data
Scores or other systematic observations in the form in which they were originally obtained.

Regression coefficient
The value of b in a regression equation. See 'Slope'.

Regression line
A line that provides the best estimate of values of a criterion variable from values of a predictor variable for all points on a scattergram graphing the relationship between the two variables.

Regression of Y on X
Prediction from a predictor variable X (values on the horizontal axis) to a criterion variable Y (values on the vertical axis).

Rejection regions
The areas in the tails of a frequency distribution that represent large differences from the mean of the distribution. As values in these regions would occur infrequently by chance, it may be inferred that when a statistic falls in these regions, it was probably due to a systematic effect of a variable (the independent variable, we hope), allowing us to reject the null hypothesis at some specified (depending on how far out in a tail the statistic fell) level of confidence.

Related *t*-test
A parametric test of the difference between means of participants in two conditions of a repeated measures (or matched pairs) design (i.e., when the same or matched pairs of participants are tested in the two conditions).

Repeated measures design
An experimental study in which the same participants receive all levels (conditions) of an independent variable.

Replication
An attempt to repeat a study. This may be as near as possible to an exact repetition (direct replication), in order to increase confidence in the results of the original study, or it may be a partial repetition (systematic replication), where some aspect of the original study is deliberately modified to test the generalizability of the findings in changed circumstances.

Representative sample
If a sample is selected from a population (of people, things or data) in a random way so that each individual has an equal chance of being selected, the sample is said to be representative of the population, and results from the sample can be generalized to the population.

Response variable
This is a way in which a dependent variable is sometimes referred because a DV usually involves a response to a stimulus variable (an IV).

Rho (standing for the Greek letter ρ)
An alternative symbol sometimes used in place of r_s. See r_s.

Robust
Probabilities associated with values of a statistic are said to be robust when they are not greatly affected by moderate departures from the assumptions of homogeneity of variance and normality.

Sample
A sub-set of a population. A random sample is considered to be representative of the population.

Scientific method
A generally sceptical attitude combined with a two-stage research strategy: the formulation of hypotheses, followed by their subjection to empirical test.

Sequential effects
See 'Carry-over effects'.

Sign test
A non-parametric test of the difference between means of participants in two conditions of a repeated measures (or matched pairs) design (i.e., when the same or matched pairs of participants are tested in the two conditions). This test considers the direction of the differences between pairs of scores, but not the magnitude of the differences.

Situational variables
Nuisance variables associated with an experimental situation (i.e., aspects of the experimental environment and procedures).

Slope (denoted by the letter b)
The number of units that a regression line moves on the Y-axis for each unit it moves on the X-axis. Also known as the 'regression coefficient'.

Social desirability
A threat to the validity of an experiment, whereby the extent to which people's behaviour appears acceptable to a participant may affect that person's responses.

Spearman's rank order correlation coefficient (r_s)
Calculates strength of linear relationship between variables. It is generally used when parametric assumptions are not met, typically with ordinal data. It ranges between 1 (perfect positive correlation) and −1 (perfect negative correlation).

Specific hypothesis
A prediction that a statistic (e.g., the difference between two means) will have a particular value (e.g., zero for the null hypothesis).

Standard deviation
The square root of the average of the squared deviations of a set of scores from their mean (i.e., the square root of the variance).

Standard score
A transformation of raw scores such that the distribution has a fixed mean and a fixed standard deviation. For example, IQ scores often have a fixed mean of 100 and a standard deviation of 15. Thus a score of 115 is 1 SD above the mean (i.e., $z = +1$. See 'z-score').

Statistic
A value calculated from a sample of data (e.g., a mean of a sample of data is a statistic).

Statistical inference
The process of carrying out operations on data to ascertain the probability that an apparent effect of one variable on another could be accounted for by the random (chance) effects of other variables.

Statistical significance
An effect (e.g., a difference between means) is said to be statistically significant when there is a low probability (by convention, a less than 5% or 1% chance) that it could have arisen as the result of random error – the chance effects of random nuisance variables.

Stimulus variable
This is a way in which an independent variable is sometimes referred to because an IV involves exposing participants to a specific stimulus.

Subject variables
See 'Participant variables'.

Subjects
The old name for 'participants', dating from a time when much experimental research in psychology was with animals.

Systematic error
This is the type of error produced by a (systematic) nuisance variable, such that its effects on the dependent variable can be mistaken for the systematic effect of the independent variable.

Systematic nuisance variable
See 'Confounding variable'.

Systematic observation
Systematic gathering of behavioural data without intervention by the researcher.

Temporal validity
The extent to which findings from an experiment can be generalized to other time periods.

Tests of association
Tests of the relationship (correlation) between variables. A significant correlation is not interpreted as indicating a causal relationship between the variables.

Tests of differences
Tests of the difference between scores obtained in two conditions of an experiment (or quasi-experiment). If the data are obtained in a 'true experiment', in which random allocation is used, and the experiment is internally valid, a significant difference is interpreted as indicating a causal relationship between an independent and a dependent variable.

Theoretical construct
A concept or 'thing' that features in a theory.

Theory
A coherent set of interrelated ideas that can account for certain phenomena and from which specific hypotheses can be derived.

Ties
In non-parametric tests, the first step often involves ranking the data. Two kinds of ties have to be dealt with. One involves cases where a participant scores the same in two conditions; these ties are omitted from the analysis. The other involves cases where different participants obtain the same score (or difference between scores); these ties are given the same rank, which is the mean of the ranks to be occupied by the ties.

Trial
When many presentations of each condition are possible in a repeated measures experiment, each presentation of a condition is referred to as 'a trial'.

True experiment
This is an experiment in which levels of an independent variable are manipulated by the researcher and there is random allocation of participants (and the times available for them to be treated) to the conditions. If the experiment is properly conducted and confounding variables are controlled, an inference that levels of the IV are the cause of statistically significant differences in the DV between conditions may be justified.

True zero
See 'Ratio scales'.

Two-tailed test
Both tails of the distribution are considered. If α is set at .05 and the value for the statistic falls among the 2.5% most extreme values in either direction, the decision will be to reject the null hypothesis ($p < .05$, two-tailed). If the statistic falls anywhere else, the decision will be to fail to reject the null hypothesis ($p > .05$, two-tailed).

Type I error
Finding a statistically significant effect when the null hypothesis is in fact true. The probability of making this kind of mistake is the value at which α was set (e.g., .05 or .01).

Type II error
Failing to find a statistically significant effect when the null hypothesis is in fact untrue. The probability of making this kind of error is represented by β, which is often set at around 0.2.

Unrelated t-test
See 'Independent groups t-test'.

Validity
The extent to which the design of an experiment and the measurements we make in conducting it permit us to draw sound conclusions about our hypothesis.

Variability
Differences between scores on a variable due to random (chance) effects of uncontrolled (nuisance) variables.

Variability, measures of
See 'Measures of dispersion'.

Variable
Anything which, in a particular research context, can take different values, as opposed to having one fixed value (such as '10-year-olds' or 'exposure time for presentation of stimuli').

Variance
The average of the squared deviations of a set of scores from their mean.

Weighted average
In the calculation of an independent groups t-test, if group sizes are unequal, the denominator in the formula for t contains an average of the variances of the two groups that takes account of their respective sample sizes.

Wilcoxon Matched-Pairs Signed-Ranks T test
A non-parametric (rank order) test of the difference between means of participants in two conditions of a repeated measures (or matched pairs) design (i.e., when the same or matched pairs of participants are tested in the two conditions).

Within-subjects design
See 'Repeated measures design'.

Yates' correction for continuity
A correction to the formula for computing Chi Square in a 2×2 contingency table that is often recommended when the expected frequencies in the cells of the table are small. The correction is designed to deal with the fact that, although the theoretical distribution of Chi Square is continuous, the obtained distribution is discrete. We do not recommend using the correction for the reason given by Howell (2002).

z-score
A particular form of standard score in which scores are expressed in number of standard deviations above or below the mean (see 'Standard score').

A BRIEF LIST OF RECOMMENDED BOOKS

Allison, P.D. (1999). *Multiple regression: A primer.* Thousand Oaks, CA: Pine Forge Press.

Campbell, D.C. & Stanley, J.C. (1966). *Experimental and quasi-experimental designs for research.* Chicago: Rand McNally.

Cohen, J. (1988). *Statistical power analysis for the behavioural sciences* (2nd edn). Hillsdale, NJ: Lawrence Erlbaum Associates.

Howell, D.C. (2002). *Statistical methods for psychology* (5th edn). Pacific Grove, CA: Duxbury, Wadsworth.

Kinnear, P.R. & Gray, C.D. (2000). *SPSS for windows made simple: Release 10.* Hove, East Sussex: Psychology Press.

Pallant, J. (2001). *SPSS: Survival manual.* Buckingham: Open University Press.

Siegel, S. & Castellan, N.J. (1988). *Nonparametric statistics for the behavioural sciences* (2nd edn). New York: McGraw-Hill.

Todman, J. & Dugard, P. (2001). *Single-case and small-n experimental designs: A practical guide to randomization tests.* Mahwah, NJ: Lawrence Earlbaum Associates.

INDEX

The index is arranged in word-by-word sequence; page numbers in *italics* refer to figures; page numbers in **bold** refer to tables.